# Mass Communications and American Empire

## Also by Herbert I. Schiller

Super-State: Readings in the Military-Industrial Complex

The Mind Managers

Communication and Cultural Domination

National Sovereignty and International Communication: A Reader, *edited with Kaarle Nordenstreng*

Who Knows: Information in the Age of the Fortune 500

Information and the Crisis Economy

Culture Inc.: The Corporate Takeover of Public Expression

Hope and Folly: The United States and UNESCO, 1945–1985, *with William Preston, Jr., and Edward S. Herman*

Triumph of the Image: The Media's War in the Persian Gulf—A Global Perspective, *edited with Hamid Mowlana and George Gerbner*

CRITICAL STUDIES IN COMMUNICATION
AND IN THE CULTURAL INDUSTRIES
Herbert I. Schiller, Series Editor

*Mass Communications and American Empire, Second Edition, Updated,* Herbert I. Schiller

*Triumph of the Image: The Media's War in the Persian Gulf—A Global Perspective,* edited by Hamid Mowlana, George Gerbner, and Herbert I. Schiller

*The Persian Gulf TV War,* Douglas Kellner

FORTHCOMING

*The Panoptic Sort: The Political Economy of Personal Information,* Oscar Gandy, Jr.

*Intellectual Property in the Information Age: A Political Economy of Film and Video Copyright,* Ronald Bettig

*The Communications Industry in the American Economy,* Thomas Guback

*The Dallas Smythe Reader,* edited by Thomas Guback

*Media Transformations in the Age of Persuasion,* Robin K. Andersen

*The Social Uses of Photography: Images in the Age of Reproduction,* Hanno Hardt

*Introduction to Media Studies,* edited by Stuart Ewen, Elizabeth Ewen, Serafina Bathrick, and Andrew Mattson

*A Different Road Taken: Profiles of Five Critical Communication Scholars,* John A. Lent

*Hot Shots: An Alternative Video Production Handbook,* Tami Gold and Kelly Anderson

# Mass Communications and American Empire

## Second Edition, Updated

### Herbert I. Schiller
UNIVERSITY OF CALIFORNIA–SAN DIEGO

Westview Press
BOULDER • SAN FRANCISCO • OXFORD

For Anita, Dan, and Zach

*Critical Studies in Communication and in the Cultural Industries*

Copyright © 1969, 1992 by Herbert I. Schiller

Published in 1992 in the United States of America by Westview Press, Inc., 5500 Central Avenue, Boulder, Colorado 80301-2877, and in the United Kingdom by Westview Press, 36 Lonsdale Road, Summertown, Oxford OX2 7EW

First published in 1969 by Augustus M. Kelley Publishers. Paperback first published in 1971 by Beacon Press.

Library of Congress Cataloging-in-Publication Data
Schiller, Herbert I., 1919–
    Mass communications and American empire / Herbert I. Schiller. — 2nd ed., updated.
       p.   cm. — (Critical studies in communication and in the cultural industries)
    Includes bibliographical references and index.
    ISBN 0-8133-1439-9. — ISBN 0-8133-1440-2 (pbk.)
       1. Communication—United States.   2. Mass media—United States.
3. Communication, International.   I. Title.   II. Series.
P92.U5S29   1992
302.2′0973—dc20                                                      92-17286
                                                                            CIP

Printed and bound in the United States of America

   The paper used in this publication meets the requirements
of the American National Standard for Permanence of Paper
for Printed Library Materials Z39.48-1984. Printed on recycled paper.

10      9      8      7      6      5      4      3      2      1

# CONTENTS

# FOREWORD TO
# THE FIRST EDITION

This book represents a substantial step toward redressing a grave imbalance in the literature on communications at a moment in time when the need for it is great.

Over the past generation, students and scholars in the communications field have been relatively undersupplied with literature which is in the "critical" research stream and relatively oversupplied with literature which is in the "administrative" research stream — to use a valuable distinction first made by Paul F. Lazarsfeld in the early 1940's.[1] By administrative research he meant research within the frame of reference laid down by the mass media themselves or by the support structure of advertisers, agencies and government. It takes for granted the basic policy assumptions of those who define the terms of reference. And while the volume of funds devoted to administrative communications research may be small as compared with the volume devoted to physical science research, it has been rising rapidly, especially because recent recognition of the politico-economic roots of "insurgency" in developing nations has given urgency to the problems of efficiency in communications diplomacy. While market research is typically designed to make the mass media function more efficiently toward their objectives as business enterprises, much research by psychologists and sociologists since World War II has tacitly assumed the same terms of reference. Beginning in the 1950's economists, political scientists and anthropologists have been drawn into administrative research on communications, especially in regard to developing nations, as the exposure of "Camelot" so dramatically revealed. *The Dissenting Academy* documents the point.

What Lazarsfeld called "critical" research remains in short supply

---

[1] Lazarsfeld, Paul F., "Remarks on Administrative and Critical Communications Research", *Studies in Philosophy and Social Science*, Vol. 9, Columbia University.

in North America. Too often work which qualifies in this category is tangential to studies centered in older fields of inquiry. One thinks in this connection of C. Wright Mills[2], Robert A. Brady[3], Thurman Arnold[4], Robert S. Lynd[5], and others. Or, as with Daniellian's book, *ATT*, the work is so obsolete as to have chiefly historical interest.

Herbert Schiller's book, *Mass Communications and American Empire*, is an excellent addition to the critical communications research literature for a number of reasons. For the first time in a comprehensive treatment, the structure and policy of mass communications in the United States are critically examined in relation to their most important functions: the economic and political. Professor Schiller has dealt with his subject realistically, drawing on a wide diversity of industrial and government sources for information as to the dynamics and structure of mass communication. Here is no idle play with econometric models but the reality which concerns board rooms and lawmakers. Finally, the point of view which permeates the book makes it relevant to the concerns which a Black Power-shocked and Vietnam-shocked American electorate is facing. These concerns in various ways center on questioning the relevance of the policies of American institutions to the grave dangers which beset the country, and through it the world. Because the mass media of communication set the agenda for the daily consideration of the issues and problems of which note should be taken, it is necessary to understand how the mass media function if one seriously proposes to alter either that agenda or the agenda-setting structure in the United States. On all of these accounts *Mass Communications and American Empire* is a valuable work. It should be required reading for undergraduate classes in all of the social sciences.

DALLAS W. SMYTHE

University of Saskatchewan
December 1968

2 Mills, C. Wright, *White Collar*, Chapter 15 (1951).

3 Brady, Robert A., *Business as a System of Power*, Chapters 7-9, (1943).

4 Arnold, Thurman, *The Folklore of Capitalism*, Chapters 7-8, (1937).

5 Lynd, Robert S., *Knowledge for What* (1939).

# A Quarter-Century Retrospective

*Mass Communications and American Empire* was written between 1965 and 1967 and first published in 1969. Seismic shifts in the balance of world power have occurred since those years. Yet the world preeminence of the American media/cultural sphere remains intact, if not more secure than ever. The war in the Persian Gulf in 1990–1991 provides a recent measure of this preeminence.

In that war, a new dimension of information monopoly and control was demonstrated. The messages and imagery that circulated nationally and worldwide were transmitted by *one* network: Cable News Network (CNN). CNN, in turn, acquired its material essentially from two sources, the Pentagon and the White House. As a consequence, most of the world's understanding of what was happening in the Gulf and what it signified came from practically a single U.S. source.[1]

How has this incomparable capability—the power to define—been sustained and *augmented* over the past quarter of a century? No less important, what differentiates the 1990s from the mid-1960s with respect to media-cultural influence? The answers to these questions constitute the substance of what follows.

The theoretical framework of *Mass Communications and American Empire* depended on three geopolitical features that characterized the period 1945–1965. One was the existence of a globally dominant United States, whose influence rested on a combination of economic, military, and informational power. A second recognized the existence of a far-flung, state-managed territory, calling itself socialist and encompassing approximately one-third of the world's

---

1. Hamid Mowlana, George Gerbner, and Herbert I. Schiller, eds., *Triumph of the Image: The Media's War in the Gulf—A Global Perspective* (Boulder: Westview Press, 1992).

population. It was assumed by all that this imposing region served as an oppositional pole to the U.S.-led sphere. Finally, there existed a vast area outside these two blocs. It was composed of nations that had recently achieved independence from the European colonial empires that had carved out huge holdings in Africa, Asia, and the Middle East. This sizable group of new states also was joined by the nations of Central and Latin America, which, though nominally independent for a century, in fact remained economic and political vassals of the United States, and earlier, Great Britain.

Together the new nations and the Latin American contingent constituted what was then called the Third World. Sometimes it was optimistically labeled the developing world and on occasion the less industrialized world. It was loosely organized in what was known as the Movement of the Non-Aligned Nations. At that time, the Non-Aligned Movement was also regarded, justifiably, as an oppositional pole to U.S. and Western dominance. Some of the movement's most militant members had led the struggles for national liberation.

Developments in the past twenty-five years have dramatically changed the features that defined the reality of the 1960s. The U.S. corporate economy, for example, has grown significantly over these years but its global position has weakened. Domestically, the industrial infrastructure has shrunk markedly while a huge increase in information-using services has largely transformed the nation's work and jobs.

No less momentous, the state socialist sector of the world has contracted sharply. The more industrialized countries in that bloc, the former USSR, Czechoslovakia, Hungary, and Poland, have mostly eliminated their state planning character and are in varying degree and tempo restoring capitalist institutions and values. Astonishingly, the main oppositional pole to world capitalism for more than seventy years has collapsed.

Another differentiating condition between the 1960s and the 1990s is the near-disappearance of the Non-Aligned Movement as a functioning entity. With its enfeeblement, the other oppositional pole to Western capitalism also, for the moment, no longer exists. The governing strata throughout what was once the Third World, with few exceptions, accept the West's market prescriptions for economic activity and allow, or can do nothing to stop, their countries from being integrated into the world market system.

In sum, these three determining features of the mid-1960s have undergone 180-degree turns in the succeeding quarter of a century. We will examine each one of these transformations in turn.

## The Changing U.S. Corporate Economy

In the mid-1960s, before the massive and disastrous intervention in Vietnam, U.S. industrial power worldwide, we now can see, was at its apex. The dollar was the ruling currency of international trade and investment. U.S. military troops garrisoned much of the world. The United Nations was still totally dominated by Western, mostly U.S., power. Made-in-America movies, TV programs, music, news, and popular culture in general constituted the imagery and message fare of much of the world.

Some, but not all of this, has changed drastically to the disadvantage of U.S. global power. What follows in this section is a consideration of the paradox that although there is a day-in and day-out relative diminution of U.S. industrial strength *internationally,* the politico-cultural influence of the corporate sector *domestically* is all-pervasive.

Beginning in the late 1960s and early 1970s, corporate America began to experience powerful pressure from two different sources. One was the return to the international market in growing force of Germany (still only the Western part) and Japan. For the past twenty years, the competition for world market share from these completely rebuilt and fully modernized economies, along with the export push of the "Asian tigers," have been at the expense of the U.S. global position.

The other pressure, less appreciated in its initial period, has been the onset of a global economic slowdown, now of some years' duration. Unemployment has been heavy in several of the industrial economies (France, Great Britain, Canada, the Netherlands, Australia, and others).

U.S. corporate efforts to cope with, or accommodate to, the foreign competition and the economic stagnation have been mostly financial and technological. The financial strategy (if it may be called that) in the 1980s, the Reagan years, was to acquire and merge huge corporate structures, financing the consolidations by the issue of debased securities, junk bonds. This was all very comfortable and extremely profitable to the deal makers as long as there was some growth in the economy. When the economic machine stalled, the capability to pay the interest on the mountain of corporate debt fell off rapidly. Write-downs and bankruptcies mark the 1990s, and there is no end in sight. The speculation and debt creation have left much of the hard-pressed corporate structure with little room for maneuver.

Corporate America's technological response to preserve its global market position has been still more destabilizing and wrenching. It has subjected the social order to an incredibly rapid upheaval, affecting industries, jobs, and the working conditions of tens of millions of Americans. This chaotic transformation has been foisted on the public as a technological blessing and has been given the mystifying but reassuring label of "the information society." With all opinion-shaping organs agreeing that the shift to an information-using society was the most exciting development since settled agriculture more than 5,000 years ago, computers have been installed in governmental agencies, factory offices and industrial processes, retail trade, and the home itself.

The computerization of the economy has been so rapid that only a little more than ten years ago I could still, naively, urge a go-slow policy in this development and recommend "the beginning of a systematic and comprehensive international effort to develop standards, codes and conditions of applicability *before* computerization is introduced into any locale . . . [further] such standards and codes will not be promulgated quickly. This is all to the good. It will afford time to think through the enormous complexities that surround advanced communication and other technologies at this stage of unequal global power and influence."[2]

This advice, given at that time, actually was after the fact. Computerization had already become irreversible. The 1980s saw its acceleration. It was accomplished after due deliberation. The

---

2. Herbert I. Schiller, *Who Knows: Information in the Age of the Fortune 500* (Norwood, N.J.: Ablex Publishing Corp., 1981).

preparations had been under way for decades in governmentally supported corporate and military projects that were the forerunners of the widespread uses that were adopted later on. Just as the Marshall Plan had been a brilliant program organized by American leadership in the immediate post–World War II years to deny Europeans the possibility of radically restructuring their economies, the development of computers and satellites (telecommunications) was an equally farsighted initiative to maintain American industrial advantage and global primacy. The origins of computerization tell the story.

For half a century, beginning during World War II, the American military has channeled enormous research and development (R&D) funds from its astronomical budget into work on new information technologies and computerization in particular.

The Pentagon's interest was far from academic. The expected (and actual) payoff was data and information processing capabilities that would enable the American military machine to be in instantaneous and continuous contact with its worldwide deployments and to monitor communications of friend and foe alike around the world. The Pentagon's expenditures on R&D flowed into corporate, governmental, and university labs. A significant fraction of these outlays were concentrated on electronics, computer science, and artificial intelligence research. From these investments came the products of the information age. They accounted in large measure for the early preeminence and worldwide leadership of American activity in this area.

Part of the stock wisdom of U.S. business and political leaders in the postwar years, elevated almost to scripture in the Reagan Bush era, is the myth of government inefficiency and the corollary that finds efficiency at its peak in the corporate sector. It is not without irony that the information society, such as it is, the alleged epitome of efficiency, owes its existence to government spending.

Douglas Noble details, for example, the great influence of the military on the development of computer-based education (CBE) and what the consequences of this relationship have been on the education of the youth. Additionally, Noble quotes sources that observe that "computer science is not a branch of military science, yet 70% of all academic research is funded by the Department of Defense."[3]

The major funding agencies for science and technology since World War II—the Office of Naval Research, the Rand Corporation, the National Science Foundation, and the Atomic Energy Commission—have all been heavily dependent on military funds.

In the 1990s this spigot has begun to be tightened. With the disappearance of the "red menace," the military budget is on the defensive. What this may mean for future research supported by government money (in military uniform) in the information and electronics fields is cloudy. But the infrastructure of the information-using economy is in place and its effects are all too observable.

## The Main Users of the New Information Technologies

The enthusiasts and promoters of the new information technologies, especially computers, have branded those who have raised questions about the uses to which these technologies have been applied as "technophobes," akin to the machine wreckers in England of the early nineteenth century. But it is not at all a question of liking or disliking the new instrumentation. The question that has to be raised is Who are the main users of the new technologies and what are they using them for? Clearly this issue relates closely to the earlier question: Where did these technologies come from and why were they so generously supported?

Who then, are the big users of computers and satellites and their related equipment? Along with the military and the intelligence services whose interest in, and employment of, high-speed global communications is self-evident, the main beneficiary of these recent new data-handling and transmission capabilities is big business. With these technologies, corporations have the means to operate not only in a national market but in an international market as well. With state-of-the-art communications—no cheap service—a company can transact business internationally as easily as locally. Data concerning any production site on the face of the earth are

---

3. Douglas Noble, *The Classroom Arsenal: Military Research, Information Technology and Public Education* (London: Palmer Press, 1991), page 283.

quickly ascertainable. Capital can be shifted from one locale to another electronically. The labor supply, wherever it is cheaply available, can be employed to do the job that the global company wants done, regardless of the costs and pain to workers in the abandoned work sites.

It is not surprising that increasing shares of global production are now accounted for by a few thousand large firms, a good but declining fraction of which are still American owned. Regarding its 1990 list of the "Global 500"—the biggest industrial corporations in the world—*Fortune* magazine reported that "the U.S. leads all countries with 167 companies on the list. That's more than Japan, West Germany and Canada combined. . . . Americans are No. 1 in 14 of the 25 industries on the Global 500." Despite this reassuring information, *Fortune* also notes, "Impressive as these figures are, U.S. dominance is slowly giving way. In 1980, 23 U.S. companies made the top 50, compared with only 5 Japanese. Now there are 17 American and 10 Japanese."[4]

The commanding role that these corporations play in global economic affairs elevates them, with few exceptions, above the authority of most governments in the world. The international balance sheets for some of the main U.S. corporate players, for example, display a condition very different from that of the government's. Although the United States overall has been suffering a dismal trade deficit for several years, American transnational companies are doing very well. Their accounts are overwhelmingly in the black and richly profitable as well.

When these companies search the world for low-cost production sites to extract the maximum profitability (economists call this "comparative advantage"), they leave behind pools of unemployment, shut-down factories, and human despair in their home base. But these are not balance sheet items and consequently do not get counted or considered when the utility of transnational corporate activity is calculated.

So the U.S.-owned global corporation is doing very well while the state languishes and its world influence recedes. In fact, up to

---

4. "The Global 500: The World's Biggest Industrial Corporations," *Fortune*, July 30, 1990, page 265.

this time the slightest effort to rectify the deepening malaise has been vigorously and successfully resisted by the corporate sector and its political representatives, who have a hammerlock on Congress and the national political process. This is the unholy interlock that is contributing to the unraveling of the American democratic project.

In the information age as presently structured, a few thousand supercorporations operate adventurously on a global scale, utilizing the most up-to-date information technologies. The domestic costs—physical and human—of these unaccountable corporate actions contribute to the downgrading of the country's essential well-being and to its lessened international strength. The political process that at one time was available to call these policies and practices to account is blocked. And the media-cultural landscape nationally is a corporate playing field.

The new information technologies—and here television, cable, and the communication satellite must be included along with computers—have enabled the corporate sector to intrude massively in the nation's culture and opinion making.

Admittedly, U.S. big business since Civil War times a century and a half ago has exercised a strong, if not commanding, position in American society. That position today, with the assistance of the new communications capabilities, has been strengthened immeasurably. Because the giant corporation is the chief accumulator of the nation's wealth, at the center of production, and the most visible presence in media and cultural affairs, its authority and resources are unmatched.

Yet big business's employment of the new information technologies for its own advantage, nationally and internationally, was *preceded* by its sweeping takeover of the domestic communication apparatus. As early as the general advent of radio in the 1920s, and deepening with the introduction of television in the late 1940s and early 1950s, the electronic apparatus has been largely at the disposal of the business system and the "national advertiser" in particular. Ever since the early days of radio, the American informational system has been more appropriately understood as a marketing system because it is in this capacity that the press, radio, and television are most heavily utilized.

The comprehensive employment of sophisticated communication facilities and ancillary services such as surveys, to the instruction and persuasion of consumers, is the foremost identifying feature of developed capitalism—that which prevails in the United States. The energies and resources that go into the study and making of consumers, the creation of the messages and imagery that are employed to realize these objectives, and the seizure of as many sites as possible where people—potential consumers—congregate have produced a commercially saturated national environment.[5]

No locale or forum is excluded from a truly obsessive effort to reach and influence consumers. Radio, television, and the press are the familiar channels for transmitting the sales message, in both programming and commercials. The process, however, hardly stops there. Sports, for example, have been brought under the marketing umbrella. The huge audiences attracted to the major professionalized sports are mobilized for the large advertisers and are structured to their, the advertisers', needs. Financing for the general sports enterprise comes from the national television networks and cable franchises, who, in turn, receive their revenues from the national advertisers, the giant companies. Some of this huge money pool filters down to the players and causes some critical comment about the preposterous salaries that some athletes now receive. Hardly a mention is made of the sums going to the owners of the professional franchises, and rare is the sports writer who would dare to mention, much less to attack, the source—advertising— that underpins this golden enterprise.

Scarcely a cultural space remains, consequently, that is outside the commercial web. Concerts, classical as well as popular, have their corporate sponsors. Street fairs and city marathons bear corporate logos. Recently the country's most prestigious scientific and cultural complex, the Smithsonian Institution, announced that corporate logos would be permitted on some of its exhibits. And, as of this writing, more than 10,000 grammar schools have accepted television programming, with commercials, into their classrooms. The justification for this educational vandalism is the specious

---

5. Herbert I. Schiller, *Culture Inc.: The Corporate Takeover of Public Expression* (New York: Oxford, 1989).

argument that the children see commercials at home so therefore it is not an extraordinary departure.

The arrogance and boldness of the corporate sponsor are breathtaking. A giant food company, RJR Nabisco, succeeded in having commercials of one of its food products printed on a U.S. Department of Agriculture government publication. A cigarette company, Philip Morris, is a major patron of the arts, sponsoring important performances and shows while discreetly pushing its carcinogenic products. There seems to be no limit to the corporate incursion into the fabric of American life. A conservative wing of the Democratic party, holding a meeting to consider its strategy for the 1992 national elections, assembled "800 delegates from all 50 states, including members of Congress, state and local officials and lobbyists for major corporations . . . the corporate backers, which included A.T.&T., RJR Nabisco and Philip Morris Companies, contributed from $300 to $25,000 to underwrite the three-day event."[6]

The capability to fill social space with corporate consumer messages and imagery is provided by the instrumentation and processes now available to those who can afford to use them. The muchheralded deregulation of communications (and other industries), begun in the 1970s and carried forward vigorously into the 1980s, is best understood as the chosen means to boost corporate profitability.[7] The new information technologies, removed from social oversight and applied to business purposes, domestically and internationally, offer lower costs of communicating, increased flexibility of managerial decisionmaking—that is, shifting production and jobs from one site to another—and freedom from accountability.

It is difficult to exaggerate the importance of social accountability. In the preregulation era, the big companies may have had things much their own way in the communication sphere. Yet the principle of accountability was acknowledged and institutionalized in the actual existence of regulatory agencies, for example, the Federal Communications Commission (FCC).

---

6. Gwen Ifill, "Democratic Group in Dispute over Goals," *New York Times*, May 7, 1991.

7. Dan Schiller, *Telematics and Government* (Norwood, N.J.: Ablex Publishing Corp., 1982).

The FCC is still in place but its social mandate has been all but abandoned. Unrestrained mergers and consolidations, total disregard of the long-standing broadcasters' obligation to serve the public interest, privatization of communication satellite systems, and a raft of other measures have given the communication industry pretty much of a free hand in their domestic and international communication activities.

The national community, as a consequence of these developments, has been transformed into an orchestrated consumption ensemble, and corporate perspectives have been substituted for the political voice of the electorate. With the support of a series of Supreme Court rulings beginning in the late 1960s and continuing into the 1980s,[8] what is called "corporate speech" has received increasing legitimation as protected expression covered under the First Amendment.

With this judicial sanction in hand, corporate access to the media system has been further strengthened, strong as it was to begin with. Because of the way television has evolved in the United States, only the deepest pockets can afford to buy time on the home screen. The deepest pockets are those of the biggest businesses. What now prevails, therefore, is the rule of money complemented with the rule of law.

## Internationalization of the Corporate Perspective

The corporate voice now extends far beyond continental limits, just as corporate operations no longer are contained within national territory. Powerful U.S. companies have used their considerable resources, in collaboration with their overseas counterparts, to achieve internationally the operational arrangements they enjoy at home. Accordingly, deregulation that was launched in the United States in the late 1970s moved across the ocean and soon became the major thrust of Thatcherism in England. Now it thrives on the continent as well. The movement is especially strong in the communication sector.

---

8. See *First National Bank of Boston vs. Bellotti*, 1978.

Not so long ago, communication in Western Europe was the exclusive domain of the state. In recent years, in one country after another, for example, England, France, Italy, and Spain, transnational and national corporate interests have privatized and liberalized (commercialized) state broadcasting and telephone services.

In varying degree, similar transformations have been effected in Latin America, Asia, and Africa, under similar stimuli. Freedom for the corporate voice, and especially for its marketing message, has been the common development in most parts of the world. Hailed, not unexpectedly, by corporate-dominated channels of information as the triumph of freedom, the benefits from these changes have gone overwhelmingly to the big global corporate companies. The paramount benefit has been the formidable growth of capital's worldwide power and at the same time the weakening of its opposition—labor, organized as well as unorganized. Corporate media-cultural influence has been no less enhanced.

There is another striking change. Whereas in the 1960s it was accurate to refer to American media and cultural imperialism, in the 1990s the term and the concept have to be recast. Twenty-five years ago, U.S. media products flooded the world. Today, there is no diminution of American popular cultural exports. In fact, the dollar and physical volumes of the outputs of the U.S. cultural industries flowing into the international market are higher than they were then.

What has changed is that the producers of these products have become huge, integrated, cultural combines. These conglomerates, which include film, TV production, publishing, recording, theme parks, and even data banks, now offer what amounts to a total cultural environment. And they offer it to a global as well as a national market. Actually, the global market is increasingly considered in the decisions of the big cultural industry corporations. Consumerism is no longer an American phenomenon with some spillover effects. It flourishes and is rooted in Europe, Japan, and numerous other enclaves around the world.

In addition, the cultural conglomerates now are not exclusively American owned. German, Japanese, French, Brazilian, English, and other national capitals increasingly are invested in these transnational enterprises. For this reason, U.S. cultural styles and techniques—acknowledged as the most popular internationally—have themselves become transnationalized, serving the ideological and marketing needs of capital, wherever its origin. The *Los Angeles Times,* for example, reported, "Euro-TV turns to Hollywood. New commercial networks on the Continent recruit U.S. writers, producers and directors to develop and guide shows. A major goal is to sell the program in America."

This account offers a good example of what the current ingredients of American cultural influence in a Europe that has become an industrial rival are:

> Paris and other European capitals have been invaded by American producers, directors, designers and writers hired by the Europeans to help them shape the new market along time-tested lines. . . . *Americans know how to capture and hold an audience.* This business can benefit from the tricks invented in Hollywood. . . . French writers are taught how to structure plots in the American way, which means inserting mini-climaxes before commercial breaks. . . . When the blockbuster European television soap opera "Riviera" debuted in France, it had a decidedly American feel to it— the plot, pacing and dialogue could have been lifted directly from an episode of "Dallas" or "Santa Barbara."[9]

Half a world away, in the same vein, a Brazilian researcher noted that Brazilian television programming is "the creolization of U.S. cultural products. It is the spiced up Third World copy of Western values, norms, patterns of behavior and models of social relations." His findings, no different from what one would conclude in the United States or Europe, is that "the overwhelming majority of Brazilian soaps have the same purpose as their U.S. counterparts, i.e. sell products."[10]

Selling products is, above all, the role of popular culture in an age of transnational corporate market domination. "Local" spon-

---

9. Rone Tempest, "Euro-TV Turns in to Hollywood," *Los Angeles Times,* July 11, 1991, page A-1. Italics added.

10. O. S. Oliveira, "Brazilian Soaps Outshine Hollywood: Is Cultural Imperialism Fading Out?" Paper presented at the meetings of the Deutsche Gesellschaft fur Semiotik, Internationaler Kongress, Universitat Passau. October 1990.

sors for Brazilian programming have familiar names: Coca-Cola, Volkswagen, General Motors, Levi's, and so on.

What these accounts confirm is the global advance of consumerism, promoted and spearheaded by the transnational corporate system, with its cultural-media sector at the leading edge. Corporate capital, insistent on full access to the informational system to propagate its commercial and ideological messages, has demanded, and achieved, the privatization of the communication sector (telephone, television, satellite, and computer) in one country after another. In France, for example, "television ad[vertising] spending tripled from 1985 to 1990." At the same time, French commercial interests still are not satisfied because, they say, "the biggest problem may be that the Government has tended to view television not as a business, but as a cultural asset."[11] It is clear that this archaic view needs to be overcome if France is to be truly and fully culturally conglomeratized.

This problem of France's has never existed in the United States. Radio and television, from their inception, were regarded, and used, as profit-making opportunities, despite some dissenting voices. Still, Europe seems to be overcoming its "problem." In 1990, though European advertising revenues had already reached an unprecedented peak, an American consultant company, Booz-Allen & Hamilton, Inc., bullishly reported: "On a per-household basis, four times as much is spent in the United States on television advertising as in Europe." The European potential, therefore, is "enormous."[12]

What has been happening over the past twenty-five years, the past ten especially, has been a phenomenal expansion of transnational capitalism and its seizure of global communication facilities—nationally based, to be sure—for its marketing and operational and opinion-controlling purposes. American cultural imperialism is not dead, but it no longer adequately describes the global cultural condition. Today it is more useful to view transna-

11. Jacques Neher, "The Battle over French TV: Profits vs Culture," *New York Times,* August 12, 1991, page C-8.

12. Leigh Bruce, "Europeans Tune In to a New Wave of Television," *International Herald Tribune,* June 11, 1991, page 1.

tional corporate culture as the central force, with a continuing heavy flavor of U.S. media know-how, derived from long experience with marketing and entertainment skills and practices.

The greatly expanded corporate activity and influence in the international arena has been affected by two other, closely related major developments: the collapse of the Soviet system and the debilitation of the less industrialized world. In both cases, a leading role was, and continues to be played by, transnational corporate media and cultural forces.

## New Frontiers for the Sales Message: The Former Soviet Sphere

What was once the Soviet Union and its Eastern European sphere of control has moved en masse out of state-managed economic systems to varied, if embryonic, capitalist forms. China appears to be moving along the same road though it is still tightly managed politically.

Although North Korea, Vietnam, and Cuba continue—for the time being—as state socialist societies, what had not so long ago been a seemingly strong and rival *global* system to capitalism has largely disintegrated. The central geopolitical feature of the post–World War II era, the U.S.(Western)-Soviet antagonism, no longer exists. A fundamental driving force for half a century in American communication policy and practice has disappeared. So too, the support for research and development of new information technologies has lost much of its earlier justification.

Each day brings fresh evidence of the triumph of American commercial culture and media values in what was once the Soviet realm. Actually this "victory" has been long under way and it is not an exaggeration to regard the American consumerist message as having had a significant role in undermining the former state socialist near-global sector. It succeeded beyond the wildest dreams of American cold war information warriors. Whatever might have been unimaginable a few years ago now is commonplace. The extent of the U.S. media-cultural conquest of Eastern Europe and Russia, at least in the immediate post-Communist period, appears to be unconditional. Consider the following:

- In July 1991, a Russian-language edition of *Reader's Digest* was introduced, with an initial circulation of 50,000. The first edition had a profile of General H. Norman Schwartzkopf, the U.S. commanding general in the Gulf War.[13] *Reader's Digest* has been a unique and successful organ of reactionary ideology in the United States since the 1920s.
- In September 1991, it was reported that "most of the fare at the movie theaters is now American . . . more than 20 American films are now showing in the city [Moscow] . . . [and] the brooding statue of Pushkin is bathed in the neon glow of a Coca-Cola billboard and the lights from the world's largest McDonald's restaurant."[14]
- Also in September 1991, a one-day rock concert featuring popular Western groups was held in Moscow, sponsored by U.S. media conglomerate Time-Warner. Executives of the company described the concert as a "celebration of democracy and freedom." One undeniable freedom was the opportunity it gave Time-Warner to make a film of the event. The company intended to screen the program on HBO (Home Box Office), one of its subsidiary cable channels.[15]
- In early 1992, the president of Warner Brothers International Television Distribution announced a project to screen American prime-time TV programs for Russian television viewers. He predicted that "this [Russia] is a market that is not yet a consumer society, but it will be. . . . We will eventually be able to put American products on the air. This is an investment for the future."[16] To cap off these developments, in early 1992 Mikhail Gorbachev became a columnist for the *New York Times,* writing about his friendship with the pope. At the same time, the weekly

---

13. *New York Times,* July 24, 1991, page C-17.

14. William E. Schmidt, "The Neon Revolution Lights Up Pushkin's World," *New York Times,* September 27, 1991.

15. William Schmidt, "Heavy-Metal Group Shakes Moscow," *New York Times,* September 29, 1991, page 3.

16. Bernard Weinraub, "Ready for Prime Time in Moscow," *New York Times,* January 22, 1992, page C-1.

"News in Review" section of the *Times* announced that it would be published weekly in Moscow.[17]

Just to reassure those who fear that Eastern Europe is being ignored by transnational corporate advertisers, it was reported in fall 1991 that streetcars in Prague will begin to "wear the colours of Marlboro and Camel cigarette packets. Every inch of the trams' surfaces are being painted at the moment to achieve what will resemble huge metal cigarette packets on wheels."[18] This foreign advertising takes place at a time when cigarette companies in the United States—the very center of consumer advertising—are on the defensive before rising criticism, including that of the surgeon general and the American Medical Association.[19]

The collapse of state socialism in the East strengthens the transnational corporate media machine in more ways than one. Most directly, it offers a new and potentially vast market for media products and services. American and Western European films, TV programs, recordings, fashions, advertising, and public relations can expect huge new outlets—if not immediately, then in the years ahead. This market will be a welcome stimulus to an already export-oriented sector.

The qualities and characteristics of American film, TV, and music (about which more will be said later) make these pop cultural products almost irresistible to audiences in the former managed societies as well as to those elsewhere.

The enthusiastic reception of American cultural product spills over into the informational and intellectual areas. Where there had once been a sharply critical view of Western standards and values, from news reportage to media content, today there is an undiscriminating willingness, even eagerness, to accept Western and U.S. perspectives in culture, law, and economics. Whatever social cost this may eventually impose on these societies, in the United States

---

17. *New York Times,* February 17, 1992, page C-5.

18. Ariane Genillard, "Freedom Brings a Free-For-All," *Financial Times,* September 4, 1991, page 8.

19. "Top Health Official Demands Abolition of 'Joe Camel' Ads," *New York Times,* March 10, 1992, page 1.

it further strengthens an already self-satisfied and status quo out-look of the dominant corporate-managerial strata. These are the perspectives that permeate the national opinion-making machinery.

Domestic criticism of the corporate media-cultural apparatus and its product, somewhat more active in the post–Gulf War period, has hardly represented a threat to established power. Such criticism is further burdened at this time by the naive enthusiasm and historical amnesia now evident in Eastern Europe and Russia and the other former Soviet Republics, which allow them to absorb, without reflection, American media product, information, and general ideology. There is a counter side to this. The end of the "evil empire" makes it more difficult for U.S. domestic reaction-aries to denounce each and every social initiative as subversive.

Additionally, the end of the "Soviet threat" (President Bush proclaimed in his January 1992 state-of-the-union message that "we won the cold war") presents some problems to the official American communication voice. And, while U.S. and Western commercial media giants move to stake out markets and invest-ments in the once inaccessible regions, the fate of official American governmental information services grows more problematic. With-out a recognizable "enemy," the function of "The Voice of Amer-ica," "Radio Liberty," and "Radio Free Europe" becomes uncer-tain. A strong imagination now must be called upon to justify the maintenance of these activities.

"Radio Free Europe," for example, argues for its future by "broadcasting regular primers on democracy and free market economics." Another suggestion is for these broadcasters to under-take "a Marshall Plan of the Mind," a variety of instructional programming for Eastern Europe.[20]

More ambitious still in the effort to maintain the facilities and jobs of the cold war broadcasters is a proposal to create a "Radio Free China." Still in the exploratory stage, the installation would "beam news to China about itself" or at least what its directors selected to emphasize about that country.[21]

---

20. William E. Schmidt, "After the Cold War, Different Times, Different Sta-tions," *New York Times*, November 24, 1991, page E-5.

21. George Lardner, Jr., "Create 'Radio Free China,' Hill Is Urged," *Washington Post*, November 22, 1991, page A-24.

Actually, the contribution these governmental and CIA propaganda services made to the demise of communism is uncertain at best. The appraisals of their effectiveness have been largely their own. More telling is one commentary that recommends the elimination of these services to save money and that notes that "Ted Turner is doing them better, anyway."[22]

The effectiveness of the commercial media is another story. In performing their daily tasks in a seemingly objective and nonideological manner, their impact on audiences everywhere has been stunning. In the post–cold war era, blanketing former socialist audiences with programming designed for market objectives can be expected to be a large and growing field of endeavor.

## The Less Industrialized World in the Post–Cold War Era

If the demise of a once powerful oppositional pole to American cultural domination has left less space inside the United States for alternative perspectives (though it has also removed the convenient battering ram of anticommunism), the effect on most of the nations in Africa, Asia, and Latin America is a near disaster. In 1969, when *Mass Communications and American Empire* first appeared, Third World opposition to American cultural (and economic) domination was at its zenith. This was a time, it may be recalled, that the impositions of colonialism were still fresh in the minds and experiences of the leaders and the peoples on these continents. They were still close to their liberation struggles. For several of these nations—Algeria, Angola, Cuba, and others—the military struggle for independence had just concluded. Their leaders had been tested in the fiercest battles.

These countries and their leadership were in no mood to accept renewed subservience, be it economic, political, or cultural. Their passion and their thinking came from Franz Fanon, Amilcar Cabral, Che Guevara, Mao Tse Tung, and Nkrumah. Additionally, class divisions that existed even at that early time of independence had not yet become rigid. The class interest was not, in many cases,

22. John W. Sewell, "Where to Find a Quick $6 Billion," *Los Angeles Times,* January 21, 1992, page B-7.

strong enough to override the powerful expectations for economic improvement and equality and sovereign control of domestic resources that the liberation struggles had generated.

It was in this relatively turbulent time of social activism, at home and abroad, that the Non-Aligned Movement of African, Asian, and Latin American nations pressed its demands for a restructured global economy (the call for a New International Economic Order) and a democratized and participatory informational environment (the New International Information Order).

For a brief moment, also, the United Nations Educational, Scientific, and Cultural Organization (UNESCO), safely under American control since its founding in 1946, became a forum for the views of its new and militant Third World constituency.[23] For most of the 1970s, meetings and resolutions of UNESCO championed the claims for changing the global economic and cultural condition to the better advantage of the ex-colonial and the longtime exploited Latin American states. At the same time, the Non-Aligned Movement pressed its even stronger views in forums outside UNESCO and helped to keep the issues high on the international agenda.

The culmination of the Third World effort to restructure the global information condition was realized in the creation by UNESCO in 1978 of the McBride Commission for the Study of Communication Problems. The commission's report, *Many Voices, One World* (1980), recapitulated many of the themes that had occupied the discussions from the late 1960s on: the power of the transnational media conglomerates; the one-way flow of media product and information from New York, Los Angeles, Washington, London, and Paris to the rest of the world; the excessive commercialization of that flow; and the need for protection of national cultural sovereignty in the face of the cultural avalanche from the West.

At the time, the McBride Commission (named after its chairman, Sean McBride, legendary fighter for Irish independence) served to

---

23. William Preston, Jr., Edward Herman, and Herbert I. Schiller, *Hope and Folly: The U.S. and UNESCO, 1945–1985* (Minneapolis: University of Minnesota Press, 1989); see also Herbert I. Schiller, *Communication and Cultural Domination* (Armonk, N.Y.: M. E. Sharpe, 1976).

legitimize the numerous information-media grievances of the Non-Aligned nations and to elevate these issues to a higher level of international attention—and, it was hoped, to achieve corrective action.

In retrospect, the formation of the commission at the high point of Third World opposition to the prevailing global informational condition was an all-too-familiar stratagem of the Western leadership, though it seemingly opposed even that measure at the time. Still, the creation of a group *to study* a problem has been a time-tested technique to defer action.

Although the United States participated only grudgingly in the McBride Commission's work and sharply criticized its practices and findings, it benefited from the commission's drawn-out hearings. It offered the West a few years' breathing space in which to prepare a many-sided counterattack against UNESCO and the militantly oppositional nations in particular. In the immediate succeeding years, Washington and its few but powerful allies used military force, political maneuvering, Western public opinion management, and denial of desperately needed economic assistance against the Third World's essentially rhetorical efforts to change the terms of its economic and cultural existence.

## The U.S. and Western Attack on the New International Information Order and Its Supporters

No nation endeavoring to create an alternative social order was left alone by the military. Threats of armed force created impossible conditions for whatever limited social experimentation was attempted. The threats often materialized into actions. Oppositional forces in the nations that initially had rejected the Western market system were given arms and financial support by shadowy groups connected to the highest political levels in Washington. In this manner, Angola and Mozambique were turned into wastelands by armed groups receiving American support. Vietnam and Cambodia were invaded by U.S. troops. Years of torching and bombing these nations left behind vast physical and human wreckage. Cuba was invaded by U.S.-supplied exiles at the Bay of Pigs. After repulsing that onslaught, the country has been embargoed and blockaded by Washington fiat for thirty years. The triumphant

Sandinistas in Nicaragua soon found themselves struggling against an army, the Contras, organized and supplied by a right-wing, illegal inner clique at the center of the Reagan administration. Other actions in other countries were no less destructive and effective in reducing the possibility of alternative social systems to the transnational corporate world.

How this global counterrevolutionary assault was presented and justified to the American public and the world at large exemplifies the definitional control that has been exercised in the past half century by the American informational machine.

Not as observable, but equally damaging, to the Third World nations that did not pay their proper respects to capital was the economic leverage employed against them. In line with the treatment meted out to the former Soviet Union from the time of its Bolshevik Revolution in 1917, Latin American, African, and Asian countries that tried to extricate themselves from the world market system were cut off from critically needed loans and capital assistance that only the main Western financial centers could supply.

In 1971, for example, the democratic socialist government (of Salvador Allende) in Chile requested a tiny sum from the international financial agencies to allow it to organize its economy. The request was denied. Two years later, Allende was killed and Chile's government was ousted in a coup that had the sanction, if not the active support, of the U.S. government.

It is not possible to judge what might have been achieved if aid had been forthcoming to the many nations that sought assistance *without* conditions attached to it. What *is* evident was the unhesitating willingness of Western leaders to allow the nations that they viewed as recalcitrant to fall into ever greater misery and improverishment as victims of economic embargo or military attack.

In the media-informational sphere, American actions against the Third World were no less harsh and uncompromising. Here the effort was directed at public opinion in the Western countries. It aimed to turn Western views against the one international forum where communications and cultural issues were aired—UNESCO.

A massive campaign was launched in the dominant Western media, mostly the press, because the issue was difficult to put into a television format. It aimed to convince public opinion that the demands of the Non-Aligned nations for information equality and the protection of their national cultural sovereignty from Western commercialized media products were indistinguishable from a program of totalitarianism. State efforts to safeguard national film, television, and publishing industries were portrayed as acts of censorship. State support for young and beleaguered cultural-informational activities was, according to the Western interpretation, a denial of freedom.

Actually, this assertion was an extension of the argument used domestically to deregulate the information sector. Government oversight of broadcasting and telecommunications was successfully attacked on the grounds that such oversight denied or limited freedom.

The unanimity of the Western media in emphasizing these themes was remarkable. Ironically, it confirmed the accusations against the Western informational system. It was an exemplary lesson in informational control in that it succeeded in making Americans believe that most countries in the world wanted one or another form of censorship. The only conclusion possible was how fortunate we as Americans were with our media institutions. The never-missed connection was that Americans were blessed with a "free" press. The main constituent of a free press, it was unqualifiedly asserted, is that it is privately owned. Without private ownership of a newspaper, radio or television station, or other medium, so this reasoning goes, there is no freedom of press.

This proposition has served as the centerpiece of the U.S. claim to be the model of a free society with a free press. It has been used, as well, to belittle and denigrate other arrangements that do not give precedence to private ownership of the media. Media owners and mangers have no uncertainty about the infallibility of this view and have no hesitation whatsoever about retailing it in their privately owned outlets. No conflict of interest is perceived.

To inculcate Americans with this view is one thing. It is another to gain acceptance for such a definition in a diverse world. Yet this in fact was the goal of the American-led attack on UNESCO, beginning in the late 1970s and rising to the level of a crusade after the election of the Reagan administration in 1980.

UNESCO, as the acknowledged forum for communication and cultural questions, was an ideal target to those determined to maintain the status quo ante in information and media matters and the structural arrangements that underlay them. UNESCO was the weakest of the UN-associated organizations and consequently the most vulnerable to the pressure of its single largest financial contributor.

After a softening-up period lasting several years—in which the Western media never lost an opportunity to focus on some alleged impropriety in UNESCO's practice (the most egregious of which was the false assertion that the organization had called for the licensing of journalists)—Western public opinion was prepared for the coup de grace against the organization. This came with the decision of the United States to withdraw from UNESCO, announced at the end of 1983 and implemented in 1984.

With this move, the United States deprived UNESCO of a significant share of its budget, severely restricting its activities. At the same time, it served as a warning to others—international organizations, national groups, and individuals—to fall into line or suffer economic, or possibly military, reprisal. All the while, this unilateral and coercive action was presented by the Western media as a principled defense of free speech.[24]

The attack on UNESCO may be understood as the generalized equivalent of the aggressions against individual Third World countries whose policies did not secure U.S. approval. In the short run, up to this date at least, American efforts have been successful. UNESCO, cowed and enfeebled, has become fully compliant with Western media interests. Its former director-general, Amadou M'Bow, was replaced by a conservative West European. M'Bow, a Senegalese, was regarded as much too Third World oriented. The organization has eliminated all references to the New International Information Order in its program and planning reports. The major communication issues of the age have been left off its agenda. The "free flow of information," the code expression for the unrestricted global movement of the products and services of the Western media conglomerates, has been enshrined once again in UNESCO's vocabulary and directives.

Many of the groups and individuals in the United States who had been vociferous in demanding that UNESCO be punished for its

24. Ibid.

alleged transgression, that is, its politicization—allowing the views of its Third World membership to be expressed—are now placated. Some, in fact, urge the United States to return to the organization. This return has not yet occurred because the American Right has been particularly obsessed with UNESCO. The Bush administration feels that this is a small price to pay for keeping a significant slice of its political support quiet. And so, the U.S. government continues to withhold sizable funds from the parent UN as well as remaining outside UNESCO. The U.S. delinquency in its dues to the UN in November 1991 amounted to nearly half a billion dollars.[25] Cynically, Washington is satisfied that its policy is working. It pays no dues but gets its way in the organization notwithstanding. Replying to an inquiry on whether the United States intended to return to UNESCO, a State Department official noted: "The price of admission is $50 million a year, and that is a lot in this day and age. . . . We have not found it a significant disadvantage to be outside UNESCO."[26]

American unilateralism and the hostility to international organizations that characterized the Reagan years have by no means disappeared. However, international institutions, the UN in particular, have provided indispensable diplomatic and public opinion-making utility to American policy, especially in the Gulf War period. The Persian Gulf "coalition," which the Bush administration rapidly put together with bribes and some arm-twisting, provided an internationalist veneer for an aggressive war that otherwise could not have been waged.[27]

For the time being, the Third World challenge in the informational and economic sphere to Western and American dominance has been repulsed. Indeed, the capitulation of African, Asian, and Latin American nations—with few exceptions—to the global market economy and its strictures has been stunning. A *New York Times* report rhapsodized about the change. It noted that "countries that

25. Paul Lewis, "U.N. Asks Billion for Peacekeeper Fund," *New York Times*, November 25, 1991, page A-3.

26. Roger Cohen, "UNESCO Comes Knocking, Seeking U.S. Help," *New York Times*, March 1, 1992.

27. Richard Falk, "Twisting the UN Charter to United States' Ends," in *Triumph of the Image*, Mowlana, Gerbner, and Schiller, eds.

were once proud economic nationalists are now attempting to forge closer ties with the rest of the world."

Why this is happening is explained in these words: "In many developing nations there is a new sense of realism, much of it inspired by the hardships of the last decade."[28] Not mentioned in this account is *who* imposed these hardships and what some of the hardships were. Armed interventions and financial strangulation are strong motivators.

No less enthusiastic is another report of developments in the Third World. *Business Week* headlines a "Global Rush to Privatize" and states that "From Tierra del Fuego to the Rio Grande, and from Eastern Germany to the [former] Soviet Union, the sale of the century is off and running . . . privatization will be a main topic of discussion as bankers from around the globe get to Bangkok for the annual meetings of the World Bank and The International Monetary Fund (on October 15–17, 1991)."[29]

The communications infrastructure of most of the Third World has been privatized and turned over either to transnational corporations or to national collaborators with transnational capital. The elimination of what was once the Soviet oppositional pole to Western (and now also Japanese transnationalist) capitalism has left Africans, Asians, and Latin Americans almost defenseless against the demands and depredations of global predators. Samir Amin expects revolutionary upheavals in these areas sooner or later.[30] The accent should be on the "later." The combination of financial and informational, not to overlook military, power employed to maintain the current global order will not be easily overcome.

Meetings of the Non-Aligned nations were rarely reported when the influence of the movement was at its peak. If mentioned at all in the Western press, such gatherings received at most a few lines, despite the attendance of scores of the leading political and cultural

28. Sylvia Nasar, "Third World Embracing Reforms to Encourage Economic Growth," *New York Times,* July 8, 1991, page A-1.

29. "The Global Rush to Privatize," *Business Week,* October 21, 1991, pages 49–56.

30. Samir Amin, "The Future of Socialism," *Monthly Review* 42, no. 3 (1990):10–29.

leaders of the Third World. Contrast this press treatment with the generally full coverage accorded a routine get-together of a handful of Western political figures.

In 1992, with Non-Aligned activities at low ebb, the *Los Angeles Times* reported on the movement's problems and noted, with a certain satisfaction, "that the ascendance of America and its allies has presented some hard options." It quoted the Algerian foreign minister's rueful comment: "It is visible to the naked eye. Their [U.S. and Western] superiority is a fact."[31]

## Peering Ahead

At the end of January 1992, President George Bush presented his annual state-of-the-union address to the U.S. Congress. Among other points, he flatly asserted: "By the grace of God, America won the cold war."[32]

Although this triumphant assertion may be accurate, the prognosis for American power in the twenty-first century is hardly favorable. Although considerable military strength still remains— at the end of 1991 "the United States had 375 foreign military installations staffed by more than 500,000 servicemen and women worldwide"[33]—by itself it is not enough to keep intact the global domain that not too long ago was unquestionably under American domination.

The vast Russian expanse, the preponderant part of which in an earlier period was the Soviet Union, for example, should now be a prime target of U.S. corporate attention. Instead, domestic crisis has prevented the initiatives that could snap up a territory of almost infinite resource wealth. This is not to say that U.S. corporations, not least of which the oil giants, are totally ignoring the economic bounty that can be had by quick and decisive action. But the scale of the takeover remains remarkably modest.

---

31. Nick B. Williams, Jr., "Nonaligned Alliance Runs on Empty," *Los Angeles Times*, February 11, 1992, page H-2.

32. *New York Times*, January 29, 1992, page A-14.

33. Joel Brinkley, "U.S. Looking for New Path as Superpower Conflict Ends," *New York Times*, February 2, 1992, page 1A.

Former president Richard M. Nixon, for his own reasons, chided the Bush administration on this matter, arguing that the United States is missing a historic opportunity. In Nixon's semantics, the United States is not sufficiently supporting Russian democracy.[34]

President Bush, in a candid admission—rare in itself—revealed the source of the difficulty: "We're living in a time of constrained resources. There isn't a lot of money around. We are spending too much as it already is. So to do the things I would really like to do, I don't have a blank check for that."[35]

Is the decline of American economic power responsible? Bush's acknowledgment may be one of the few instances where the government is telling the truth, albeit reluctantly. Still, it is useful to remember that the American economic machine remains a mighty engine, for all its faltering. A near-$6 trillion economy cannot fail to be a tremendous force in the world system. And it is. Yet it is also a declining force.

Two of the factors that bear on this condition rely heavily on informational and definitional control. One, surprisingly enough, is still regarded as an element of systemic strength. It is the unqualified insistence of American managers and owners on uninhibited freedom of decisionmaking. This condition is given precedence over all other considerations, whether national, social, or individual. It is undeniable that this insistence can sometimes promote energetic economic growth. It was certainly a successful formula—with considerable social costs—when the United States was a rising power in the late nineteenth century and again when it was practically the only power on the international stage at the end of World War II. It is a far less serviceable philosophy and practice when other, increasingly formidable industrial competitors are pressing for enlarged shares of the global marketplace. Yet this perspective continues to dominate American political discourse.

The second factor, closely related to the first, is the doctrine of self-advantage as the mainspring of individual behavior. With these

34. Thomas L. Friedman, "Nixon Scoffs at Level of Support for Russian Democracy by Bush," *New York Times*, March 10, 1992, page 1.

35. Thomas L. Friedman, "Bush Cites Limits on Aid to Russia," *New York Times*, March 12, 1992, page A-1.

two principles deeply embedded in U.S. national consciousness, American capitalism has achieved long-standing ideological mastery of the citizenry and global primacy. But now these powerful behavioral organizers threaten to lead to systemic dysfunctionality because they block the fundamental institutional restructuring that many thoughtful observers of the American scene consider obligatory.[36] That is, this restructuring is obligatory if the unraveling of the social and economic fabric is to be halted, much less reversed.

Additionally, the possibility of undertaking the social renovation that is required is thwarted at the outset by the one sector of the economy that is not in decline and is more robust than ever: the media-cultural sphere. Perhaps its vigor is overstated because there are more than enough problems facing media enterprises today, especially the press and television. Some of these problems will be considered. But, overall, the cultural industries in the United States cannot be compared with Detroit and the automobile industry.

The makers of film, television programming, and recorded music are improving continuously their already astonishing capability to attract and compel viewers and listeners. A whole new subindustry has developed: that of special effects, which creates new sounds, new imagery, new emotional and visceral shocks. It has become an integral part of the cultural industry because it serves a crucial imperative of the overall economy as it is presently structured.

The greatly increased use of special effects is a function of the insatiable needs of the marketing imperative. Because all media are employed primarily to catch and hold audiences' attention for the sales message, there is an unrelenting frenzy to produce new, different, and overpowering sensory stimuli. The special effects industry performs its commercial assignment brilliantly. Its superlative work assists in no small measure in maintaining and perpetuating the prevailing ideological framework. The special effects industry contributes, in its own way, to forestalling a desperately needed national dialogue about the directions of the economy and the society. It does so by shattering attention, diverting audiences, and reducing rational thought. None of this, it needs be said, is done deliberately. Marketing develops and uses these techniques to

---

36. See, for example, Jacques Attali, *Millenium* (New York: Random House, 1991).

sell goods. The accompanying effects are seen, if they are considered at all, as the characteristics of postmodernity.

This condition is not limited to the domestic sphere. The international flow of American films, TV programs, music, and other cultural material succeeds in raising the stimulation level wherever these products are seen and heard and, at the same time, creates the expectation and the demand for similar qualities in local media-cultural production. Thus, American pop culture, which once sought markets overseas by "dumping" product at lower-than-cost prices, has added a new ingredient to its wares—a wide-ranging assortment of special effects stimuli.

Yet special effects are costly to produce and the prices of American-made films and TV programs are sky-high in comparison with national outputs elsewhere. Accordingly, the foreign market for U.S. media product is no longer, as it once was, a windfall benefit. In the 1990s, the external market has become essential in order to help finance the out-of-sight production costs.

What follows from this is a U.S. media-cultural sector that continues to be the main, though no longer exclusive, source of product for the international market, with the resulting impact on values and behavior of audiences everywhere. Because the overriding objective of this product is to publicize, promote, and sell consumerism, it is the ideal instrument of the transnational business system. Its American origins account for its style and production values. Yet its utilization is no longer limited to U.S. transnational corporations. It is now the *generic* material for all transnationals, whatever their ownership base. Sony, Siemens, Philips, Nestle (Japanese, German, Dutch, and Swiss companies) alike rely on TV to bring their marketing messages to audiences around the world.

A curious situation now exists. In addition to entire U.S. industries being practically eliminated by foreign competition, American-owned media are being acquired by foreign industrial rivals. Philips, the giant Dutch transnational, for example, bought an interest in Whittle Communications, a Time-Warner subsidiary. Another chunk of Time-Warner went to Toshiba and Itoh, big Japanese electronic companies. Similar acquisitions have resulted in the buying up or out of major American film studios, book publishers, and advertising agencies.

For the most part, these companies that were acquired were not ailing. They were vigorous and successful transnational enterprises. The buy-outs reflect the weakening of the general American economy, not its media-cultural component. In real terms, this sector has been doing better than ever. Its products are in wide global demand, and its management and creative talent have been equally successful.

When the Japanese electronics conglomerate Matsushita bought out one of the Hollywood "majors," MCA/Universal, in 1990, it made a special point of retaining American creative and managerial talent. Sony, in its earlier acquisition of U.S. media properties, acted similarly. The Japanese, German, and other purchasers of American cultural industries recognize talent and ability. They also can afford to pay for it.

What was once uncontested worldwide American media domination, therefore, has become increasingly transnationalized in its ownership. The new directors, however, retain the American quality and form of the media product because they have demonstrated their extraordinary ability to do the job—to grab the attention and stir the emotions of the audiences.

This ability is duly noted by Hollywood. A *Los Angeles Times* reporter offered this appraisal of current American media exports:

> Although America's political power may be eroding, there is no sign of any erosion of the cultural impact of Americana throughout Europe. "Generally speaking, America's [cultural] influence in France has never been stronger than it is today," said D. Moisi [codirector of the French Institute of International Relations in Paris]. "Burger King has been accepted as a part of our culture." The picture is similar elsewhere. German mail-order houses advertise a variety of American goods from Los Angeles Lakers rooters caps to star-spangled children's lunch boxes. Second German Television (ZDF) program buyer Manfred Schuetze says the number of U.S. TV productions is down, but the level of films remain at about 75% American. And the only German rock band with global impact—the Scorpions—performs strictly American hard'n'heavy rock in English.[37]

_____

37. Tyler Marshall, "Bye-Bye American Pie—and Troops and Power," *Los Angeles Times,* February 4, 1992, page H-2.

Yet there is more strength in the American cultural-informational position worldwide than mere pyrotechnics of production. It is supported by the powerful role of language itself, for the language of international discourse today is English. One scholar puts it this way: "English seems to have entered the stage of a self-expanding global lingua franca, connecting all supranational and many national languages in a network of communicative interdependence that constitutes the emerging world language system."[38]

Many factors account for this phenomenon but the influence it confers on Anglo-U.S. informational and image outputs is immeasurable. For example, a study conducted of a large sample of non-U.S. mathematics journals revealed that of 32,000 articles published during 1970, 1975, 1980, and 1985 "the proportion of English articles increased in dominance from 52% of all articles examined in 1970 to 65% in 1985. At the same time, the proportion of French articles decreased from 17% to 10%, the German from 13% to 7%. Russian increased from 13% to 16%." (This increase took place *before* perestroika. It is hard to imagine that it has not fallen since then.)

In France, more striking still (considering the country), three journals published in 1989 by the Institut Pasteur in Paris decided to change the journal titles from French to English. It was, as one writer put it, "the loss of language."[39]

Further evidence of the same trend comes from Eugene Garfield, president of the Institute for Scientific Information. In 1983 he noted the astonishing preponderance of scientific articles, published in 122 Third World countries, that were written in English. The percentage increased from 85 in 1973 to 92 in 1981.[40]

The ascendancy of English as the world's scientific language is not the outcome of a universal recognition of the language's supe-

38. Abram de Swaan, "Notes on the Emerging Global Language System: Regional, National and Supranational," *Media, Culture and Society* 13 (1991), pages 309–323.

39. Virgil Diodato, "The Use of English Language in Non-U.S. Science Journals: A Case Study of Mathematics Publications, 1970–1985," *Library and Information Science Research* 12 (October–December 1990), New York.

40. Eugene Garfield, "Mapping Science in the Third World," *Science and Public Policy* 10, no. 3 (June 1983).

riority or of its neutrality. It has occurred mainly as a consequence of the astronomical expenditures over the post–World War II years by the U.S. military, channeled through the scientific establishment, to extend American power in military, scientific, and financial spheres. (It also is the beneficiary of an earlier century of British imperial domination, which transported English to Asia, Africa, and the Middle East).

It is little wonder that a good part of the scientific literature of recent decades is published in English. The vast outpouring of the findings of military-funded American research between 1945 and 1990 is the source of American scientific data bases that are now accessed globally. One writer summed it up this way: "By some measures, the cold war was the best thing that ever happened to research. . . . Since 1955, the Government has spent more than $1 trillion on research and development of nuclear arms and other weaponry."[41]

The use of English worldwide has been abetted further by American media product that has swept over the world in this same period—and that continues to flow massively.

It is now incumbent on professional, governmental, scientific, and business strata around the world to develop proficiency in English in order to follow scientific, administrative, military, and cultural developments *and to be included in the dialogue, even if in a subordinate role.*

In no way, however, does this development represent a movement to a participatory, shared, and disinterestedly beneficial world common language. Given the economic and political disparities that now exist inside and between nations, English becomes instead the channel through which hegemonic patterns, perspectives, and values are transmitted, passing mostly unremarked to receptor nations, groups, and individuals.[42]

Further extending this basic definitional privilege conferred by the primacy of language on world business, intellectual, and cul-

41. William J. Broad, "Swords Have Been Sheathed But Plowshares Lack Design," *New York Times,* February 5, 1992, page A-1.

42. Herbert I. Schiller, "La Langue de la Science et la science de la domination," *Enjeux,* edition AFNOR, no. 40 (October 1983), Paris, pages 39–41.

tural affairs is the rapid development of computerization in the past twenty years. The creation of electronic data bases that assemble vast data holdings in scores of special fields and disciplines—including medical, biological, chemical, humanities, and social science—are possible only with computerization.

But in addition to the rich range of data now available, *at a price*, voluminously and instantaneously, are less visible but no less important characteristics of much of the data. These are the *selectors* that are used to organize, categorize, and present the data. Inevitably these are conditioned by the dominant social practices and beliefs, conscious or not, of those who have made the generally costly effort to do the assembling. The central assumptions of the selectors and data organizers, their views of what is and what is not important, and their choices in identifying, organizing, and ranking material are always present but rarely fully explicit.

This is not to claim that data bases, in general, are unreliable or deliberately manipulated. It is to suggest instead that the creation and character of data bases are affected, sometimes more, sometimes less, by underlying structural forces whose influence is generally unacknowledged.

The amount of weight that should be given to this elusive factor in assessing the question of information control in the electronic age is clearly a tricky matter. But it would be foolhardy to brush it aside as inconsequential. In any case, in 1990 the United States produced 70 percent of the world's total of data bases (3,982 from the United States and 1,707 from the rest of the world).[43]

The revenues to U.S. owners of these bases, from sales of information services abroad, amounted to $9 billion in 1990. These revenues are expected to increase at an annual growth rate of 20 percent through 1995[44]—again, hardly the mark of a declining industry or a receding global influence.

It is interesting that despite Japan's development into an economic powerhouse in recent decades, "only 226 Japanese databases

---

43. Martha E. Williams, "The State of Databases Today: 1991," *Computer-Readable Data Bases: A Directory and Data Sourcebook,* 7th ed. (New York: Gale Research, 1991), page ix.

44. *Information and Interactive Services Report, 1991* (Washington, D.C.: BRP Publications, October 11, 1991), page 2.

were available overseas in 1991—surprisingly few given the international interest in Japan. . . . *The main reason for this imbalance is language.* While most Japanese read English to some extent, very few people outside Japan read Japanese. Therefore data bases must be translated to be commercially viable, an initial investment few Japanese database producers have been willing to risk."[45]

These kinds of statistics—production and ownership of data bases—change substantially from year to year. This is especially true in the relatively new and rapidly growing sector of electronic information generation and dissemination. All the same, U.S. information companies now derive a hefty return from their strong international position in the data-holding and -management sphere and it is not likely to diminish in the next several years. The expanding use of English may well improve further the current American information-supplying edge.

Perhaps of greater and longer-lasting significance, the *social influence* that inheres in providing information and data that have been, wittingly or not, molded in the likeness of prevailing American (or transnational?) capitalism is incalculable. Because more than two-thirds (68 percent) of all U.S. data bases in 1990 were commercially or industrially produced, these holdings can probably be regarded as containing a transnational as much as an American business focus and perspective.

This strong U.S. position in the media-informational sphere led Joseph Nye, Jr., in 1990 to write[46] that "the United States is likely to retain a broader range of power resources—military, economic, scientific, cultural and ideological—than other countries [in the twenty-first century] (p. 155). In particular, Nye emphasized what he terms "soft power," defined as relying on "instruments such as communications, organizational and institutional skills, and manipulation of interdependence" (p. 158). Soft power, according to Nye, "occurs when one country gets other countries to *want* what it wants. . . . The ability to affect what other countries want tends to

---

45. Glenn Hoetger, "An Overview of the Japanese Information Industry," *Information Today* 9, issue 1 (January 1992), page 25 (italics added).

46. Joseph S. Nye, Jr., "Soft Power," *Foreign Policy*, no. 80, Fall 1990. Italics in the original. See also Joseph S. Nye, Jr., *Bound to Lead: The Changing Nature of American Power* (New York: Basic Books, 1990).

be associated with intangible power resources such as culture, ideology and institutions. . . . The United States has more co-optive power than other countries" (p. 168). It is "American domination of popular communication" and control over a good chunk of the world's information resources that Nye views as the constituents of power in the 1990s and beyond.

Here then, is a former high State Department official, currently director of Harvard University's Center for International Affairs, proclaiming and confirming what *Mass Communications and American Empire* set out in 1969. What separates the two analyses is that Nye recommends using the instruments of cultural imperialism, "soft power," for holding onto the global dominator's position, whereas *MCAM* sought to give support to those who challenged it.

Yet in the few years since Nye's views were published, changes in world power relationships have accelerated. Germany has been reunified on its own terms and is now the overriding force in Europe, West and East. The Soviet Union has disappeared as a political entity and what has replaced it is still in flux. Whatever emerges will be, for a long time to come, a greatly diminished world power. Japan has continued its economic advance, its trade balances larger than ever and its influence across the Pacific growing apace. The United States, along with most other industrial states, is in painful economic recession. (No one has the courage to say the "D" word—depression.) Additionally, in the short-lived but violent Persian Gulf War, launched by the United States for geopolitical and economic advantage, American military power was once again convincingly on display. However, the lack of economic strength to support it also was embarrassingly evident. The president and secretary of state were compelled to go on a global fundraising tour to meet the costs—which they succeeded in doing, on this occasion.

What can be made of all this? The United States remains a (the only) military superpower. It also continues to be a mighty, though declining (relative to its main rivals), economic force. It disposes of a nearly $6 trillion economy, however lopsided, and a world-girdling electronics apparatus that maintains instantaneous and continuous global surveillance and eavesdropping. Its soft power is awesome, though also increasingly at the disposal of its major competitors. How do these relate to an age whose future characteristics are not yet clear? Will the world, for example, be divided into vast regional blocs with constellations of states surrounding central nodes of influence and power such as Europe, Japan, North America, and China? Will the Japanese continue to bankroll what could be regarded as a fragile U.S.-Japanese alliance?

The main pillars of the current American global position are military and cultural. How long can these be maintained if the economy continues to falter? Already the clamor to cut the military budget rises as vital social needs increasingly go unattended. The Pentagon and the civilian administrators of empire talk and plan for a downsized armed force that can still intervene quickly wherever social change threatens the system's privileged holdings. Can even this less ambitious strategy be pursued? And should there be a significant reduction in the military expenditures, under public pressure, does any stimulus exist to keep the American economy from falling back into permanent stagnation and crisis—the condition that existed prior to World War II and was overcome only with the stupendous arms budgets of the past fifty years?

Actually, the Pentagon and its friends in the military-industrial complex still retain more ambitious, if unrealistic, aims. In a policy statement made public by the *New York Times* in March 1992, the Pentagon outlined its hope: "Our first objective is to prevent the reemergence of a new rival . . . to U.S. global leadership." In short, "we [the United States] will retain the preeminent responsibility for addressing selectively those wrongs which threaten not only our interests, but those of our allies or friends, or which could seriously unsettle international relations."[47] The statement was disavowed after a public storm erupted. But, given its endorsers, the matter can hardly be at an end.

Adding to the uncertainty is the central problematic of a "free-market" world now hailed so euphorically by leaders almost everywhere. Can this mean anything other than the extension of the practices of the "old" market forces, whose historical consequences are apparently forgotten? The "new thinking" of many West European industrialists sounds very familiar. Carl H. Hahn, chairman

---

47. "Prevent the Re-Emergence of a New Rival," *New York Times*, March 8, 1982, page 4.

of Volkswagen, for example, addressed these words to working people: "Labor in Western Europe is thinking in terms of the first half of this century. . . . We have to shed the traces of a certain socialism that exists in the West even as it has gone under in the East."[48]

Can this statement be interpreted as a call for the restoration of nineteenth-century capitalism and its ruthless exploitation of the work force? It is clear that this outlook now prevails in what were once the state-managed societies of the East. Yet what does a market-forces philosophy, unchallenged by significant opposition—in fact, intensified with the demise of state socialism—imply for the conditions of life, the global resource base, and the future of the planet?

In fall 1991, a group of world-renowned intellectuals met in Mexico and issued a declaration. In it they noted and indicted the waste and despoliation of the earth's resources, calling attention to a grotesque distortion in global resource allocation whereby "20% of the world's population consumes 80% of its wealth and is responsible for 75% of its pollution."

The symposium focused on the source of this shocking phenomenon: "We deplore the cultural pollution and loss of tradition which have led to global rootlessness, leaving humans, through the intensity of mass-marketing, vulnerable to the pressures of economic and political totalitarianism and habits of mass-consumption and waste which imperil the earth."[49]

Yet, more than any other force, American capitalism, now thoroughly transnationalized, has contributed to this condition. It has done so, in its quest for markets at home and abroad, by continuously improving, and employing, the means of persuasion and the techniques of mass marketing. American expertise in mass salesmanship and audience and consumer stimulation has led the way in the construction of the consumer ethos around the world. This,

---

48. Quoted in Roger Cohen, "The New East Meets the Old West, Dollars Apart," *New York Times*, February 5, 1992, page C-4.

49. "Approaching the Year 2000," the Morelia Symposium Declaration, reprinted as an advertisement in the *New York Times*, November 1, 1991, page A-18. Apparently it was not considered a newsworthy story: Its organizers had to pay to get the declaration into the nation's foremost newspaper.

allied with the pressure from American and foreign big businesses for total access to the new communications technologies—the drive for deregulation—has permitted a worldwide flood of imagery and messages since the end of World War II. Initially this could be seen as American cultural imperialism. More recently, it has become transnational corporate cultural domination.

Today's world market economy has evolved from, but retains the central characteristics of, the original American pattern. Now it is a global system with many nationally based transnational corporations employing the communication and cultural practices and processes that originated, and continue to prevail, in the United States. *Business Week* described these developments this way:

> World corporations represent a dramatic evolution from the U.S. multinational, alternatively feared and courted since the 1960s. . . . As cross-border trade and investment reach new heights, big global companies are effectively making decisions with little regard to national boundaries. Though few companies are totally untethered from their home countries, the trend toward a form of "stateless" corporation is unmistakable. The European, American and Japanese giants heading in this direction are learning how to juggle multiple identities and multiple loyalties.[50]

With the aid of the new information technologies, world companies can "make almost daily decisions on where to shift production."[51] This capability eludes the national work force wherever it may be based. Its welfare, and the community's well-being as well, is excluded from such decisions.

Yet "statelessness" has its limits and German and Japanese companies, despite their rapidly expanding activities in the international market, regard themselves as nationally affiliated. More indicative of the weakening U.S. economic position is that the national label, for some American companies at least, now seems to be a burden. The U.S. commissioner for American participation

---

50. William J. Holstein, "The Stateless Corporation," *Business Week*, May 14, 1990, page 98.

51. Ibid., page 101.

at Expo '92 in Seville reported that companies like Time-Warner, CNN, and DuPont "considered themselves global and transnational and didn't want to be pegged as an American company." Their reason for such bashfulness was that "the products they sell will not be seen as high quality if they are seen as American."[52]

In this uncertainty of the future character of the global business units, *Business Week* posed the central question: "Are all industrial nations part of one big happy global economy where nationality doesn't matter? Or are they merely entering a new stage of intensified competition?"[53]

One global "happy family" of nations is hardly on the horizon. What is on the upcoming agenda are mass marketing and intense media use, destined to reach still higher levels across most of the world. At the same time, the need for protection of the global public against these messages and imagery is barely at the threshold of recognition. Accompanying the drive for markets and the creation of consumers by the global companies in each of the supranational blocs in formation will be, in all probability, rising chauvinism as one core economy or another falls behind in the global competition and as the clamor and migratory efforts of the excluded, the world's majority, rise.

The U.S. free-flow-of-information policy and practice since the end of World War II has been remarkably successful. Contested briefly in the late 1960s and the 1970s, it has prevailed. The world has been exposed to a tidal flow of made-in-America images and messages. American pop culture has captured the youth in countries around the earth. The products and services that are inherent in, and promoted by, that culture either have been adopted, or longed for, by people everywhere. The "buying ethos" has conquered.

Now the cultural industry corporations that produced this worldwide standard are being bought out or bought into by the giant firms in the rival economic blocs. Where does this leave the Amer-

---

52. "World-Class Flop in Seville," editorial, *New York Times*, February 4, 1992, page A-14.

53. Holstein, "The Stateless Corporation," page 104.

ican media empire of yesteryear? It is still strong—far from dismantled. It is, in fact, reinforced by an in-place global electronics network that transmits billions of data bits daily. The crisis affecting American global power and influence does not originate in the media-informational sector, although it is certainly abetted by this sphere. It derives from the resistance to any and all efforts to restructure the dominant institutions that determine the social and economic priorities in American life. In a word, a privately owned and directed economy, concentrated in relatively few hands, that recognizes nothing but profit as a legitimate objective has been able to protect itself from serious scrutiny and challenge. Domination of the informational system has been a crucial factor in this achievement to date.

Given the continuing, actually growing, strength of the image and message apparatus and the determinedly resistant politico-economic institutions, what may be expected? All too likely, as the general economic condition of the nation either deteriorates or stagnates, an increased use—already evident—of the informational system for social control and pacification may be expected.

This social use would include in varying degree, and according to the exigencies of the moment, the use of media and technology as a further diversion, through endless sports, more MTV, and the expansion of theme-park projects. The informational system can also be used for surveillance of the citizenry—a technique already far advanced and facilitated by the social security number, the credit card, the telephone number, and a wide and growing assortment of techniques to secure personal information.[54] It would also continue transforming the news and analysis service into happy talk and fractured bits purveyed by heavily managed sources. The Persian Gulf War was a chilling exhibition of the latter. The emergence of MTV "news" is a foretaste of the three-second news story.[55]

---

54. Oscar H. Gandy, Jr., *The Panoptic Sort* (Boulder: Westview Press, forthcoming).

55. Karen De Witt, "MTV Puts the Campaign on Fast Forward," *New York Times,* February 8, 1992. De Witt reported, "The [news] reports are about three or four minutes long and begin with snippets of interviews with a few young people. The cuts are fast. A couple of words. Then a change: A reporter. A candidate. A question. *Three seconds each*" (italics added).

Will these developments pass by unchallenged? Hardly! There exist in the country many local and a few national enclaves of independent and alternative media. There are also considerable numbers of disaffected professionals in the big commercial media companies. More critical for achieving a significant level of opposition, however, is to get the attention and support of the American working class.

There has been a uniform media effort to claim that the only workers in the country are blue collar and that they have been largely eliminated by the disappearance of heavy industry. In political campaigns, all candidates refer to the "middle class." Yet this category overwhelmingly contains working men and women in all kinds of jobs that are not necessarily industrial. The middle-class designation comes from either the higher pay for some kinds of work or, more likely, the fact that two or more wage earners are needed to keep life tolerable in the family unit. In either case, the United States possesses a large working class, however deceptively it is defined and presented.

The American working class has been uncharacteristically passive in recent decades for reasons that need not detain us here. Yet historically the American working class yields to none in militancy. There is every reason to believe that militancy will reassert itself as the conditions of life worsen or, at best, stagnate.

In sum, the years ahead are sure to be stormy. *Mass Communications and American Empire* no longer fully describes the global condition. Transnational cultural combines, largely utilizing American marketing techniques, are turning the world into a shopping mall for those with sufficient disposable income. The rest, the large majority, are to be kept quarantined in their poverty. The instability and explosive anger that this way of organizing the world will generate, and already is generating, can hardly be imagined. But it is happening! Meanwhile, the media power that American commanders applied to the rest of the world for the past fifty years is now being directed more intensely at domestic targets. But Americans have had more familiarity than others with the messages and images of the corporate and political governors. This experience may serve well in the coming years and help turn advantage away from the sponsors and to the "middle," aka the working, class. Still, it is safe to conclude that the (dare it be said?) class conflict to come will contain a strong focus on the media-cultural institutions that bear such a large, though not ultimate, responsibility for the maintenance of an unjust and dysfunctional social order.

# CHAPTER 1

## Electronics and Economics
## Serving an American Century

It is now more than a quarter of a century since Henry Luce in a *Life* editorial, urged Americans "to accept wholeheartedly our duty and our opportunity as the most powerful and vital nation in the world and in consequence to exert upon the world the full impact of our influence, for such purposes as we see fit and by such means as we see fit." What is more, he said then that "it now becomes our time to be the powerhouse from which the ideals spread throughout the world. . . ."[1] It was appropriate that the arrival of an *American Century* should have been announced by the controller of one of the most powerful communications complexes in the United States. As its director, Luce understood, earlier than others, that the fusion of economic strength and information control or image-making, public opinion-formation, or call it what you will, is the new quintessence of power, international and domestic.

*Fortune,* another Luce publication, put the international significance of the matter squarely before its readership in a 1944 war-time article on "World Communications." It stated: "Upon their (U.S.-owned international communications) efficiency depends whether the United States will grow in the future, as Great Britain has in the past, as a center of world thought and trade . . . Great Britain provides an unparalleled example of what a communications system means to a great nation standing athwart the globe. . . ."[2]

---

[1] "The American Century", Henry R. Luce, Farrar & Rinehart, Inc., New York, 1941, p. 23.

[2] *Fortune,* "World Communications", May, 1944, pp. 129 and 178.

To "own" a century is to own an empire. Yet this is no simple matter in a world only now escaping from unabashed colonialism and in which the patterns of the past are still vivid in the minds of former subjects still alive. How difficult would be the task of a new usurper of national independence behaving as a traditional conqueror? What small prospects for success would face a society which openly announced its intention of imposing a second imperial tutelage on a newly-liberated people? Imperial domain is an inconvenient and troublesome notion also to most Americans who have long regarded themselves, quite justifiably, as the children of the first anti-colonial outburst.

All the same there are some offsets to what otherwise would be a trying situation for a fledgling empire-accumulator. The world leadership syndrome which has been so prominent in American decision-making in the post-World War II years has had a unique instrument to support its inclinations. Unavailable to expansionists of earlier times, modern mass communications perform a double service for their present-day controllers. At home, they help to overcome, by diversion in part, the lack of popular enthusiasm for the global role of imperial stewardship. Abroad, the antagonism to a renewed though perhaps less apparent colonial servitude, has been quite successfully (to date) deflected and confused by the images and messages which originate in the United States but which flow continuously over and through local informational media. The domestic and international sides of the imperial coin are thus both distinct and related.

Domestically, the realm is governed confidently by a propertied managerial-industrial corps, instructing a consumer community stratified by income and race. A combination of media supply the primary ideological ingredient of the affluent society; the concept of the good life.

The period of capital accumulation in America which emphasized prudence, restraint, thrift and saving has long since terminated. The developed and glut-prone state has found new virtues to dignify and explain popular behavior operating in a high-capacity market economy. The mass media, openly in its advertising and less obtrusively in its general "entertainment" features, inform and instruct their audiences on the social patterns that are indispensable for relieving the unbearable pressure on market-oriented enterprises. Consequently, a high premium is placed on personal economic reactions favoring impulse and immediacy. Spending and asset acquisition are stimulated and, for a quarter of a century at least, they have with some slight pauses, served to keep the factories running.

The entire operation, bordering often on psychic chaos and material indigestion, is presented to the average citizen as a reasonable and unmanipulated system. Moreover, its beneficiaries reassure both the public and themselves that the apparent lack of direction, and the billions of individual (and generally insignificant) decisions that make up the national demand and supply maps, are evidence of the country's freedom. Commercial television, for instance, which literally sells its audiences to goods producers with carefully-determined ratios of so many thousands of viewers per advertising dollar, warns against those who would tamper with "free" television.

The impact abroad of the domestic pattern is equally far-reaching, though some time has had to elapse for its effects to be manifest. An American international domain, represented by a visible 55 billion dollars of private capital invested overseas (and untold billions not identified) and another 55 billion dollars of annual foreign trade, is organized by an extremely concentrated group of commercial commanders. Extending across all continents, the sphere grows significantly larger year by year. A powerful communications system exists to secure, not grudging submission but an open-armed allegiance in the penetrated areas, by identifying the American presence with freedom—freedom of trade, freedom of speech and freedom of enterprise. In short, the emerging imperial network of American economics and finance utilizes the communications media for its defense and entrenchment wherever it exists already and for its expansion to locales where it hopes to become active.

Communications material from the United States offers a vision of a way of life. The image is of a mountain of material artifacts, privately furnished and individually acquired and consumed. The emphasis in the programming and advertising is on the first and last elements in the American tryptych. The private character of production is generally though not always overlooked. The imagery envelops all viewers and listeners within the range of electronic impulses patterned after the American model and that radius is untiringly being enlarged. Simultaneously, the behavioral sciences in the United States supply the expertise for the great promotion and academic research turns its attention to these matters with great vigor.*

What is the nature of the post-colonial world that so readily adapts itself to American influence and penetration? Some very powerful historical currents have contributed to the onrushing tide of American power.

The international community that has emerged in the last quarter-century presents a vastly different complexion from the one prevailing before World War II. The new age is defined by a massive shift in the global distribution of power points. More than matching the recession of European authority, once exercised internationally, has been the upsurge of American industrial strength. Alongside this sweeping power transfer have occurred two other significant developments. One is the extension of the state-directed sector from the isolation of its initial, quarantined Soviet base to a position that embraces half of Europe and much of Asia. The countervailing influence on world affairs of this, for the most part, vast and contiguous territory, which applies some principles of social planning, is considerably diminished in recent years, as evidence of its own serious disagreements on development policy have become worldwide knowledge.

There is also the transition of a good portion of the rest of the world from a state of formal *total* subordination, colonialism, to a condition of *political* independence and national sovereignty. Following the breakdown of the Western European colonial system twenty-five years ago, scores of new states have emerged. The membership of the United Nations, reflecting these changes, has doubled since its founding in 1945. Independence notwithstanding, the frontiers, the human and material resources and the social structures of the new nations continue to reflect their colonial experience and past servitude

---

*A recent issue of *Broadcasting* reported about the research to be undertaken at Wayne State University in Detroit. It asked this question: "Will some of the next major advances in creative programming and advertising come out of the university laboratories of the nation before they are discovered in the broadcast studio or advertising agency?" It noted some of the research that will be undertaken at Wayne State: "subliminal advertising techniques in television . . . (and) "compressed, and expanded, speech and music. Newly refined and rather expensive equipment is now available to make long commercials or short ones fit a prescribed time precisely . . ."
Broadcasting magazine, June 5, 1967, p. 56

Diminished European strength, an expanded but defensive Socialist geographical and material base and the newly-independent but economically feeble "third" world provide the environmental setting in which the contemporary expansion of American power occurs. What lends sophistication to the still-youthful American imperial structure is its dependence on a marriage of economics and electronics, which substitutes in part, though not entirely, for the earlier, "blood and iron" foundations of more primitive conquerors.

Recognition that economic might and communications know-how could complement each other to effectively promote the creation of an American century evolved slowly. The acceptance of United States economic power as an instrument of international influence came first. Communications possibilities were appreciated much later. In 1944, while the war still was being fought, J. B. Condliffe, in a paper titled prophetically "Economic Power As An Instrument of National Policy", called the attention of the nation's economists, assembled at their annual meeting, to what was going on before their unseeing eyes. He noted that "For the first time in many decades—indeed for the first time since the earliest years of the enfant republic-attention is now being paid by soldiers and political scientists, but little as yet by economists, to the power position of the United States in the modern world."[3]

Actually, what may not have been apparent to American academic economists was certainly no secret in London and Washington. British leaders for some time had been aware of the hard and driving edge of American economic power, exhibited during their war-time negotiations for United States economic assistance. More than one commentary at the war's end mentioned the tough, uncompromising objectives of American business and governmental representatives, itching to put their weakened English competitors to the financial wall.[4]

The outlines of a national expansionist economic policy, evident in the bits and pieces of war-time negotiations, took some time to be

---

[3] J. B. Condliffe, "Economic Power as an Instrument of National Policy", Papers & Proceedings of the 56th Annual Meeting of the American Economic Association, Washington, D. C., January 1944, p. 307.

[4] Read for instance the views of J. M. Keynes and L. S. Amery, two Englishmen of very different outlooks, who agreed on what the English were up against in their dealings with America.

formulated into an all-embracing theoretical structure. By 1947, however, the patterns were firm and secure and capable of being articu-
lated comprehensively. To an appreciative audience, gathered at
Baylor University in Texas in March, 1947, President Truman addressed himself publicly, and with the unmistakeable accent of
authority to the new American world role. He began by noting that
"We are the giant of the economic world. Whether we like it or not,
the future pattern of economic relations depends upon us. The world
is watching to see what we shall do. The choice is ours." The President's words are worth quoting in some detail because their message,
it will be seen, has been the basis of American policy-making for an
uninterrupted twenty-year span and continues to illuminate and
guide national decisions. Unequivocally, Truman declared that
"There is one thing that Americans value even more than peace. It is
freedom: freedom of worship—freedom of speech—and freedom of
enterprise." He made it quite clear that it was the last freedom (of
enterprise) which weighed most heavily on his mind at that moment,
and which, incidentally has been determining in United States economic relationships throughout the last four presidential administrations. Freedom of speech, however, interpreted to signify the unrestrained opportunity for the dissemination of messages by the
American mass media in the world arena, has developed in the years
since Truman spoke as an equally significant support in the American imperial arch.

Truman called for a pattern of international trade that would be
"most conducive to freedom of enterprise . . . one in which the major
decisions are made not by governments but by private buyers and
sellers, under conditions of active competition, and with proper safe-
guards against the establishment of monopolies and cartels. Under
such a system", he stressed, "buyers make purchases, and sellers make
their sales, at whatever time and place and in whatever quantities
they choose, relying for guidance on whatever prices the market may
afford. Goods move from country to country in response to economic
opportunities. Governments may impose tariffs, but they do not
dictate the quantity of trade, the sources of imports, or the destina-
tion of exports. Individual transactions are a matter of private choice.
This is the essence of free enterprise." Americans valued these arrangements, Truman asserted, higher than peace—a curious prefer-
ence, we might observe, in a nuclear age. Any other value scale, he

noted parenthetically, "is not the American way. It is not the way to peace."[5]

What assistance communications could provide to these objectives the President didn't specify. All the same, his declaration viewed in retrospect, included arguments that could and later would be made explicit. In this respect, if "information" or "communications" is substituted for "trade" in the passages of the Truman-Baylor speech, we have a clue to the contemporary mechanics of American expansionism. Arranged thusly, we are seeking a pattern of *international communications* that would be "most conducive to freedom of enterprise . . ." et al. That there are grounds for regarding this a warrantable substitution, consider the recent words of Robert Sarnoff, RCA's president, who predicts a time, not far in the future, when "information will become a basic commodity equivalent to energy in the world economy" and that "it will function as a form of currency in world trade, convertible into goods and services everywhere."[6]

Information moving between nations on the basis of "economic opportunities" and "competition", unimpeded by other national or cultural considerations, affords American communications media the same advantages American commerce now receives from "free" world trade patterns that are also minimally controlled by national states. Accordingly, the material interests of American commerce and American mass communications find their expression in the early postwar presidential declarations of freedom of speech and freedom of enterprise. Their joint interests are further promoted when, over time, it became apparent that the championing of freedom of communications (or speech) most often had as an indirect benefit, the global extension of American commerce and its value system. But more of this later.

Truman's conception of a well-arranged international economic order, though newly-announced as American doctrine in 1947, had an earlier counterpart in another world-embracing system. Writing about English national policy in the latter part of the nineteenth century, two English economic historians used the felicitous phrase "free trade imperialism."[7] The concept of empire, they noted, can-

[5] Harry S. Truman, Address, March 1947, Baylor University.

[6] Address by Robert Sarnoff, president, R.C.A., May 1, 1967, to the International Communications Association.

[7] J. Gallagher and R. Robinson, "The Imperialism of Free Trade", *The Economic History Review*, Second Series, Vol. VI, No. 1, August 1953.

not be judged by *formal* empire alone. "Refusals to annex are no proof of reluctance to control." The mechanics of informal empire, in the British experience, these writers found, "was the treaty of free trade and friendship made with or imposed upon a weaker state."[8] The policy as they describe it was "trade with informal control if possible, trade with rule when necessary." A brilliant opportunity for the practice of free trade imperialism was offered to the English in Latin America after that area's breakaway from Spain in the early 1800's. Canning, the British minister in 1824, put the issue in terms that are stunningly contemporary. "Spanish America is free", he said, "and if we do not mismanage our affairs sadly, she is English."[9]

A century and a half later, American leaders view the dissolution of the British, French, Dutch and Portuguese empires with equal enthusiasm if less candor. Moreover, the opportunities for informal control affording paramount interest in the newly-independent nations are irresistible to the youthful American power complex. One may accept Landes' bland explanation of American practices ". . . as a multifarious response to a common opportunity that consists simply in disparity of power", and that "whenever and wherever such disparity has existed, people and groups have been ready to take advantage of it."[10] More illuminating perhaps is the Baran and Sweezy analysis that "capitalism has always been an international system. And it has always been a hierarchical system with one or more leading metropolises at the top, completely dependent colonies at the bottom and many degrees of superordination and subordination in between."[11] In either case, the United States is at the top of the power pyramid that exists today and scores of recently independent states are at the bottom.

To believe that the commercial and informational connection points that join these economically feeble nations to the technologically powerful American economy are beneficial to both sides of the union is to outdo Voltaire's good doctor Pangloss. If free trade is the mechanism by which a powerful economy penetrates and dominates

---

[8] *Ibid*, p. 11.

[9] *Ibid*, p. 8.

[10] David S. Landes, "Some Thoughts on the Nature of Economic Imperialism", *The Journal of Economic History*, December 1961, Vol. XXI, No. 4, p. 510.

[11] P. A. Baran and P. M. Sweezy, "Monopoly Capitalism", Monthly Review Press, 1966, New York, p. 178.

a weaker one, the "free flow of information", the designated objective incidentally of UNESCO, is the channel through which life styles and value systems can be imposed on poor and vulnerable societies. If the perils that unrestricted trade pose to developing nations are now fairly widely recognized, the significance of communications flows as elements in international control are only barely beginning to be appreciated, even in the United States itself. Perhaps a special sophistication is required to comprehend the material benefits that accrue to the transmitter nation from the intangible messages and information it processes for weaker, receiver societies. To those long accustomed to mercantilist beliefs in which *hard* exports at least must be matched with *hard* imports, the returns to information export are uncertain and inconclusive. But belated as recognition has been, communications are now a major factor in decision-making throughout the interlocked American power complex. Business has been aware of and has utilized mass communications with great vigor since the advent of radio forty years ago. Now the executive and military bureaucracies have seized enthusiastically the possibilities offered by information control.

The television editor of the *New York Times,* Jack Gould, writes that "President Johnson believes that the governmental priorities of the days ahead may well be defense, foreign affairs and communications."[12] A congressional committee in 1967 considered the issues of "Modern Communications and Foreign Policy" in its hearings, significantly titled, "Winning the Cold War: The U.S. Ideological Offensive."[13] Testimony before the committee, asserted flatly that "To a significant degree what America does will shape the emerging international communications system. . . To a very large degree other countries will imitate our experience and will attach themselves to the institutions and systems we create. . . Given our information technology and information resources, the United States clearly could be the hub of the world communication system."[14]

Another witness before the Committee, John Richardson, Jr., President of Free Europe, Inc. [Radio Free Europe] claimed that

---

[12] *The New York Times,* July 3, 1966.

[13] Modern Communications and Foreign Policy, Report No. 5, Subcommittee on International Organizations and Movements of the Committee on Foreign Affairs, 90th Congress, 1st Session, Washington, 1967, House of Representatives.

[14] *Ibid,* p. 53.

"the subject matter [modern communications and foreign policy] is the most important question now before the U.S. Government. It is one of the most important matters that could possibly attract the attention of leadership in America both private and public."[15]

More efficient control of communications is also a major concern of the military establishment for very practical purposes. Behind the verbal inducement and material enticement that American expansionism first displays to the out-lands lies the traditional regulator of international domination—military force. One hundred and fifty military bases outside the continental United States attest to the vigilance which is maintained for the security of the spreading American involvement over the planet. Strong American garrisons are strung out across the Pacific, onto the Asian mainland, in Western Europe, Latin America and the Middle East.

In a world split as much by a North-South poverty line as by an East-West ideological divide, the expectations of regional and local violence against an intolerable status quo are high. Former Secretary of Defense McNamara, perhaps as part of his occupational interest, found a startling association between poverty and social violence. "There is a direct and constant relationship", he stated, "between the incidence of violence and the economic status of the countries afflicted."[16]

What conclusions do the purveyors of and defenders against violence draw from this relationship? Not surprisingly, the U.S. military establishment implements the civilian decision to control the rate and character of the change in the poor world, and modern communications techniques find their most admiring practitioners among the war games specialists. Instantaneous connections to men in the most inaccessible field locations are benefits already available to combat strategists. For some time, communications and space satellites have been providing intelligence that is of great tactical value in what is now euphemistically called "counter-insurgency." The Director of Telecommunications Management in the President's Executive Offices, former General O'Connell appeared before a Congressional committee in 1966. He compared current United States' requirements for international communications with its "non-empire"

---

15 *Ibid*, p. 53.
16 *The New York Times*, May 19th, 1963.

with Britain's needs of an earlier time which in some instances still carry over to the present. O'Connell put the nation's international communications demands in a sympathetic and unaggressive setting. "The United States does not have a farflung empire or common-wealth of nations", he stated, "but at this point in our history we have a great community of interest with the many free and independent nations of the world whose rights of self-determination, progress toward higher living standards, governmental strength, stability and ability to resist the forces of externally sponsored subversion are of great interest to us as a nation." For this reason, then, "the rapid growth of our International Telecommunications System is a matter of the greatest importance in strengthening our mutual interest and understanding . . . In this connection it is interesting to note that the British Commonwealth still has a somewhat larger international complex of communications than does the United States."[17] As a spokesman for a society so concerned with denying its imperial position, the general's comments are notable both for their appreciation of the British world role and his difficult task of reconciling United States' communications requirements for professed unselfish purposes with England's colonial utilization of the same or similar resources.

Ironically, as a result of their powerful communications capabilities, American policymakers have come to accept the legitimacy of a position that once was highly regarded by the Soviet leadership of an earlier time. Appealing directly to the people over the heads of a nation's governmental bureaucracy was once the revolutionary stock-in-trade of Russian Communists. From the very beginning of the 1917 Revolution, Lenin had emphasized the value of getting the ear of the "masses" in other nations and circumventing the tiresome and generally unsympathetic channels of the bourgeois state. A half-century later, the combination of prolonged economic prosperity and communications sophistication have produced comparable sentiments in the American command community. A report of the congressional committee concerned with "Winning the Cold War" and "Ideological Operations and Foreign Policy", elaborates the new approach:

---

[17] Government Use of Satellite Communications, Hearings before a subcommittee of the Committee on Government Operations, House of Representatives, 89th Congress, 2nd Session, August and September, 1966, p. 284.

"For many years military and economic power, used separately, or in conjunction, have served as the pillars of diplomacy. They still serve that function today but the recent increase in influence of the masses of the people over governments, together with greater awareness on the part of leaders of the aspirations of people, brought about by the concurrent revolutions of the 20th century, has created a new dimension for foreign policy operation. Certain foreign policy objectives can be pursued by dealing directly with the people of foreign countries, rather than with their governments. Through the use of modern instruments and techniques of communications it is possible today to reach large or influential segments of national populations—to inform them, to influence their attitudes, and at times perhaps even to motivate them to a particular course of action. These groups, in turn, are capable of exerting noticeable, even decisive, pressures, on their governments."[18]

The opportunity to address a national, if not a world audience grows continuously. Leonard Marks, the director of the United States Information Agency, reminded his listeners at the national press club in early 1967 that the number of nations with television already had reached 104, and the number of sets around the world totalled 182 million and was climbing spectacularly. Radio receivers numbered well over half a billion, and international broadcasting, increasing steadily, has now reached 24 thousand hours weekly.[19]

Small wonder then that since the end of the second World War the American technological supremacy, and its leadership in communications in particular, has been receiving wider and wider appreciation inside the domestic business, military and governmental power structures. Understandable, too, has been an assumption of additional responsibility by the communications apparatus for these interest groups. An intra-governmental committee on international communications, including representatives of the Federal Communications Commission, the Office of Telecommunications Management, and the State, Justice and Defense departments, reported in (April) 1966 that "telecommunications has progressed from being an essential

---

[18] Committee on Foreign Affairs, Report No. 2 on "Winning the Cold War. The U.S. Ideological Offensive," 88th Congress, House Report No. 1352, April 27, 1964, pp. 6-7.

[19] Leonard H. Marks, "International Communications a National Imperative", National Press Club, Washington, D. C., February 23, 1967.

support to our international activities to *being also an instrument of foreign policy.*"[20] (Italics added)

The more active role accorded to communications activities in behalf of the governmental and private interest has prompted some attempts at creating a philosophical underpinning, to distinguish contemporary American practices from efforts by other societies to achieve imperial hegemony at other times through broadly defined cultural operations. To this task, Charles Frankel, professor of Philosophy at Columbia University and formerly Assistant Secretary of State for Education and Cultural Affairs, recently addressed himself. Frankel believes that "we are entering an era of educational and cultural relations" which "offer instruments for diplomacy and foreign policy whose potential ability is enormous and has as yet only begun to be felt." He distinguishes three separate stages in the history of cultural exchange between states and peoples. At the beginning, in the first and longest stage, ". . . cultural exchange was simply an accidental by-product of the contact between different groups. It was not usually sought, and it was frequently resisted." Stage number two, according to Frankel, which had its climax in the 19th century, consisted of the "triumph of one's own culture over the culture of others. (It) was not accidental, but was deliberately sought and promoted. It was a motive as well as a consequence of war, of commerce, of imperial organization and imperial rivalry . . . This is the period of the great explorations and of colonization." For Frankel, this period is dead and done with. We are now, still according to Frankel, in the third stage, one that in his calculation, began only twenty years ago, almost coincidentally with the date of Mr. Luce's recognition of an American Century.

What characterizes the "new era" (not to be confused with a similarly termed period that enthusiasts applied to the 1920's, prior to the Great Collapse) ? Frankel lists several features that identify the current cultural scene and make it, in his estimation, qualitatively different from preceding periods. There is the volume and intensity of the cultural traffic. It is heavier and it penetrates more deeply than the earlier flows. There are more organized social institutions—churches, universities, foundations, voluntary associations and gov-

---

[20] Report and Recommendations to Senate and House Commerce Committees, Submitted by the Intra-Governmental Committee on International Telecommunications, April 29, 1966, Executive Offices of the President, April 1966, p. 1.

ernments—that participate in the informational flow. And, finally, Frankel suggests that for the first time, there is a two-way flow between the rich and the poor, the more powerful and the less powerful nations and peoples. Furthermore, spectacular scientific and communications revolutions are continuously accelerating the already high level of social intercourse.[21]

The facts are much as Frankel describes them. Their interpretation is another matter. For him "the height of the period of cultural imperialism, in which the richer nations moved out toward the poorer ones" terminated in the 19th century. To less officially-oriented observers there can be a different reading which sees an agressive and powerful industrial-electronics complex working to extend the American socio-economic system spatially and ideologically. The intense volume of messages that Frankel calls attention to only highlights the expanded capability of modern communications over which the United States is in command. The numerous social institutions participating in the traffic do not in any way dilute the system's major message. Churches, universities, foundations and governments have with few exceptions, uncomplainedly carried the official, industrial-governmental outlook. The ease, for instance, with which the CIA enlisted voluntary conduits, which still affirm their "independence", suggests the near total triumph of the imperial idea in the American "pluralistic" society. In most instances, conviction, not force, persuaded these various institutional groupings to follow the official course.

The two-way flow of "information, attention and trouble" between the powerful and the less powerful nations that Frankel considers to set the age apart from preceding epochs is still more apparent than real and certainly not evenly balanced. Who for example, would claim that the "information, attention and trouble" contributed by the United States to Latin America is reciprocated? It is appropriate, too, that "trouble" is mentioned by Frankel as one of the ingredients of this new era. What is "trouble" to American power-wielders may be anything but trouble to less developed states and their populations. Generally, the efforts of the inarticulate to express themselves constitute "trouble" to already-established and privileged groups.

---

[21] Charles Frankel, "The Era of Educational and Cultural Relations", Department of State Bulletin, June 6, 1966.

Satisfaction with and support of the American international cultural offensive is of a piece with current attitudes to the country's economic expansion and global penetration. Yet self-delusion has never been a national monopoly. Our English friends not so long ago colored the world's maps with their own particular hue, indicating their far-reaching paramountcy—all the while exclaiming that their steadily expanding empire was indeed even a surprise to themselves. As one English chronicler of the late 19th century put it, "We seem, as it were, to have conquered and peopled half the world in a fit of absence of mind."[22]

Since that time of innocence, we have overtaken and surpassed the British in many fields, not least of which is apologetics. American explanations of what has been unfolding on the international scene in recent decades substitute concern and cultural exchange for absent mindedness as the motivating elements in the nation's overseas behavior. Beginning a long line of self-justifications, President Truman in his 1949 inaugural address, for example, anticipated by two decades Frankel's evaluation, when he affirmed that "The old imperialism-exploitation for foreign profit has no place in our plans. What we envisage is a program of development based on the concepts of democratic fair-dealing."[23]

Academics likewise have assured us of our benevolence as well as how much we differ from this century's earlier predators. One writes, "It is certainly misleading to describe by the same word 'imperialism' both the European statesmen who plan ruthlessly to overrun a country in Asia or Africa and the American company building an automobile assembly plant in Israel."[24] Another asserts that "what was regarded as exploitative imperialism about a half-century ago is now regarded on almost all sides virtually as benevolences extended to economically backward nations starved for development capital . . .

---

[22] J. A. Seeley, "The Expansion of England, 1883", quoted in A. P. Thornton, "*The Doctrines of Imperialism*", John Wiley & Sons, Inc., New York, 1965, p. 23.

[23] Harry S. Truman, President, in Department of State, General Foreign Policy Series, No. 18, p. 8.

[24] Daniel H. Kruger, "Hobson, Lenin and Schumpeter on Imperialism", *Journal of the History of Ideas*, Vol. XVI, No. 2, April 1955, p. 252.

Hobson's imperialism is dead, which is not the same, of course, as to say, as some scholars do, that it never existed."[25]

Yet academic and official agreement over the death of imperialism, both economic and cultural, seems somewhat premature when considered alongside the behavior and the openly expressed views of the power complex itself. Read, for example, the words of former Deputy Secretary of State for Economic Affairs (and now U.S. Representative to the United Nations) George W. Ball, delivered to the New York Chamber of Commerce in May 1967. He noted that "it has been only in the last twenty years that the multinational company has come fully into its own. Today the lines between domestic and overseas business are no longer very distinct in many corporations." Ball sees "few things more hopeful for the future than the growing determination of American business to regard national boundaries as no longer fixing the horizons of their corporate activity." With realism and candor, Ball carefully divides up the non-socialist portion of the world between the United States and the industrialized and capitalistic Common Market countries. "In practice this would mean an American recognition of the primacy of the European interest in Africa — and consequently the primacy of European responsibility for the economic assistance, education, health and defense of the African people. We would, in other words, recognize that Africa was a special European responsibility just as today the European nations recognize our particular responsibility in Latin America."[26]

This is hardly the model of a two-way flow of "information, attention and trouble" that Charles Frankel sees as the indication of the new era in cultural exchange. The multinational corporations that Mr. Ball extolls, are the engines that give the thrust to American expansionism. The communications apparatus which these industrial giants have at their disposal provides the methodology without which the new imperial surge would be ineffective, coming as it does on the heels of political liberation in so many former colonial territories.

The character of the United States communications complex is significant then, not only for its tremendous importance domestically

---

[25] B. Semmel, "On the Economics of Imperialism", in *Economics and the Idea of Mankind*, Bert F. Hoselitz, editor, Columbia University Press, New York, 1965, p. 193.

[26] Address by George W. Ball, before the New York Chamber of Commerce, New York, May 5, 1967.

in influencing the lives and organizing the daily behavior of Americans. Less apparent at home but increasingly felt abroad is its contact with the international community. The structure, character and direction of the domestic communications apparatus are no longer, if they ever were, entirely national concerns. This powerful mechanism now directly impinges on peoples' lives everywhere. It is essential therefore, that there should be at least some familiarity with what the American communications system is like, how it has evolved, what motivates it and where it is pointing. These are the subjects for our further consideration.

CHAPTER 2

# The Rise of Commercial Broadcast Communications

The development of broadcast communications in the United States affords perhaps the most damaging as well as the most recent evidence of how an exciting new possibility for human enlightenment and satisfaction can be transformed into a stultifying spiritual swamp by a web of retrogressive social institutions. Writing more than forty years after the introduction of radio broadcasting in the United States and seeking support for public television, the President of the Ford Foundation, McGeorge Bundy warned that "...the nation must find a way to a wholly new level of action in this field—one which will release for our whole people all the enlightenment and engagement, all the immediacy and freedom of experience which are inherent in this extraordinary medium and which commercial services —as they freely admit—cannot bring out alone."[1]

Abuse of a great national resource, the radio spectrum, for more than four decades, makes Bundy's statement sound pathetic as well as reminiscent of similar high hopes expressed two generations ago. Dan Lacy in his book, *Freedom and Communications,* wrote in 1961 that "What we need is a communications system that gives the individual consumer the greatest resources to satisfy his needs for information and enrichment, and that strengthens his capacity to achieve personal development and autonomy of judgment. We need a communications system whose built-in 'lean' is toward increasing the range of information and of different sources of opinion and of dif-

---

[1] McGeorge Bundy, letter to the Federal Communications Commission, August 1, 1966, In the Matter of the Establishment of domestic non-common carrier communications satellite facilities by non-governmental entities. Docket No. 16495.

63

ferent cultural experiences that are simultaneously, and conveniently available to each user. . ."[2]

This is what we need. Bundy and Lacy are right, indeed. But what do we have and why do we have it? Lacy also has something to say about this. He notes that we "use . . . many of our major resources for communication not as a link between persons with something to say and an audience with a cause to listen, but rather as a marketing device, with the needs of marketing rather than the creative impulses of authors or the needs of listeners as the determinant of content."[3]

Certainly there is no secrecy in what has happened. Textbooks on communications state flatly that "Advertising is the lifeblood of broadcasting."[4] No sudden coup, therefore, captured broadcasting for commerce and turned American radio-television programming into the soul-destroying wasteland it is. The discovery of radio (and later television) came out of inventive minds but the development of these media was determined at all points by the market system which surrounded them. Business balance sheets, intent on profitability and unconcerned with human realization, enveloped broadcast communications.

## Broadcasting and Economic Development

Helpful in the interpretation of the evolution of the American broadcasting pattern is the perspective of nations now facing some of the choices that were made in the United States decades ago. The American radio-television experience is useful to countries beginning their developmental march at this time, not so much for what they may wish to imitate but for what they may recognize as avoidable mistakes.

The market economy provided the institutional climate in which the contours of American broadcasting gained their early character as well as their more durable features. In an environment distinguished chiefly by the private ownership of income-producing property and a state with limited economic powers, the market then, as

---

[2] Dan Lacy, *Freedom and Communications*, University of Illinois Press, Urbana, 1961, pp. 78-79.

[3] *Ibid.*, p. 76.

[4] Robert E. Summers and Harrison B. Summers, *Broadcasting and the Public*, Wadsworth Publishing Company, Inc., Belmont, California, 1966, p. 100.

now, possessed a dynamic of its own. The patterns produced are just as strong and longlasting as those of any centrally-organized agency of economic direction, yet it is usually difficult to trace the subtle forces that shape the course of events. Often the impression is created that the conditions that develop are natural and inevitable. In early American broadcasting history, the critical market forces were the manufacturing companies in their dual roles as producers and broadcasters, the consumers who purchased the radio sets, and the rising pressure to find sales outlets for all lines of national industry. The interaction of these elements accounted in large measure for the broadcasting pattern with which we are familiar today. It is a natural and inevitable pattern only insofar as the market forces were left to themselves, neither channelled nor pushed in predetermined directions.

The impact of broadcasting on economic development has been obscured by historical circumstance. Radio was one of the accompaniments of successful industrialization in Western Europe and the United States. Its utilization and expansion in the North Atlantic area occurred *after,* not alongside of, initial national economic growth. Its applicability to developmental needs remained unrealized. Broadcasting came to populations already largely literate and to states well-launched on their developmental paths. Other natural resource conservation was of slight concern. The United States in 1920, despite frequent warnings by concerned individuals, continued to consider North America a rich and inexhaustible continent. Western Europe still had at its disposal the mineral wealth of Asia and Africa. In these circumstances, there was minimal regard in Europe and America for the radio spectrum as a resource useful to general development or as a helpful instrument in the conservation and maximization of other resources. To the contrary, in the United States, radio quickly became an adjunct to the mass production way of life, accommodating itself quite easily to the requirements and priorities of its developers and promoters.

## The Development of Radio in the United States

The existing institutional structure in 1920 treated the new natural resource just as any other commodity whose value was to be determined exclusively by market considerations. In the judgment of the market, radio's commodity value was first comprehended in units of equipment sold. The possibilities of retailing broadcast time appeared soon after as an even more attractive source of income. This made the private possession of radio channels a prime objective of property-holders. These criteria for evaluating the new medium made it inevitable that the radio spectrum's physical characteristics would be largely disregarded, that its social importance would be unappreciated and that radio's general applicability to national purposes would be gravely distorted. From the outset, there was no element in the society capable and sufficiently influential to protect the national and popular interest in the new resource. Instead, corporate complexes struggled for monopolistic control of the broadcasting medium while the public was considered first only as a consumer of equipment and later as a saleable audience.

Minuscule governmental interest in broadcasting gave the initial period of radio's growth a permissive quality that verged on total irresponsibility. No license controls, other than the perfunctory approval of the United States Department of Commerce, existed. By 1924, three years after the beginning of regular broadcasting, "over a thousand licenses to broadcast had been issued",[5] and radio broadcasters were "scattered throughout the United States in a haphazard and uneconomical way, with very little regard for the needs of the public and amount of interference caused."[6] Most stations served urban areas because broadcasters were interested in concentrated audiences.

The wastes of competition were heavy. A little more than one-half of the stations established in the first three years dropped out.[7] By 1927 the overlapping use of frequencies had created such chaos in the spectrum that listening was a frustrating experience. The private broadcasters were compelled to seek governmental regulatory assistance in allocating frequencies.

The apparent freedom of entry into broadcasting and the large number of radio stations lightly shielded an underlying structure of

---

[5] William Peck Banning, *Commercial Broadcasting Pioneer, the WEAF Experiment, 1922-1926*, Harvard University Press, Cambridge, Massachusetts, 1946, pp. 232-233.

[6] Hiram L. Jome, *Economics of the Radio Industry*, A. W. Shaw Company, Chicago, 1925, p. 70.

[7] *Ibid.*, p. 71.

tightly-held corporate control. Patent rights for the manufacture of radio equipment and for the transmission of signals were vested in two influential business groups, each vying with the other for total domination in the expanding industry. The "radio group", whose membership included the two giant electrical equipment manufacturers, General Electric and Westinghouse, and their jointly-launched protégé, R.C.A., represented one faction. On the other side was the American Telephone and Telegraph Company, a powerful aggregation even then. A.T. & T. had the unannounced, ambitious objective of achieving exclusive control of radio broadcasting while protecting, at the same time, its substantial investment and leading position in telephonic communications.[8]

Though control of broadcasting was the ultimate aim of both of these corporate groupings, the surge of public interest in radio threw the emphasis temporarily to the production of radio sets and equipment. An influx of small firms into radio manufacturing produced a brief atmosphere of dynamic competition, but the patents held by R.C.A. and the radio group afforded them a privileged position in production as well as the ability to claim royalties from the other producers. Much more significant, though related to the early entrenched position of monopoly power, were the consequences of the frantic emphasis on set production in the first years of the new medium.

Since radio is essentially a *means of communication* and only incidentally a manufacturing activity, the development of the industry in the United States completely reversed what might be considered rational priorities and subordinated communications objectives (whatever they might be regarded to be) to the manufacturing and sales of receiving sets. As one account put it, "the founders of the Radio Corporation of America consortium had been less concerned with what would come out of the magic receiving sets than with who would sell them".[9] The degree to which early broadcasting was dominated by the manufacturing interest is only partially indicated by the 222 manufacturers of radio and electrical equipment who were

---

[8] N. R. Danielian, *A.T. & T. The Story of Industrial Conquest,* The Vanguard Press, New York, 1939, p. 121.

[9] L. White, *The American Radio,* University of Chicago Press, Chicago, 1947, p. 12.

also broadcasters in 1923. The stations owned by the manufacturers were the most influential transmitters.

The expectations of the manufacturers, that sales would be stimulated if broadcasts were expanded, were well-founded. Despite their stations' fading and clashing signals, popular enthusiasm rose spectacularly. From 1922 to 1925, the number of families with radios increased from .2 percent to 10.1 percent of the population. The value of sets produced grew from $5 million in 1922 to $100 million in 1926 and even more rapidly thereafter. The stream of sets coming onto the market satisfied the public's demand for immediate participation in the wondrous new world of radio, and provided manufacturers with more than satisfactory profits. That the future of radio in America also was being determined, however inadvertently, by the millions of individual purchase transactions was not so apparent. Yet once the number of set-owners reached into the millions, a chain of events had been concluded, and the new medium assumed what is now a very familiar and conventional role inside the American home —that of the salesman.

The large radio audience constituted an unsuspecting but willing market for the high capacity industries that had grown up in the country. The needs of manufacturers to dispose of goods were rapidly linked with the desire of set-owners to hear something on their newly-acquired receivers. Commercial broadcasting was the product of those two widely separate interests. A chronicler of early radio wrote: ". . . the public in general did not realize that radio broadcasting must find some means of self-support or perish. Manufacturers of radio might have an incentive to broadcast until the radio boom should have passed its crest, but so soon as profits might be endangered by the expenses of broadcasting they too must close their radio stations."[10] The newly-constituted Federal Radio Commission in its first formal statement of intention in 1927, yielded completely to market forces when it noted that "advertising must be accepted for the present as the sole means of support of broadcasting, and regulation must be relied upon to prevent the abuse and over use of the privilege."[11]

Sales of broadcast time created the conditions and the prospects

---

[10] G. L. Archer, *History of Radio to 1926,* The American Historical Society, New York, 1938, p. 286.

[11] Federal Communications Commission, *Public Service Responsibility of Broadcast Licensees,* March 7, 1946, Washington, D. C., p. 41.

for considerable profit-making. The ownership of radio stations in choice market areas offered attractive investment opportunities. And though the air has always been a natural resource owned by all the people, the practice of granting licenses for station-holding which are never revoked and allowing, at the same time, the sale of stations, "did in fact treat channels as private property."[12]

The market economy pushed radio communications first into the hands of the equipment manufacturers and then into the arms of commercial broadcasting. Other interests, whatever their merits, were powerless. Radio became an effective participant in the accelerating produce-and-consume cycle. Until the arrival of television, it was the most persuasive and, accordingly, highly paid salesman in the nation.

## Educational Radio

Intentions, and there were many, to use broadcasting for educational purposes found the market place a less than friendly environment. The mass production of sets had created a national audience in half a decade. Programming, costly even when atrocious, received its commercial support only by appealing to the widest listening public.

Talent too moved, however sheepishly, in the direction of the fatter commercial payrolls. Laboring against this national pattern of broadcasting, educational radio with its shoestring budgets was helpless. It could not meet either its own requirements or compete with the popular qualities of its commercial rival. Of the 202 educational station licenses that had been granted between 1921 and 1936, 164 were permitted to expire or were transferred to commercial interests, most of them prior to 1930.[13] Accordingly, in the critically formative first two decades of its utilization, the radio spectrum had only the most limited opportunity to demonstrate its capabilities for human resource enhancement.

Incorporated into the prevailing national pattern of resource utilization, radio served instead as an extremely effective agent for the further promotion and extension of that pattern. By the time its

---

[12] Erik Barnow, "A History of Broadcasting", Volume 1 to 1933, Oxford University Press, 1966, p. 178.

[13] L. White, *op. cit.*, p. 101.

potential for human improvement was more widely recognized and numerous educational stations were established on a sounder basis, its adult audiences had been lost to the newer and even more compelling medium of television. The contributions of the later noncommercial radio stations generally have been limited by compartmentalization into formal educational channels with narrow appeal. Public service broadcasting has been isolated from the bulk of the listening audience which has long since been conditioned by commercial programming.

## Early Television Experience in the United States

Despite two decades of disappointments and unfulfilled promise in radio, television practically repeated radio's developmental pattern. As in the earlier era, private decision-makers sought quick gain and used public interest in the new medium to press for narrow advantage. In 1945, the Federal Communications Commission accepted the position of some of the more influential members of the electronics industry to approve a pre-war technical standard for television. There was no time, these industrial leaders argued, to develop the UHF portion of the spectrum which was then almost unoccupied. Though many had warned against putting television broadcasting into the already crowded VHF portion of the spectrum, this was where R.C.A. and other potent members of the radio industry had made their pre-war investments on research and development and they were anxious to capitalize quickly on them. The public, fascinated with the new product in communications, eagerly purchased sets. Once again, production of equipment took precedence over, indeed eliminated, concern with the content of the medium. The retail value of factory output of television sets from 1946 thru 1967 totalled 23.3 billion dollars.

To induce consumers to make the investment decision that the purchase of a receiver represented, stations had to offer steady schedules of programming. Television broadcasting from the beginning was entirely dependent on advertising revenues for its support and the few years of uncertainty that characterized radio's infancy were absent. Commercially oriented, television sought mass audiences to attract billings from sponsoring advertisers and to entice new customers as well. Its successes can be measured in the rising curve of its time sales, climbing from less than $9 million in 1948 to $1,835 millions in 1966, at which point its total time sales were double that of radio's ($912 million) .[14]

Not unexpectedly, the resource enhancing capabilities of the spectrum in the television frequencies have suffered the same neglect in TV's growth period as they did in the first years of radio. It is probable that resource wastage has been, if anything, more excessive and damaging in the latter period. Combined visual-auditory stimulation has produced an overwhelming impression-and-image-creating force. The emotional and educational implications of *what has been offered* on commercial TV are just as significant as what has not been provided on weak or ineffectual or nonexistent educational television.

## Educational Television in the United States

Educational Television's (ETV) early experiences paralleled those that enfeebled non-commercial radio. Unable to secure generous financing, it was no match for the private TV networks which sent signals across the country. Furthermore, ETV had a major technical disadvantage in addition to its weak competitive situation.

The original FCC decision which placed television broadcasting in the VHF portion of the spectrum was a serious engineering error. More space was needed and it could be obtained only in the higher bands, the so-called UHF. In 1952 the FCC opened up 70 channels in the UHF frequencies, reserving many of them for educational stations. Unfortunately, the set manufacturers were not disposed to produce receivers that could accommodate both VHF and UHF channels. More costly to manufacture, the industry was reluctant, it said, to put higher priced units on the market in any great volume, fearful of the impact on its overall sales.

The net effect of this tangle of commercial interests was to make ETV almost inoperative in the UHF frequencies to which most of its stations had been assigned. In 1962, it was estimated by the FCC that "of some 52 million television receivers throughout the country, only 8.7 million (less than 17 percent) are capable of receiving television signals which are broadcast in the ultrahigh frequencies (UHF) ."[15] Nearly 80 percent of the assigned frequencies in the UHF

[14] *Television Fact Book,* 1968-69, pp. 51a and 55a.

[15] N. Minow, Chairman, Federal Communications Commission, before the Sub-Committee on Communications, Committee on Commerce, U.S. Senate, February 20, 1962, Hearings on All-Channel Television Receivers, 87th Congress, 2nd Session, on S. 2109.

range went unused throughout the 1950s.[16] Only in 1962 did Congress finally approve legislation that compelled television manufacturers to produce sets, after April 30, 1964, that could receive all channels, the 12 VHF and the 70 UHF as well.

The modest developments in the last few years of non-commercial radio and educational television have been unable to overcome the initial setbacks. Though chairmen of the Federal Communications Commission continuously have deplored the fact that "educational television should permanently struggle for subsistence,"[17] financing remains an urgent unsolved problem. Another difficulty that is an outgrowth of the commercial system of broadcasting is the separation of programming into educational (non-commercial) and recreational (commercial). This division totally undermines the educational offerings and reduces their impact to marginal benefits.

In assessing the failure to maximize television's potential for human resource improvement, a former president of the National Association of Educational Broadcasters declared: "With regard to education's rights in the electro-magnetic spectrum, I am impressed with the past record of neither the FCC, the Congress, the trade press, nor industry."[18] To insist upon a single explanation for this poor performance in resource utilization would be misleading. Yet one conclusion from the experiences of American broadcasting seems unavoidable. This is the market economy's demonstrated inability to provide the comprehensive treatment that reasonable resource performance in a modern interdependent society requires.

For some resources, and this is especially true of the radio spectrum, *some* planning is an indispensable prerequisite for their physical utilization. Overlooking the allocation of frequencies, for instance, can quickly produce chaos in the spectrum, as it did in the 1920's, making it unusable for all. Again, the characteristics of electromagnetic waves make them most useful for specialized purposes. Fore-

---

[16] Noting this, Representative Oren Harris, the Chairman of the House Committee on Interstate and Foreign Commerce, declared that ". . . one of the most valuable resources that we have in the world is the spectrum . . . perhaps one of the most glaring examples of waste of a resource is the present utilization of some parts of the spectrum." *Hearings on H.R. 8031*, 87th Congress, 2nd Session, March 5, 1962, p. 29.

[17] *New York Times*, October 3, 1964.

[18] H. J. Skornia, "A Pandora's Box of Dissent and Challenge", *Audio-visual Instruction*, April 1964, p. 224.

thought is necessary to match end use with the physical qualities of the resource, so that if television belongs in the UHF frequencies it ought not be placed in the VHF bands. Once technical decisions have been made, they may be changed only at great expense and inconvenience; e.g., those with VHF sets, cannot shift to UHF without an additional financial outlay. The social consequences of unplanned resource use remain to plague us for generations.

In 1937, the Federal Communications Commission reviewed the course of radio broadcasting to that date and concluded: ". . . the existing radio broadcast system is the product of a new art which like other new industries have developed in advance of complete understanding of its social significance."[19] Since that time, radio has made much technical progress and an entirely new and more influential use of the spectrum has been developed with the advent of television. It can no longer be maintained, if it ever could, that the social significance of these powerful communications media is uncomprehended. In fact, it is comprehended all too well by the most influential elements in this privately-organized economy. Broadcast communications, using the people's property, the air waves, have been monopolized for private enrichment. More perilous still, the mass audiences of radio-television broadcasting are continuously persuaded by the materials offered them of the desirability of the cultural, political and economic status quo. David Potter wrote that the impact of commercial broadcasting is "to make the individual like what he gets—to enforce already existing attitudes, to diminish the range and variety of choices, and, in terms of abundance, to exalt the materialistic virtues of consumption."[20]

Communications, which could be a vigorous mechanism of social change, have become instead, a major obstacle to national reconstruction. They have been seized by the commanding interests in the market economy, to promote narrow national and international objectives while simultaneously making alternate paths seem either undesirable or preventing their existence from becoming known.

---

[19] Federal Communications Commission, *Report on Social and Economic Data Pursuant to the Informal Hearing on Broadcasting*, Docket 4063, Beginning October 5, 1936, G.P.O., 1938, p. 11.

[20] David Potter, *People of Plenty*, The University of Chicago Press, Chicago, 1954, p. 188.

# CHAPTER 3

# The Domestic Communications Complex

Part 1 — *Militarization of the Governmental Sector*

"One of the bulwarks of a free society is freedom of communications. Its commerce, its education, its politics, its spiritual integrity, and its security depend upon an unimpeded and unsubservient exchange of information and ideas." Telecommunications—A Program for Progress, a Report by the President's Communications Policy Board, Washington, March 1951.

The growth of American power in this century has been tied inextricably to war—preparing for war and waging war. The great depression of the 1930's was liquidated only by the outbreak of the second world war. Ten million American workers, it will be remembered, were unemployed after a decade of economic stagnation, on the eve of war in 1939. Moreover, since Hiroshima, the United States has spent almost a thousand *billion* dollars on producing the instrumentation of violence and in financing military involvements which have included two sizeable wars (Korea and Vietnam) and numerous small-scale engagements (Greece, Lebanon, the Congo, Cuba and the Dominican Republic). A schizophrenic national condition has been created which finds mounting material well-being for large numbers of the population alongside of and largely dependent on omni-present and numbing terror.

At the base of what some have termed a "Garrison Economy",[1] is the American business system, which almost instinctively interprets social change at home or abroad as a threat to its opportunities for

---

[1] Terence McCarthy, *The Garrison Economy*, Columbia Forum, Fall, 1966.

uninterrupted money-making. Since most of the world has been caught up in social ferment whose consequences and end are nowhere in sight, the probabilities of conflict are incredibly high and enduring. It is a matter of American leadership, as it views the world, selecting which one of several current "threats" is the most perilous.

In such an atmosphere it is small wonder that President Eisenhower, in his farewell address to the American people in 1961, detected the emergence of a "military-industrial complex" which, he noted, influenced decision-making at every level of national life. More ominous still, half a dozen years and two Administrations later, the former Science Advisor to Presidents Kennedy and Johnson, Jerome Wiesner, writes that "The Cold War is Dead, But the Arms Race Rumbles On".[2] He attributes this paradox to the military-industrial-technological coalition, which along the way has picked up additional powerful friends in Congress and the press.

Eisenhower cautioned the people and their governmental representatives to remain vigilant to the threat that the years of continuous emergency living imposed:

"In the councils of Government we must guard against the acquisition of unwarranted influence, whether sought or unsought, by the military-industrial complex. The potential for the disastrous rise of misplaced power exists and will persist. We must never let the weight of this combination endanger our liberties or democratic processes. We should take nothing for granted. Only an alert and knowledgeable citizenry can compel the proper meshing of the huge industrial and military machinery of defense with our peaceful methods and goals, so that security and liberty may prosper together."[3]

Knowledgeability is essential to the citizen in a democracy. If the people are informed presumably they will be alert to any potential threats to their liberties. What happens, however, if the military-industrial power enclave has grown up strongest in the informational apparatus itself? What may be expected, if the alarm system, so to speak, has been disconnected by those very elements it was designed to signal against?

The influence and importance of communications in a complex mass society need constant re-telling. Special access to information

---

2 Jerome Wiesner, "The Cold War is Dead But the Arms Race Rumbles On", *Bulletin of the Atomic Scientists,* June, 1967.

3 *The New York Times,* January 18, 1961.

justifiably has been recognized as a corridor to power. The control of communications is generally a primary step in the acquisition of political authority. Situated at the center of modern organization, the informational apparatus distributes messages in a far from random way. At the same time, the volume, form and speed with which current electronic systems transmit intelligence have produced a qualitatively new factor in human and group relationships. Telecommunications are today the most dynamic forces affecting not only the ideological but the material bases of society.

Attention in recent decades has fastened on the overt marks of a semi-mobilized economy. Defense contracts, the draft, overseas bases, local wars, governmental price-wage "guidelines", and similar phenomena are the recognizable features of the state neither fully at war nor at peace. What may be less familiar to some is the structural transformation of society itself as it accommodates its routine functioning to a prolonged state of emergency.

At the core of the changing social order is the domestic communications apparatus, itself undergoing a profound restructuring while at the same time promoting shifts in the community-at-large by virtue of its compelling informational authority.

Three changing elements can be distinguished in the machinery of American communications since World War II. There is the growing military influence on the national governmental communications system. There is the continuous enlargement of the *civilian* military-industrial communications bloc. There is the special role of American *military* communications in securing the international status quo. This chapter concerns itself with a review of the changing communications activity *within* the national government itself.

## The Evolution of United States Governmental Communications Structures

Practically since radio's introduction in the United States, the utilization of the radio spectrum has been divided between the private and the governmental sector. Private transmission except for a brief and chaotic period of almost total laissez-faire, has been regulated by federal authority. The regulatory responsibility was exercised first by the Federal Radio Commission from 1927 to 1934 and since then by the Federal Communications Commission (FCC).

Governmental activity in radio is directly under the authority of the President of the United States. The allocation of radio frequencies and the character of government broadcasting are therefore immediate Presidential concerns. The satisfaction of governmental users' needs for frequencies is a matter requiring the chief executive's sanction.

Though the President is responsible for all governmental broadcasting, since 1922 he has been assisted by an intergovernmental committee that has assigned frequencies to claimants. Originally a voluntary grouping, the Interdepartment Radio Advisory Committee (IRAC) has had what amounts to an almost uninterrupted forty-five year history inside the federal bureaucracy. Accordingly, IRAC's position and influence within the governmental structure has generally determined the direction of governmental communications policies, and sometimes matters affecting, but moving beyond, communications interests.

The character of a single governmental structure may often illuminate a wide slice of the social process. Communications developments in this technically progressive society may be better understood by studying the changing composition of the IRAC and also by noting the place that the IRAC has occupied in the overall governmental structure throughout its history.

Twenty-five years of war and international tension find their reflection in the distribution of decision-making *within* the IRAC as well as in the IRAC's location in the total administrative machinery of the national government. To be sure, the expanding role of government in the national economy and the application of an advanced communications apparatus to all areas of governmental activity have contributed to the work load of the IRAC and have made its frequency allocation decisions of mounting importance to the governmental departments that comprise it. But apart from, and dwarfing, the steadily increasing general demand for spectrum space has been the pressure of the military services for radio frequencies.

A recent estimate indicates that the Armed Forces account for about three-fifths of *government's* share of the spectrum.[4] Just what proportion of the *total* spectrum is at the disposal of the military is difficult to discover. Technical and security factors prevent a sharply-

---

[4] Paul T. Miles, Office of Telecommunications Management, reported in *Telecommunications Reports*, Vol. 32, No. 28, June 20, 1966, p. 24.

defined division of the spectrum from becoming publicly available. One writer states that "fully half of the total spectrum is now given over by a rule of thumb never formalized, to government and military services, outside the FCC's purview. No one knows whether this division is just."[5]

Another appraisal, made a few years earlier, put the portion of the radio spectrum that is available to non-governmental users at only 30 percent, with "the remaining 70 percent being Government agency controlled, with about 40 percent exclusively Government and totally withdrawn from citizen use."[6]

Whichever the estimate, it seems evident that a very substantial segment of the radio spectrum is reserved for governmental use and that the preponderant share of that portion is in the hands of the military services. This is the hard rock fact that has shaped the evolution of the body that passes on frequency allocations among government users. Within IRAC itself is revealed the growing eminence of the Armed Forces vis à vis other users of telecommunications.

When IRAC was established in 1922 on a voluntary basis by those departments and agencies of the federal government having an interest in radio communications, it resided for bookkeeping and accounting purposes, in the business-oriented Department of Commerce. The unit worked in cooperation with the Secretary of Commerce, and for the first eleven years of its existence, IRAC's Chairman was a representative of the Department of Commerce. Throughout this period the President was assisted in his responsibility of assigning radio frequencies to governmental users by the Secretary of Commerce and the Secretary in turn was advised by IRAC.

With the creation of the Federal Communications Commission in 1934, the President requested its chairman to assist him in his communications responsibilities, maintaining, however, the advisory services of the IRAC in frequency assignment duties. The Chairmanship of IRAC was assumed by a representative of the FCC where it remained uninterruptedly until 1941 when it returned for two years to a Department of Commerce representative.

---

[5] "Breaking TV Out of Its Box", by Lawrence Lessing, *Fortune*, September 1964, p. 178.

[6] Testimony of Donald C. Beelar in, *Space Communications and Allocation of Radio Spectrum*, Hearings before the Communications Subcommittee of the Committee on Commerce, U.S. Senate, 87th Congress, 1st Session on Space Communications and S. J. Res. 32, August 1, 23, 24, 1961, Washington, D. C., p. 168.

Prior to World War II, IRAC was an interdepartmental body comprised of the many governmental users of the radio spectrum, but firmly anchored to civilian leadership and administrative authority.

During the war years, 1941-1945, executive orders created first a Defense Communications Board and later a Board of War Communications, to both of which the IRAC served as an advisory committee. In the brief interlude between the end of the war and the outbreak of the Korean War, IRAC remained under the FCC budget appropriation with its own earmarked funds, as it had since 1938 when it received its first independent appropriation. Its chairmanship shifted, in this period to a representative of the War Department in 1946, back to Commerce in 1947, to Interior in 1948, to Navy and State in 1949, to Treasury and Commerce in 1950, and to Commerce in 1951.

## Military Take-Over of IRAC

Only five years after World War II's end, the economy moved back into a state of partial mobilization. Insofar as communications were concerned, "the conflict in Korea and the tenseness of the world situation brought about a significant increase in frequency requirements for defense purposes."[7]

The permanent transformation of IRAC from essentially a civilian intergovernmental agency into an adjunct of military planning and mobilization, appears to coincide with the waging of the Korean War from 1950 to 1953. The impact of the war on IRAC was direct and observable. One sign of the times, the Central Intelligence Agency (CIA), newly established in 1950, "surfaced" briefly to place representatives on IRAC in 1951 and 1952 before it returned to the befitting shadows.

An executive order of President Truman (E.O. 10297) in October 1951, established a Telecommunications Advisor to the President. The order stipulated that the IRAC should report to and assist the Telecommunications Advisor. In the same year, as a result of increased activities, which strained its limited resources, IRAC had a budget crisis. It was "settled" when the newly-appointed Telecommunications Advisor "prevailed upon the Department of Defense

---

[7] "The Interdepartment Radio Advisory Committee", Executive Office of the President, Office of Emergency Planning, Office of the Director of Telecommunications, August 2, 1965, p. 2.

to make available $29,270 to augment the IRAC funds for the remainder of Fiscal Year 1952 . . ."[8]

So began IRAC's administrative and financial dependence on the military services. Failing to secure an adequate budget for its activities in the fiscal year 1953 while still under FCC auspices, the Telecommunications Advisor, acting upon instruction from the President, "called a meeting of member agencies and recommended a schedule of subscription based upon the number of radio frequency applications submitted to the IRAC for processing by each agency and an estimate of each agency's interest in national telecommunications matters."[9] The proposed schedule was put into effect and the IRAC received its funds for fiscal year 1953 and 1954 from the pro rata subscriptions of its members. With this method of financing, the Department of Defense, already the largest user and most insistent applicant for frequencies, became the chief source of IRAC's budget.

Another executive order by President Eisenhower in June 1953 (E.O. 10460) transferred to the Director of Defense Mobilization the telecommunications advisory function. Under this order, IRAC moved administratively from its former civilian shelter, the FCC, to the first of a series of administrative structures heavily concerned with defense and military questions.

Accordingly, IRAC's appropriation request was transferred to the budget of the Office of Defense Mobilization. It has remained in the successor agencies, the Office of Civil and Defense Mobilization (OCDM) and the Office of Emergency Planning (OEP), respectively, to this date. Somewhat earlier, in October 1953, FCC membership in IRAC was discontinued; however, joint IRAC/FCC meetings were inaugurated in which a liaison representative would speak for FCC. As one observer noted, this scarcely developed as a relationship of equals.[10]

Predictably, IRAC's growing financial and administrative dependency on the Government's military segment had its reflection in the internal organization and in the direction of its activities. A former Army representative assumed the chairmanship of IRAC in 1952 and

---

[8] *Ibid.*, p. 15.

[9] *Ibid.*, p. 16.

[10] Victor G. Rosenblum, "Low Visibility Decision-Making by Administrative Agencies: The Problem of Spectrum Allocation", *Administrative Law Review*, Vol. 18, Fall, 1965, pp. 19-54.

1953 as the designee of the Telecommunications Advisor to the President. Then, from 1954 to 1965, the Interdepartment Committee's chairman was W. E. Plummer. Plummer, a CIA representative to IRAC in 1951, was appointed as the representative, in turn, of ODM, OCDM and finally OEP, the various mobilization agencies that have succeeded each other since the early 1950's.

IRAC became the channel through which the Department of Defense's communications programs became national policies. In 1960, for instance, the military representatives on IRAC, submitted to the Committee proposals drafted in the Department of Defense in anticipation of the International Radio Conference scheduled to convene in Geneva in 1963:

". . . The Department of Defense representatives on IRAC (Interdepartmental Radio Advisory Committee) made comprehensive studies during 1960 which led to the formulation of drafts of possible U.S. proposals for frequency allocation to be considered at the forthcoming ITU Conference. These drafts resulted in a formal proposal to the IRAC early in January 1961. These formal proposals were then amended by IRAC to incorporate the views and requirements of other agencies, including NASA and were informally coordinated with the liaison representative of the Federal Communications Commission. . ."[11]

U.S. negotiators at Geneva in the fall of 1963 secured an agreement on this draft which originated in the Pentagon. Fifty megacycles of the radio spectrum were reserved for the exclusive use of space communications, an allocation generally regarded by American experts as useful only for military purposes. The military aim of the DOD was to use these frequencies for space communications for mobile transmitters in their counter-insurgency campaigns in progress and anticipated.[12]

While the work of IRAC as well as its financing, composition and location in the bureaucracy moved steadily closer to the military establishment, a parallel communications development was occurring at the highest levels of government.

---

11 Space Communication and Allocation of Radio Spectrum, *op. cit.*, pp. 185-186. Statement of Admiral M. E. Curts, Director of Telecommunications Policy, DOD.

12 *Satellite Communications — 1964*, Part I, Hearings before a Subcommittee of the Committee on Government Operations, House of Representatives, 88th Congress, Second Session, August 6, 10, and 11, 1964. pp. 193, 109-110.

## Formation of the National Communications System

An awakened recognition of telecommunications' importance to the nation's domestic and international power position amidst the continuing global tension stimulated debate in and outside of Congress on the necessity for a "national" policy on telecommunications. Dr. Harold Brown, at the time director of research for the Department of Defense urged:

> "It is . . . important to recognize that our domestic and international telecommunications systems are critical factors both in our military posture and in the cold war struggle and, indeed, throughout the whole spectrum of conflict. We cannot today consider our communications systems solely as civil activities merely to be regulated as such, but we must consider them as essential instruments of national policy in our struggle for survival and establish policy and organization consistent with our situation. . ."[13]

The relatively relaxed arrangements for allocating frequencies in the radio spectrum by informal decision-making of IRAC, with FCC participation, seemed to many inadequate and outdated. The great growth in demand for spectrum space by both private and governmental users eliminated the goodnatured atmosphere of abundance that formerly served to ease conflicting demands. It was unclear how objective allocation judgments could be made by IRAC when the Committee consisted of a group of users, each of whom had his own special interest to press.

Also puzzling was the split authority by which FCC administered the private, non-governmental allocation function and IRAC handled the government agencies' requests for spectrum space. How were these sectors' demands to be reconciled on a basis of equity, efficiency and essentiality? A State Department spokesman explained the predicament:

> "We are in a peculiar situation here. You see, most countries abroad have a ministry of post, telegraph and telephone, where they sometimes are unified under a minister. Here we have a divided house, of course. On the one hand we have the Government and on the other hand we have

---

[13] "Space Communications and Allocation of Radio Spectrum", *op. cit.*, p. 184.

private industry, and private industry, of course, is sub-
servient to the Federal Communications Commission, and
the Government, of course, is represented in IRAC by
OCDM. But there is no overall planning of our communications system, both government and private, by any super-
body. . .[14]

Whatever their motivation, these concerns had solid justification.
Despite its division into two compartments, one governmental and
the other private, the radio spectrum remains a natural resource
which, to be utilized effectively, must be regarded as a unity and
treated comprehensively. The division violates this unity and makes
disagreements and inefficiencies inevitable. Demands on both sectors have been increasing steadily and the supply of frequencies,
enlarged though they have been through technological advances,
remains finite. The spectrum has become more crowded with users
and frequency allocation is no longer an easy matter. Also troublesome is the matter of rapidly changing technology which often makes
equipment obsolete. Sometimes it suggests newer and better uses for
the frequency assignments made in the past. When the spectrum is
artifically separated into governmental and private bands, modifica-
tions and shifts in utilization are correspondingly more difficult to
secure, since vested positions are tenaciously defended.

Unification thus became the quest of the communications studies
that proliferated in the 1950's, but the fragmented condition in
American utilization of the spectrum was not overcome. President
Truman's Communications Policy Board, established in 1950, suggested and the President accepted the creation of a Telecommunications Advisor. The Advisor resigned, however, in 1953 and his functions were reassigned, first to the Director of the Office of Defense
Mobilization, and in a second reorganization in 1958, to the Office
of Civil and Defense Mobilization. Communications responsibilities
remained divided and unsatisfactory.[15]

---

[14] *Ibid.*, p. 195, Statement of Francis Colt de Wolf, Chief, Telecommunications
Division, Department of State.

[15] See, Special Advisory Committee on Telecommunications, (Cooley Committee) Report, December 29, 1958, reprinted in *Spectrum Allocation*, Hearings
before a Subcommittee of the Committee on Interstate and Foreign Commerce,
House of Representatives, 86th Congress, First Session, June 8 and 9th, 1959,
pp. 40-46.

Limited unification, when it came at last, was effected under the aegis of the Armed Forces. If the Korean War, beginning in 1950, had helped to produce a military complexion in the composition and the administrative organization of the IRAC, a decade later the Cuban-American encounters of 1961 and 1962 were the sources of a second, more pervasive militarization of United States governmental communications.

The chronology is important. On February 16, 1962, President Kennedy, by executive order (E.O. 10995), established the position of Director of Telecommunications Management in the Office of Emergency Planning (OEP), the mobilization agency that had succeeded the Office of Civil and Defense Mobilization (OCDM) in 1961. The Director of Telecommunications had in addition a second responsibility as the Assistant Director of the OEP. IRAC was placed under the jurisdiction of OEP in an advisory capacity to the newly-created position of Director of Telecommunications.

The President's order, which began "Whereas telecommunications is vital to the security and welfare of this Nation and to the conduct of its foreign affairs . . .",[16] grew out of the crisis atmosphere generated by the continuing Cuban-American emergency. The communications problems of concentrating the United States military and diplomatic effort during the Bay of Pigs invasion had revealed many weaknesses in the national communications network. The executive order designed to overcome these deficiences marked the first serious effort since Truman's unsuccessful attempt a decade earlier to establish a unified center for communications decision-making in the executive branch of the government.

In Congressional hearings the question came up as to why the control of all governmental telecommunications was placed under the administration of a mobilization agency. To the query, "Why would the peacetime function of frequency allocation be in the Office of Emergency Planning", the Director of Telecommunications responded: "Well, I do not know that I can give a good reason for that. It just evolved there through a series of changes which started back in 1951 and then evolved into the Office of Civil and Defense

---

[16] Executive Order, No. 10995, February 16, 1962. Federal Register. February 20, 1962 (1519) (27F.R.).

Mobilization, and when that became the Office of Emergency Planning it became a part of its responsibilities."[17]

The appointment of a Director of Telecommunications, who served as an Assistant Director of the OEP as well, unquestionably centralized the government's communications. To what extent it also militarized them could be appreciated only later. Related measures followed quickly. The Administration seemed to feel that a rising global social revolution for the moment centered in Cuba. Lt. General Starbird, at that time Director of the Pentagon's Defense Communications Agency, which tied together all Department of Defense communications, testified:

> "When the Cuban situation arose, there was the necessity to concentrate all communications rapidly in a particular place.
> Representative Flood: In the Bay of Pigs or the build up later on?
> General Starbird: The build up (deleted)
> Latin America is an area which has not had much advancement in the communications field. . ."[18]

The Government's concern for having immediate communications with distant "trouble" spots became a high priority item on its national security agenda. Confirmation was supplied by the Department of State before another congressional committee:

> "The Interdepartmental Committee on Communications, known as the Orrick Committee was set up at the time of Cuban crisis in accordance with a National Security decision, endorsed by the White House. Mr. Orrick, then Deputy Under Secretary of State for Administration, was named chairman as the Department of State was having particular difficulty with its communications."[19]

---

[17] *Satellite Communications—1964* (Part 2), *op. cit.,* Hearings before a Subcommittee of the Committee on Government Operations, House of Representatives, 88th Congress, Second Session, August 6, 10 and 11, 1964. Statement of Lt. General James D. O'Connell, Special Assistant to the President for Telecommunications, p. 752.

[18] Hearings before the Subcommittee on Department of Defense Appropriations of the House Committee on Appropriations, 88th Congress, Second Session, *Department of Defense Appropriations for 1965*, p. 699.

[19] *Satellite Communications—1964* (Part 1), *op. cit.,* p. 353.

The final report of this special committee recommended the creation of a national communications network, and President Kennedy
on August 21, 1963, in what was then a classified memorandum to the
heads of executive departments and agencies, established a National
Communications System. The emergence of the National Communications System marked the formal assumption of control of all governmental communications (at least those of a long-line nature) by the
Department of Defense.

The President's memorandum was couched in terms of military
urgency, although in the overall network of federal communications
there was a sizable portion of circuitry which had no military significance.[20]

> "The objective of the NCS", the policy statement went,
> "will be to provide necessary communications for the Federal
> Government under all conditions ranging from a normal
> situation to national emergencies and international crises;
> including nuclear attack. . . Initial emphasis in developing
> the NCS will be on meeting the most critical needs for com-
> munication in national security programs, particularly in
> overseas areas. As rapidly as is consistent with meeting criti-
> cal needs, other Government needs will be examined and
> satisfied, as warranted, in the context of the NCS."[21]

The Director of Telecommunications Management, created by the
President's February 1962 executive order, was made responsible "for
policy direction of the development and operation" of the system.
Sharing authority along with the Director of Telecommunications
Management was an *Executive Agent* of the National Communications System whose task was to design the system, carry on long-range
planning and research and development and work with all the user
agencies on their needs and priorities.

---

[20] The National Communications System which is now in operation involves an
annual operating cost of over $900 million, excluding the more than $200 million
expended annually for research, development, test and evaluation. Of this amount,
$143 million represents the long-haul, point-to-point communications of networks
of other Government agencies outside the DOD but associated with the NCS. In
terms of governmental communications annual expenditures, almost 85% is
accounted for by the DOD. Appropriation Hearings, DOD., 1965, *op. cit.*, p. 706.

[21] Memorandum to the Heads of Executive Departments and Agencies, entitled
"Establishment of the National Communications System", August 21, 1963, The
White House, reprinted in Satellite Communications, *op. cit.*, pp. 592-594.

## Militarization of the NCS

The fate of the new agency was settled when President Kennedy designated the Secretary of Defense as the Executive Agent of the National Communications System. Since 24 of the 30 million channel miles of communications circuitry found in the NCS are owned or leased by the DOD,[22] it was to be expected that the military establishment would be well-represented in the new system. What was surprising was the willingness of the Administration to turn over completely to the military services the entire governmental communications apparatus. Though the Director of Telecommunications Management was responsible for policy direction and guidance of the NCS, the day-to-day work of the system and the immediate decision-making rested entirely with Mr. McNamara, then the Secretary of Defense. To begin with, Secretary McNamara appointed Lt. General Starbird to be the manager of the National Communications System. The general at the same time was also the Director of the Defense Communications Agency in the Pentagon. General Starbird was authorized by Mr. McNamara to use the military personnel of the Defense Communications Agency as the staff of the new National System, while the DCA received an increase in personnel for this purpose.[23] Somewhat later on, General Starbird described his task: ". . . I am required to perform somewhat the same function for the civil operating agencies of the NCS as I perform in my capacity as director, DCA, for the Department of Defense."[24]

The takeover of the National Communications System by the administrative and executive machinery of the Department of Defense was so thorough that it prompted one Congressman on the House Subcommittee on Appropriations to inquire:

"Why didn't the Defense Communications Agency take over total responsibility? You have great communications ability.

[22] *Satellite Communications,* Report prepared by Military Operations Subcommittee, Committee on Government Operations, 88th Congress, Second Session, House of Representatives, Washington, 1964, p. 82.

[23] Testimony of Lt. General Starbird, Hearings before Subcommittee on Department of Defense Appropriations, 88th Congress, Second Session, February 5, 1964, p. 688.

[24] National Communication Satellite Programs, Hearings before the Committee on Aeronautical and Space Sciences, United States Senate, 89th Congress, Second Session, January 25, 1966, p. 12.

Why was it necessary to set up an additional office and staff?" To which query, the Acting Director of the Defense Communications Agency replied: "I believe, this is my opinion . . . it is more palatable to the nonmilitary agencies to have separate treatment of their communications requirements. In short, they were concerned they would disappear within the military concern about its requirements."[25]

It is difficult even now to evaluate the extent of the qualitative shift in governmental authority that occurred with the assignment of the Secretary of Defense as Executive Agent of the NCS in 1963. For years, the Department of Defense's preemption of a large chunk of the radio spectrum has concerned many other claimants for frequencies. Even before the formation of the NCS, a former director of telecommunications management, Irvin Stewart, had questioned the military assessment of its *own* spectrum needs, much less, passing on the claims of other governmental users. Stewart asked: ". . . should the military assessment of its communications needs and the best way of meeting them be accepted without question?"[26] As Executive Agents, the Secretary of Defense is able to unilaterally judge the frequency needs and the suitability of the communications planning of all the other government users. Such authority seems sweeping even to the DOD's warmest supporters. Indicative was a recent House Military Operations Subcommittee report which rather timidly noted that:

> . . . The committee pointed out in an earlier report that the Department of Defense, as a major claimant on telecommunications resources, is not in the best position to identify and evaluate other Government user requirements for communications or to make policy decisions affecting them. We recommend (ed) that this responsibility be assumed by the director of Telecommunications Management.[27]

---

25 Hearings before a subcommittee of the House Committee on *Appropriations for 1966 the Department of Defense,* 89th Congress, First Session, February 26, 1965, p. 658.

26 Irvin Stewart, "Telecommunications Management: The Strategy of Organizational Location", *Public Administration Review,* September 1963, p. 153.

27 Government Use of Satellite Communications, Forty-Third Report by the Committee on Government Operations, 89th Congress, Second Session, House Report No. 2318, October 19, 1966, Washington, p. 10.

Further enhancing the Secretary of Defense's job as Executive Agent for the NCS was the fact that the Directorship of Telecommunications in OEP was unfilled throughout the first year of the new system's operation. In effect, the only office excepting the Presidency to which the Secretary of Defense was responsible administratively was vacant throughout the NCS's first year of functioning. When, for instance, delicate, three-sided negotiations between the newly-established Communications Satellite Corporation (Comsat), the United States Government and dozens of other interested governments were being held in 1963 and 1964, concerning the feasibility of certain types of communication satellite facilities, Secretary of Defense McNamara was negotiating as the representative of the United States Government, under his authority as Executive Agent of the NCS. This delegation of authority was the subject of an interchange between Congressional Counsel Roback and the later-appointed Director of Telecommunications, James O'Connell.

> Counsel Roback asked; "Now, could Secretary McNamara, have signed an agreement, and would that have committed the government, or did that have to in a sense be approved by you or the President or what?"
>
> General O'Connell: "No. It was my understanding that he could have signed an agreement and that he had been delegated authority to do so."[28]

The position of Director of Telecommunications and Special Adviser to the President on Telecommunications was finally filled when President Johnson on April 8, 1964, nominated Lt. General James D. O'Connell, U.S. Army retired, to the post. General O'Connell had been the Chief Signal Officer of the U.S. Army from 1951 until his retirement in 1959. When his appointment came before a Senate Committee for consideration, Senator Cotton of New Hampshire inquired:

> ". . . You have a long and distinguished career as a professional soldier, from West Point to Lieutenant General and top of the signal activities of the Armed Services. You may be called upon in this new position to be the judge or referee between possible, even probable conflicts of interest or disputes between the armed services, federal agencies, and civilian organizations in the use of satellite systems.

---

[28] *Satellite Communications—1964* (Part 2), *op. cit.*, p. 758.

Do you feel that with your background, your military background, that you are in a position to be completely objective in dealing with possible conflict of interest or differences of opinion between them?" General O'Connell answered: "I have given this matter considerable thought, Senator Cotton, and I feel that I can be objective. I think it is very important to be completely objective in this position."[29]

Representative Holifield likewise voiced uneasiness at the thought of a retired general entrusted with overlooking the activities of the Secretary of Defense in governmental communications. He asked:

"This would not preclude you from advising the President of your personal judgment on a matter concerning this system even though the judgment might be contrary to the Secretary of Defense?" And again, General O'Connell answered: "No. I would have no hesitation to do this."[30]

All the same, two years later, when asked if he thought the duties of the NCS's Executive Agent should be transferred from the Secretary of Defense to his own office, the Office of Telecommunications Management, General O'Connell flatly declined the suggested extension of his authority—unusual behavior for a bureaucrat. O'Connell seemed quite satisfied with the division of labor in which Secretary McNamara made the critical decisions.[31]

The extent to which both the military and civilian reins of control over governmental communications had been put into the hands of General O'Connell, (along with Secretary of Defense McNamara,) was most succinctly presented in this dialogue:

Government Counsel Roback: "The President is Commander in Chief, so he has a defense responsibility, and under the Communications Act of 1934 he had to allocate Government frequencies, right?"

---

[29] Hearings before the Committee on Commerce, U.S. Senate, 88th Congress, Second Session on Nomination of James D. O'Connell, Director of Telecommunications, Office of Emergency Planning, May 5, 1964. Serial 61, U.S. Government Printing Office, p. 30.

[30] *Satellite Communications—1964* (Part 1), *op. cit.,* p. 498-499.

[31] Government Use of Satellite Communications, Hearings before a subcommittee of the Committee on Government Operations, House of Representatives, 89th Congress, 2nd Session, August and September, 1966, Washington, pp. 348-349.

> To which, General O'Connell replied: "And that has been delegated to me."[32]

Stated differently, the machinery of government communications has been so structured under recent Administrations that the control over governmental users of the spectrum has been concentrated in the Office of the Secretary of Defense and in the Office of the Director of Telecommunications. The latter office is itself in a mobilization agency, the OEP, and it is administered by a former general officer in the Armed Services.

The events described above relate to the envelopment of *government* communications facilities by military-dominated administrative structures. Years before these developments, complaints had been made about the increasing portion of the spectrum falling outside FCC control and regulation. In 1961 one observer unhappily noted that "Over the years the independence of the FCC has been gradually diluted with the increase in Government agency uses of radio; and the quantum of the radio spectrum remaining under the FCC's residual independence has become less and less."[33]

The FCC itself had earlier indicated its unreserved willingness to accept the demands of governmental users, and in particular those of the Department of Defense, regardless of the impact on non-governmental users. In 1959, the FCC's Chairman, Mr. John C. Doerfer, declared:

> "I think that the concept here which has created some misunderstanding is that the Executive and the military and the Defense have a specialized function which is different to varying degrees from that of the entire country. If I may make a statement, I think the day is past when every single person in this country is not a soldier in the next war for sure, whether it is hot or continues to be a cold one.
>
> We all have to recognize that. And we have to put national defense first. That's the first consideration that the FCC makes. All these other things fade into relative insignificance."[34]

Though this is the view of one individual it is not unrepresentative of the FCC's longstanding readiness to abandon its obligation to pro-

---

[32] *Satellite Communications—1964* (Part 1), *op. cit.*, p. 500.

[33] "Space Communications and Allocation of Radio Spectrum", *op. cit.*, p. 168.

[34] "Spectrum Allocation", *op. cit.*, p. 65.

tect the public interest in the civilian sector of the radio spectrum's use.[35] FCC Commissioner Nicholas Johnson, in his minority dissent against the ITT-ABC merger in December, 1966, put it this way: ". . . The Federal Communications Commission has the well-earned reputation of being less than a thoroughly vigilant agency. . ."[36]

In much the same vein, Professor Harry Skornia, first regular president of the National Association of Educational Broadcasters recently wrote that "the regulatory structure which controls [private] broadcasting in the United States would be a farce if it were not so tragic in its failure to protect the interests of the public."[37] A study of the administrative machinery of governmental communications in the late 1940's voiced the concern that "in this small but important area of public policy . . . the principle of civilian authority over the military services was endangered."[38] The creation of the National Communications System in 1963 consolidated and extended the already deep penetration of military influence in the communications system of the United States.

What is more, the civilian sector that continues to reside outside of the centralized decision-making of the National Communications System is itself surrounded by a formidable industrial-military sheath and its guardian, the FCC, is something less than a strong protector.

---

[35] Other examples of the "subservience of the FCC to IRAC decisions" are found in Victor G. Rosenblum's article "Low Visibility Decision-Making by Administrative Agencies: The Problem of Radio Spectrum Allocation," *Administrative Law Review*, Volume 18, Fall 1965, pp. 19-54.

[36] The ITT-ABC Merger Case, Docket No. 16828, Dissenting Opinion of Commissioner Nicholas Johnson, December 21, 1966.

[37] Harry J. Skornia, "Television and Society", McGraw-Hill Book Company, New York, 1965, pp. 69 and 81.

[38] Murray Edelman, *"The Licensing of Radio Services in the United States, 1927 to 1947*, The University of Illinois Press, Urbana, 1950, p. 218.

CHAPTER 4

# The Domestic Communications Complex

## Part Two—*The Military-Industrial Team*

Considered by itself, the military encirclement of governmental communications could be minimized, perhaps, as a temporary consequence of a continuing international emergency. What has been happening, though, gives little support to the notion that this is a transient condition, an interlude that will eventually disappear in a not-too-distant, more settled time. The same forces that have produced the military-industrial complex in American society-at-large have accounted for the rise of a powerful sub-sector, but by no means miniature, complex in communications.

The growth of the electronics industry has been phenomenal. The heavy governmental research and developmental expenditures, under the stimulus of anticipated military advantage, have been concentrated especially in the communications field. As reported in *Business Week* in 1967, "More than half the total R & D done by profit-making corporations this year will be concentrated in two industries —aerospace, and electrical machinery and communications. And these are the two industries in which the National Aeronautics and Space Administration and the Defense Department sink huge sums of research and development money."[1]

In addition to the massive governmental expenditures for technological improvement that have promoted growth in the big private companies, there is also the enormous guaranteed market made available to these same concerns by the continuing military purchases of hardware and systems. Eighteen electronics and communications

---

[1] *Business Week*, May 13, 1967.

95

corporations are represented among the top fifty industrial defense contractors in 1967. More would be included if transport, aircraft and missile-producing companies with substantial electronics production were included.

Finally, the dynamics of industrial growth have produced a concentration in the electronics industry, in both its hardware and broadcasting sides, that affords an economic leverage difficult to assess but not wise to underestimate. Along with their major manufacturing activities, the electronics equipment producers have been deeply involved in the informational broadcast field as well. The Radio Corporation of America (RCA), for example, was an offshoot in the early 1920s of the Westinghouse, General Electric and American Telephone and Telegraph companies. Since then it has grown into a two billion dollar-plus electronics manufacturer including the ownership of the National Broadcasting Company. NBC, in turn, is a mammoth radio and television concern that owns some of the most influential television and radio stations in the major cities of the country. It operates the second largest TV network in the nation over which its programming reaches into practically every home.

In 1965, the International Telephone and Telegraph Company (ITT), another two billion dollar producer of communications equipment, announced its intention to merge with the American Broadcasting Company (ABC), the nation's third largest radio-television corporation. Though this merger was not consummated, it served to alert whoever chooses to pay attention to the far-reaching pyramiding of information control that is taking place. It is not only a matter of large-scale economic power blocs that exclude competitors in critically sensitive areas. The three national broadcasting companies, CBS, NBC and ABC, for example, exercise "an almost complete concentration of economic and cultural control — a virtual 'monopoly' or 'triopoly', if you will, of production and procurement of television programs."[2]

Still more significant, though certainly related, is the emergence of a monopolized informational apparatus which is tightly bound up with an industrial producer interest, itself inseparably connected to

---

[2] Second Interim Report of the Office of Network Study, *Television Network Procurement Part II*, Federal Communications Commission, Washington, D. C., 1965, p. 13.

the military establishment. In this interlock of powerful interests, the objectivity and reliability of the output of the entire communications machine comes increasingly into doubt. No one seems to know to what extent the military-industrial "partnership" affects the public's access to and the quality of information. One of the chief issues of the contested ITT-ABC merger was the almost disregarded subject of the control and objectivity of electronically-provided news. One pertinent question, asked by the Chairman of the Senate monopoly subcommittee, Senator Gaylord Nelson, touched on this vital matter. "Is it possible", Nelson queried, "That ITT, in view of its large foreign investment in so many nations, will tailor its news commentary and reporting so as to minimize any conflict with local governments?"[3]

Senator Wayne Morse saw another aspect of the problem: "The assurances of ITT that its foreign interests would not in any way interfere with ABC's news coverage is pretty hard for any realistic person to swallow, when the television industry is well known for its very prompt response to the economic pressure of its advertisers."[4]

And, FCC Commissioner Nicholas Johnson, in his dissenting opinion against the merger, cut through the legal niceties and took up the jugular issue. He wrote: ". . . scarcely a day can be found in which ITT's economic interests are not affected by some big news event at home or abroad . . . there is only one example of a licensee whose business interests and broadcast properties present a situation in any way comparable to that which we create by this merger. That is the case of RCA's ownership of NBC. That ownership, however, antedated this Commission's existence. It certainly cannot be cited as excuse for allowing a second network to come under the control of a similar company. To say that, since RCA owns NBC, ITT must be allowed to acquire ABC, is to say that things are so bad now there is no point in doing anything now to stop them from getting worse. *I, for one, can see great virtue in having only one-third rather than two-thirds of the major networks owned by corporations heavily engaged in domestic defense and space work and in foreign countries. Perhaps we should consider requiring RCA to divest itself of NBC,* but nothing could be more absurd than the majority's suggestion that

---

[3] Gaylord Nelson, letter to Rosel H. Hyde, Chairman, Federal Communications Commission, September 22, 1966.

[4] Senator Wayne Morse, *Congressional Record,* Senate, January 19, 1967, p. 572.

'We could not in good conscience forbid ABC to merge with ITT without instituting proceedings to separate NBC from RCA.' "[5]

The pressures and interest groups involved in the military-industrial communications complex are stronger than the conventional business biases of advertising sponsors. *Variety* too, has touched on the roots of the danger in a few reportorial commentaries. Headlining the problem on its first page in one issue, the paper declared: "There is a deep undercurrent of concern among critical observers of broadcasting over the strong profit allegiance between the Government and broadcasters through multi-million dollar defense contracts—How, observers are asking, can such special interests be justified when radio and TV stations have become the most important force in mass media news; and especially at so critical a point in history when discerning assessment of Government news is essential . . . ?"[6] Some months later, returning to the same subject, another *Variety* reporter wrote: "Today's broadcast titans, by virtue of parental ties, are simply too enmeshed in war contracting and national-international business."[7] And again, in a comment titled "War Contracts and News Objectivity", the weekly paper of show biz flatly asserted: ". . . it's not unreasonable to conclude that none of the broadcast subsidiaries of war-contracting corporations acquitted its news obligations in a way upsetting to the contractor, the Defense Department."[8]

The web of connections that constitute the communications military-industrial coalition is at the same time formal and unstructured, individual and institutional. Consider, for example, the composition of the Committee on Communications of the National Citizens' Commission on International Cooperation.[9] This ad hoc body of five members, appointed by the President in 1965, to review and report on the role of communications in international cooperation, included three representatives of the most powerful industrial triumvirate in electronics: Harold Geneen, Chairman of the Board and President

---

[5] *The ITT-ABC Merger Case*, Docket No. 16828, Dissenting Opinion of Commissioner Nicholas Johnson, December 21, 1966. Italics added.

[6] *Variety*, February 23, 1966, p. 1.

[7] *Ibid.*, Dec. 28, 1966, p. 1.

[8] *Ibid.*, June 7, 1967.

[9] National Citizens' Commission, *Report of the Committee on Communications*, November 28—December 1st, 1965, Washington, D. C.

of the International Telephone and Telegraph Corporation, Frederick R. Kappel, at the time Chairman of the Board of the American Telephone and Telegraph Company, and General David Sarnoff, Chairman of the Board of the Radio Corporation of America. These were very special citizens indeed to be advising the nation about the future of international communications.

As another instance of the concentration of influence that has emerged in the communications structure of the country, the situation of Mr. Frank Stanton, president of the Columbia Broadcasting System (CBS) is instructive. Until very recently, Mr. Stanton wore, all at once, some very intriguing hats. In addition to being president of the nation's most powerful broadcasting system with network connections and radio-tv station-ownership, Mr. Stanton served also as the Chairman of the United States Advisory Commission on Information. The Commission comprises a four-man panel, which, under congressional authorization and presidential appointment, assesses the operations of the United States Information Agency (USIA), the propaganda arm of the American Government overseas, and proposes recommendations for its future.[10]

For ten years, and until early 1967, Mr. Stanton was also the Chairman of the Board of the Rand Corporation, a non-profit California research organization funded almost entirely with Air Force money. The Rand "think-tank" has occupied itself over the years with such questions as "the best way to drop an H-bomb", and "classified counter-insurgency research" among other esoteric subjects.[11]

A fourth hat, still donned by Stanton, is his chairmanship of the Executive Committee of Radio Free Europe. RFE is a private organization which operates broadcasting facilities in Western Europe which are used to transmit programs, for inspiration and "liberation", to Eastern Europe and the Soviet Union. In 1967, Radio Free Europe was uncovered as a conduit for the Central Intelligence Agency and a brief flurry arose in the CBS command about continuing to donate time for R.F.E.'s spot announcements and its requests for contributions.

What do Mr. Stanton's activities as president of a great broadcasting system, as well as chairman of a governmental propaganda agency

---

10 See, for example, *Twenty-Second Report of the U.S. Advisory Commission on Information*, 90th Congress, 1st Session, House Document No. 74, Washington, 1967.
11 *The New York Times*, June 12, 1967.

review panel, a Department of Defense-financed research organization and an unabashed anti-communist broadcast intelligence service signify? No one can be sure and misinterpretation is always possible. But who can feel confident of the character and direction of information transmission in the United States when such conflict-of-interest assignments are simultaneously undertaken by one individual, so influential in the nation's communications structure? Fred Friendly, in reviewing his sixteen years at CBS, the last two of which were as president of CBS News, mentions often Stanton's interventions and his reservations about CBS News programs and reports. Referring to a half-hour interview with Senator Fulbright about the war in Vietnam, Friendly quotes Stanton as saying: "What a dirty trick that was to play on the President of the United States . . . I didn't know about it until I saw the news release." About CBS coverage of Vietnam in general, Friendly reports that Stanton objected to such broadcasts because of "his concern that too much 'dove-hawk' talk unsteadied the hand of the Commander-In-Chief."[12]

More illuminating, perhaps, is Friendly's admission of the constraints under which *he* worked and which were internalized in his own decision-making. Writing of his reactions to management's unceasing interventions, he concludes: "Looking back now, I suppose I was subtly influenced to do controversial subjects in a non-controversial manner." And, ". . . I must confess that in my almost two years as the head of CBS News I tempered my news judgment and tailored my conscience more than once."[13]

Stanton's assignments, conflicting as they were and are, are still the duties of a single individual, and men come and go. Accordingly, only the *flavor* of enormous concentrated influence can be extracted from a single biography, however important the subject may be. More difficult to minimize is the evidence of *structural organization* designed to influence the character and the content of American communications. The existence of permanent, organizational forms with clearly stated objectives introduces us to the visible world of pressure and influence.

The organic fusion of the American electronics industry and the military establishment is realized as well as symbolized in a very

---

[12] Fred W. Friendly, *Due to Circumstances Beyond Our Control*, Random House, New York, 1967, pp. 216-217.

[13] *Ibid.*, pp. 135 and 265.

special organization, the Armed Forces Communications and Electronics Association (AFCEA). David Sarnoff, board chairman of one of the giants of the electronics industry, the Radio Corporation of America, member of the Citizen's Committee on Communications for International Cooperation, and a former president as well as a permanent director of AFCEA, in an address to the Association remarked on ". . . the working alliance of industrial and military leadership represented in this organization". He observed that "It took nearly two centuries and several prolonged conflicts to teach us that the absence of this vital alliance in time of peace could be costly in time of war." Furthermore, Sarnoff noted: "AFCEA has fashioned a community of interest so closely interwoven that whatever affects the progress of one partner is reflected in the progress of the other."[14]

General Sarnoff was not overstating the case. *Signal Magazine,* the organ of the Association, claims that it "serves the industry military team." Founded in 1946, AFCEA is dedicated, in its own words, "to the military-civilian partnership concept." The Association, according to a recent statement of its aims and organization, includes over 60 chapters located throughout the United States, with some overseas chapters as well. A local chapter's primary purpose "is to promote closer personal relationship between its military and industry members and thereby cultivate a more intimate understanding of their mutual problems."

Membership in the Association is open to individuals in the Armed Services as well as individual citizens interested in the objectives of the organization. Although individual annual dues are quite modest ($5.00), the Association apparently relies for most of its financial support on corporate sustaining memberships offered at $1,000 each and on corporate group memberships, each available at $500. Sustaining memberships currently are held by the American Telephone and Telegraph Co. (Long Lines Department), General Dynamics Corporation, International Telephone and Telegraph Co., Litton Industries, Inc., New York Telephone Co., North American Philips Co., Radio Corporation of America, the Western Electric Co. and Western Union Telegraph Co. Group memberships number well over 150

---

[14] Address by David Sarnoff at the Annual Convention Banquet, Armed Forces Communications and Electronics Association, Washington, D. C., May 26, 1965.

United States corporations, most of whom, but by no means all, are engaged in the electronics and communications business.[15]

Not unexpectedly, the officers and directors of the Armed Forces Communications and Electronics Association represent the highest corporate and military echelons and occupy as well the most important governmental posts in these areas. Amongst the directors of the Association are: Lt. General Gordon A. Blake, formerly director of the National Security Agency; Clovis E. Byers, Vice-President of General Telephone and Electronics Corporation; Lt. General Harold W. Grant, USAF, Director of Telecommunications Policy in the Department of Defense; David Sarnoff, Chairman of the Board, RCA; James R. McNitt, President of I.T. & T. World Communications; Frederick R. Lack, former vice-president of the Western Electric Company; and Lowell F. Wingert, Vice-president of A.T. & T. The current president of AFCEA is Dr. John T. Planje, vice-president of North American Philips Co. Amongst the six vice-presidents of the Association is Lt. General R. P. Klocko, who is also the director of the Defense Communications Agency and, at the same time, the manager of the National Communications System.

The recent work experience of a current AFCEA director, Lt. General Gordon A. Blake, USAF (ret.) illustrates the interlocks that now characterize the Association's connections with the many layers and segments of the American communications community. General Blake, before his retirement from the military establishment was head of the National Security Agency. Coincident with his departure from this post, he was made director of a study, undertaken by the Stanford Research Institute, to review all the aspects of international communications. The Stanford project was commissioned by General O'Connell of the Office of Telecommunications Management in the Office of Emergency Planning (see pp. 46-48) . It was financed largely by the Department of Defense.[16] Upon completion of this report, General Blake was named a consultant to Comsat, the communications satellite corporation,[17] half of whose stock is owned by A.T. & T., R.C.A., I.T. & T. and a couple of other electronics concerns.

---

[15] *Signal*. August, 1966, pp. 67-68.

[16] *Government Use of Satellite Communications*, Hearings before a subcommittee of the Committee on Government Operations, House of Representatives, 89th Congress 2nd Session, August and September 1966, pp. 90, 266.

[17] *Telecommunications Report*, October 3, 1966, p. 14.

In calling the attention of prospective exhibitors to its annual convention in the nation's capital, which is also an electronics show, AFCEA points out that "For the exhibitor, here is where industry really meets the men who know—prominent government and military leaders who have the power of decision. In other words, industry brings its products to the doorway of defense."

The voluntary symbiosis visible in AFCEA, of the military establishment and the electronics industry evolved and is sustained in the market-place. Here the nation's electronics producers find a continuously growing outlet for their wares, provided in large part by an obliging military demand that is seemingly insatiable. The industry sold well over 60% ($12.2 billions) of its output of approximately $23 billion in *1967* to the national government, the overwhelming share of which went to the Armed Forces. It is predictable that one would find that "The great majority of companies manufacturing electronic products are involved in some phase of work for the military"[18] though the percentage of defense business to total revenues varies widely from firm to firm. When government sales are taken to represent military consumption,[19] the dependency of private industry on the military establishment is striking. The volume of this business for some important electronics producers in 1964 is indicated in Table I.

---

[18] Standard & Poor's, Industry Survey, Electronics-Electrical, Basic Analysis Oct. 14, 1965, (Vol. 133, No. 4P, Sec. I) , P E-12.

[19] In the fiscal year 1966, the sales of the electronics industry to the Government totaled $9.06 billions. Of this, $7.35 billions were DOD purchases, $1.6 billions expenditures of the National Aeronautics and Space Administration (NASA) and $110 millions, purchases by Federal Aviation Industry. NASA's work, it should be added, moves in the twilight zone between military and non-military activity. Source: *Electronic Industries Yearbook*, 1965.

Table I
1964 Revenues of Leading Electronics
Companies and Percentage Represented by Government Sales
In millions of dollars

| | Total Revenues | Percentage of government sales to total |
|---|---|---|
| General Electric | 4,941 | 19% |
| IBM | 3,239 | 10 |
| Westinghouse | 2,271 | [1] 20 |
| RCA | 1,797 | 25 |
| [2] Sperry Rand | 1,248 | 40 |
| [3] Bendix | 742 | 64 |
| Honeywell | 667 | 32 |
| TRW | 553 | 46 |
| Raytheon | 454 | 85 |
| Burroughs | 390 | 11 |
| Ling-Temco-Vought | 323 | 92 |
| Magnavox | 227 | 21 |
| General Precision Equipment | 219 | 75 |
| [3] Emerson Electric | 219 | 12 |
| Beekman Instruments | 101 | 24 |

[1] Includes atomic energy product sales. [2] Fiscal year ended March 31, 1965, 1964. [3] Fiscal year ended September 30, 1964, 1963. [4] Fiscal year ended June 30, 1965, 1964.

Source: Standard & Poor's, Industry Surveys, Electronics-Electrical October 14, 1965, p. 312.

In the late 1950's, with a far less intense mobilization effort than today, a Department of Defense official estimated that "Over 50 percent of the output of the entire electronics industry is currently involved in the military effort and at least 60 percent of all electronic engineers in the country are now engaged in some degree of work on military programs."[20]

## The Impact of Research and Development

A factor sometimes overlooked in the dynamics of the military-industrial alliance is the ability of the power-concentrate to continuously extend itself. This occurs as a natural consequence of the forces already in motion. Take for instance the matter of research and development. Receiving a great share of the funds appropriated

[20] Statement of Mr. Paul Goldsborough, Special Assistant to the Assistant Secretary of Defense, in Spectrum Allocation, Hearings before a subcommittee on the Committee on Interstate and Foreign Commerce, House of Representatives, 86th Congress, First Session, June 8 and 9, 1959, Washington, 1959, p. 181.

for scientific inquiry,[21] Department of Defense contract researchers will produce, it is to be expected, a large portion of the new scientific and technical knowledge becoming available. One consequence of this pattern is that entirely new fields of study, as well as their practical application, become the exclusive preserves of the Armed Forces. The question naturally arises: Is this a custodianship in which a democratic society can have confidence? Military control of the discovery process automatically confers on the controller proprietary rights. When the security and survivability of the nation can also be invoked, an even tighter control is exerted. The knowledge sooner or later is applied practically and becomes functional in plants and equipment. At this point, economics takes over. The resultant facilities constitute the fixed costs that in themselves become a great inertial force, repulsing further efforts at change. Certainly this has characterized the scientific study of the radio spectrum to date. First, there is the advantage that discovery confers. The testimony of a former Administrator of the Federal Aviation Agency is instructive:

> ". . . As you expand the use of the spectrum, you do so in large blocks, so to speak. You don't eventually find a means of using a discrete frequency; you develop a technique of using a broad band of frequencies. Now if the experience of the future follows the experience of the past, it is going to follow that the Government is going to find ways and means of using the unusable parts of the spectrum. It follows that the agency of government that develops a means or a technique to use an unused portion of the spectrum will assume ownership thereof. . ."[22]

The "agency of government" that will be developing new portions of the spectrum, in all likelihood, already is the Department of Defense.

On another occasion, FCC Commissioner T. Craven told a congressional committee how the application of newly-discovered technology quickly freezes the pattern and makes alternate arrangements extremely difficult, if not, unthinkable:

---

[21] In the President's budget for fiscal year 1967, the military component of the research and development category amounted to well over 80 percent of the total amount requested. *Science,* January 28, 1966.

[22] Testimony of General E. R. Quesada, Administrator, Federal Aviation Agency, in *Spectrum Allocation,* op. cit., p. 198.

"Some time after World War II, when the problem (of unifying the control of governmental and private communications facilities) became acute, because during the war it was necessary for the military to utilize the then World War II technology to increase their communications systems, they found there were billions of dollars of investment that is very hard to undo. That is one of the major problems, as I see it, in spectrum management—what do you do with the invested capital?"[23]

In short, the mechanics are simple and automatic. Control of research enjoys an already-privileged position that is powerful enough to secure the research appropriations in the first place. The fruits of discovery further strengthen the existing power structure and, when applied practically, the material investment becomes a new obstacle to further change and flexibility.

Intolerable conditions in a changing world are defying American efforts at stabilization. The possibilities of social revolution across the globe are interpreted by American business as so many threats to its own existence and expansion. At the same time they are presented to the American public as a danger to the national security. Annual defense appropriations have risen to where they begin to approach the levels of all-out spending in World War II. These huge expenditures offer a large and secure outlet to some of the nation's most powerful businesses, producing goods and services (of broadcasting) in the most technologically advanced sectors of industry. The mutual reinforcement that the military and the communications industry power concentrates offer each other is strengthened additionally by their deep penetration into the highest levels of the governmental bureaucracy. Their extraordinary positions of authority are yet further advanced by control over the most sensitive and influential of the 20th century's power mechanisms. They dominate the nation's informational apparatus and its mass communications. In this setting of almost total electronic omnipotence, challenges to the direction and thrust of American policy, domestic and international, need desperately to find new channels for expression.

---

[23] Statement of FCC Commissioner T.A.M. Craven *Space Communications and Allocation of Radio Spectrum*, 1961 *op. cit.*, p. 82.

CHAPTER 5

# Communications for Crisis Management:
# The Application of Electronics
# to Counter-Revolution

In the fall of 1965 Lin Piao, commander-in-chief of China's Armed Forces and second in authority only to Mao, made a public pronouncement outlining the shape of the future as he (and presumably Mao) viewed it. Speaking in metaphorical terms, he presented an image of North America and Western Europe as "cities" encircled by the indigent and rebellious "rural areas of the world", Asia, Africa and Latin America. Basing his analysis on China's revolutionary experience, the prospects were excellent, according to Lin, that the destitute "country-side", in the not-too-distant future would envelop the prosperous and "selfish" North Atlantic enclaves.

Dismissed in the mass media of the West as wishful thinking, the Chinese leader's thesis has received a surprising amount of unintended support from sober and responsible American spokesmen. George D. Woods, for instance, until recently president of the World Bank, described a very bleak picture of the conditions of mankind in an article enumerating the desperate differentials in living standards between the rich and the poor nations.[1] Former Secretary of Defense McNamara's outlook has been no less anguished. Reviewing the economic plight of the low income world, McNamara declared, "The conclusion to all this is blunt and inescapable: Given the certain connection between economic stagnation and the incidence of violence, the years that lie ahead for the nations in the southern half of the globe are pregnant with violence."[2] Finally, the reactions of Senator

---

[1] *Foreign Affairs,* January, 1966.

[2] *The New York Times,* May 19, 1966.

107

William Fulbright, Chairman of the Senate Foreign Relations Committee, are even more grim: "We delude ourselves further," he writes, "if we suppose that the forces of change in the emerging nations are likely to be consummated everywhere without violence and profound social dislocation."[3]

If it is true that there are no inevitabilities in history, it is also evident that certain courses of action or inaction can be said to have predictable consequences. Consider the implications of these items:

—It is estimated that seventy-five per cent of the world's population lives under conditions that would be described in the United States as abject poverty or worse.[4]

—In 1965, total personal income in the United States increased $35 billion over 1964, or almost $180 per person. Putting this in a comparative global context, one year's incremental advance in the United States exceeds, for its individual citizens on a per capita basis, the total annual income of a billion and a half people in the less-favored nations.

—As the incomes and wealth in the few industrialized nations have increased in recent years, economic assistance from the well-to-do to the less-developed societies has declined both proportionally and absolutely.

—Arms expenditures in the well-off western arc of the world now approximate 100 billion dollars annually, a sum at least ten times larger than the region's yearly allotment of economic assistance to the poor world.

The itemization of the seeds of catastrophe could be extended. High birth rates and growing external debt in the low-income nations are two other agents intensifying the developing international crisis.

One conclusion from these depressing facts seems certain. The status quo that produces this imbalance with all its social misery cannot long endure. Some other judgments also seem warrantable. The United States has been unwilling to take steps consonant with the magnitude of the problem. Its foreign economic assistance has been token. Its efforts to restructure its domestic institutions to smooth the development of the have-not states are non-existent. At the same time, Washington has not been prepared to allow the poor

---

[3] *St. Louis Post-Dispatch*, September 26, 1965.

[4] Escott Reid, *The Future of the World Bank*, Washington, D. C., 1965.

nations to move along paths of their own choosing if those roads are regarded as injurious to American private interests or this country's notions of social progress. Recognizing the dilemma this behavior produces, Robert Heilbroner asked: "Is the United States fundamentally opposed to economic development for the poor world?" His answer: "It must be said aloud that our present policy prefers the absence of development to the chance for communism—which is to say, that we prefer hunger and want and the existing inadequate assaults against the causes of hunger and want to any regime that declares its hostility to capitalism."[5]

The Secretary of State has declared that the United States is not "the policeman of the universe"[6] but for twenty years, since the enunciation of the Truman Doctrine in 1947, Washington has determined unilaterally with its own critera when communism is "aggressive", when peace is threatened and when an American intervention is required.

Where does this leave us? If we are not prepared to make an assistance effort that really matters and if we won't permit the impoverished states to move out on courses of their own choosing and, if the status quo is intolerable, we must then reconcile ourselves to interminable conflict over much of the earth's surface. And if these outbreaks are to be beaten back, "extinguished" in the parlance of current military jargon, we must develop what the London *Economist* calls "the art of crisis management."[7] Furthermore, since local insurrections are devilishly hard to quell or even to contain once they have commenced and they have acquired widespread popular support, or at least tolerance, reliance must be placed on the most developed *technical* means of reducing the initial advantages to the local insurrectionists. It is to these purposes, among others, that America's mastery of communications technology has been applied. The nation's electronic sophistication, a product of massive research and development supported by huge federal expenditures, has been commissioned to oversee and sometimes to overpower primitive economies steeped in social misery if they give any sign of rebellion.

---

[5] Robert L. Heilbroner, "Counterrevolutionary America", *Commentary*, April, 1967.

[6] *The New York Times*, February 19, 1966.

[7] *The Economist*, June 18, 1966, p. 1307.

Communications media of course, are neutral. The purposes to which they are put are not. Frantz Fanon has shown that modern communications can be given a revolutionary role. He traced the reversal of radio's function in a colonial area once the Algerian liberation war had begun. Fanon described how broadcasting became a means of enlightenment, hope, and national unity, contrasted with its earlier service as a source of cultural domination and pressure.[8] If Radio-Algiers in the colonial period represented "Frenchmen talking to Frenchmen", once the national revolution began, it became the instrument of public information for the illiterate Algerian masses. Radio set acquisition jumped dramatically with the establishment of the Voice of Free Algiers. "Since 1956, the purchase of a radio in Algeria has meant," Fanon wrote in the middle of the war, "not the adoption of a modern technique for getting news, but the obtaining of access to the only means of entering into communication with the revolution."[9]

At this point, Fanon noted how easily the former stubborn resistance of the family structure to group listening disappeared and how the entire household unit grouped itself eagerly around the receiver to obtain some news of the national resistance movement. Instantaneously aware of the changed mood, the French Administration prohibited the sale of radios and batteries to the local population, began to jam the Voice of Free Algeria and destroyed in the Army's raiding parties whatever radio equipment it could lay its hands on. "All at once, radio became as essential as arms to the people in their actions against the colonial system . . . Psychologically, before 1954 . . . the radio was an evil object, anxiogenic and accursed. After 1954, the radio assumed totally new meanings."[10]

If Fanon viewed broadcasting as a revolutionary instrument, the United States, given the predicament in which it finds itself globally, pursues a different communications orientation. The U.S. Department of Defense, for instance, regards the potential of the radio spectrum strictly as a military asset, useful in overcoming the very conditions that excited Fanon's enthusiasm. A Pentagon spokesman in the late 1950's gave this appraisal of what modern electronics offer:

---

[8] F. Fanon, *Studies in a Dying Colonialism*, Monthly Review Press, New York, 1965, p. 72.

[9] *Ibid.*, p. 83.

[10] *Ibid.*, p. 85.

". . . The military services are using electronics and the radio spectrum as an integral part of the weapons system . . . People are paid to invent new ways of using electronics in this way. The constant objective of developing new ways of exploiting electronics to meet military needs accounts for the fact that military requirements for spectrum space have been increasing and will continue to increase. This is an imperative of modern military readiness. The speed and devastating consequences of modern warfare are such that the nation cannot afford to be in a position of having an inadequate communications-electronics posture. It is necessary, in order to maintain a state of operational readiness adequate to meet any potential threat to the United States —and at the *same time sufficient to support international commitments—that U.S. military services have the capability of employing modern weapons systems anywhere in the world where the need might arise.*"[11]

## Communications and Counter-Insurgency

Communications for counter-revolution, or counter-insurgency as the modern terminology puts it, has been a concern of military thinking for some time. In recent years, counter-insurgency has been elevated to national policy and the employment of communications for counter-revolution has developed along a broad and varied front.

In the summer of 1962, for example, the State Department, supported by the Department of Defense, came before a senatorial committee to recommend a curious amendment to the Communications Act of 1934. The Under Secretary of State, George W. Ball, requested that the Act be changed to grant the President the power "to authorize a foreign government to operate a radio transmitter at or near its mission in Washington when that government had provided reciprocal privileges to the United States to operate a radio station within its territory."[12]

---

[11] *Spectrum Allocation,* Hearings before the subcommittee of the Committee on Interstate and Foreign Commerce, House of Representatives, 86th Congress, 1st Session, June 8 and 9, 1959, Washington, 1959. Statement of Paul Goldsborough, Special Assistant to Assistant Secretary of Defense and formerly Director of Telecommunications in the Department of Defense, page 181, italics added.

[12] Statement of Hon. George W. Ball, Under Secretary of State, to the Subcommittee on Communications, Committee of Commerce, U.S. Senate, 87th Congress, 2nd Session, Hearing on *S.3252, A Bill to Amend the Communications Act of 1934 as amended, August 29, 1962,* p. 19.

The problem to which the proposed legislation was directed was not the need or the desire of foreign nations to have additional radio facilities in the nation's capital. The objective of the suggested amendment was to enable Washington to communicate more rapidly and effectively with its representatives abroad. The Under Secretary informed the Committee:

> "Our problem is the development of improved communications with many of the newer posts throughout the world, particularly in Africa, Asia and Latin America. The ability to communicate promptly with these areas is an essential element in our conduct of international relations. Time and time again we have found our ability to cope effectively with crises in the less developed areas impeded by lack of modern communications facilities. For instance, a telegram sent by commercial facilities to the Congo, Vientiane in Laos, or to Algiers may take as long as 20 hours. Today in all these areas hourly developments can have an important bearing on our interests."[13]

Ball reassured the Committee that "We do not believe that many of the foreign embassies in Washington would wish to avail themselves of this opportunity." Washington had adequate commercial facilities that were cheaper than installing new equipment, and, more to the point, "most embassies do not have the volume of traffic associated with U.S. missions abroad."[14]

The Department of State's request received the endorsement of the Department of Defense. Admiral Curts, Director of Telecommunications Policy in the Office of the Secretary of Defense, observed: "Recent events have focused attention upon the increasing requirement for closely coordinated efforts between the Department of Defnse and the Department of State. Effective coordination requires rapid, reliable and secure communications. Enactment of this bill will materially assist in providing better communications in many places where better communications are needed."[15]

Securing information and communicating policy to diplomatic representatives abroad is hardly an illegitimate function of govern-

---

13 *Ibid.*

14 *Ibid.*, p. 22.

15 *Ibid.*, p. 28.

ment. But alerting the nation's armed forces stationed overseas to intervene in areas in the throes of social revolt is quite another matter. Unfortunately, it has been this second, counter-revolutionary role for communications that has enlisted the Pentagon's interest, motivated the government's international diplomacy, and stimulated federal funds for communications research and development.

Unparalleled opportunities for instantaneous intervention are provided by the new space satellite technology. This has not passed unnoticed in the corridors of the Department of Defense. One official of the Aerospace Corporation, the nonprofit company supported extravagantly by the Armed Forces, noted:

> "Communications has historically been a military weakness. Limited war anywhere in the world, the advent of nuclear weapons, and rapid delivery methods have aggravated the weakness. Space and communications satellites offer the military a superb opportunity to correct this weakness. It should not be passed up."[16] It has not been.

While the use of communications satellites for commercial, educational and economic developmental purposes have been in the forefront of public attention,[17] the military possibilities of satellite communications have received the solid resources and diplomatic assistance of the United States Government. The officer in command of the Pentagon's Defense Communications Agency and also the manager of the National Communications System, testified to the Department of Defense's interest:

> "It is most desirable that we have means of establishing, on the shortest time-scale, reliable communications to out-of-the-way areas where tension develops—that is to say flexibility to extend rapidly into new areas. . . Any system which will give a rapid, instantaneous, reliable communication to a new, troublesome, out-of-the-way area will have a tremendous advantage in the future. Of all the potentially new communications media means, the communications satellite

---

[16] *Satellite Communications—1964* (Part 1), Hearings before a Subcommittee of the Committee on Government Operations, House of Representatives, 88th Congress, 2nd Session, August 1964, p. 190.

[17] Statement of the President of the United States on Communications Satellite Policy, July 24, 1961, reprinted in Satellite Communications, *op. cit.*, p. 590.

appears to offer the greatest promise of providing the improvements required in the Defense Communications System. . ."[18]

The ability to bounce a signal off a body in space and have it come down to any other point on the globe is the military establishment's dream realized. It offers a technique for communicating to a unit deployed anywhere on the earth's surface without having to worry about wires being cut. Electronic interference is still possible but an increasingly refined technology can be expected to cope with such a problem sooner or later. Here is counter-insurgency in a new dimension.

Predictably, the military feasibilities of space communications have been put foremost in the development of communications satellites. They have shaped the international negotiations by which spectrum space has been obtained for space communications. They have influenced and sometimes determined the design of the space satellite system. They have directed the continuing research on space technology.

## Counter-Insurgency and Space Communications

The military interest of the United States Government in international space communications became evident at the seventy-nation, International Telecommunications Union's meeting in Switzerland in 1963 (The Extraordinary Administrative Radio Conference to Allocate Frequency Bands for Space Radio Communications). Detailed planning years in advance of the event, until recently a rarity in American governmental behavior, preceded the Geneva Conference. Recognition that this meeting might be used to national advantage for consolidating and even extending America's electronic lead, prompted careful interdepartment governmental preparations. The Conference's task was the allocation of frequencies for space communication, a need felt by few nations in 1963 and, in fact, of importance probably to the United States alone.

---

[18] Hearings before a Subcommittee of the Committee on Government Operations, House of Representatives, 88th Congress, First Session, April 23, 1963—*Military Communication Satellite Program*—Statement of Lt. Gen. Arthur D. Starbird, U.S. Army, Director, Defense Communications Agency, p. 8.

The American proposals for the conference were formulated originally in the Department of Defense and subsequently moved through interdepartment governmental channels for coordination and redrafting.[19] More discussion followed and further revisions were made after the recommendations were submitted to industry scrutiny and eventually to the Department of State. However, the proposals were born in the Department of Defense where parenthood was acknowledged. "Whenever any scientific endeavors depend in part upon the use of radio frequencies, the Department of Defense has tried to anticipate the frequency needs and make provision for them through the IRAC (Interdepartment Radio Advisory Committee) at the earliest possible date." So testified the Department of Defense's Director of Telecommunications Policy.[20]

The Geneva meeting richly rewarded the diligent American preparatory efforts. Amongst the accepted proposals was the approval of the United States request for a narrow band of frequencies for space communications exclusively. The full import of this frequency allocation is described by the president of the Communications Satellite Corporation (Comsat), Dr. Charyk, who was a member of the United States negotiating team:

> ". . . for communications satellites, agreement was reached on 2,800 megacycles of frequency space. In other words, 2800 megacycles of frequency space were devoted to the use of communications satellite systems, but not exclusively . . . these frequencies are also used by various ground communication networks, in particular microwave relay systems, and out of the total 2800 megacycles only 50 megacycles were reserved exclusively for communications satellites for transmission in the earth-to-satellite mode."

The significance of the exclusive frequencies was elaborated by Dr. Charyk:

> "Now, the National Communication's System requirements have as their key element the fact that the government

---

[19] *Space Communication and Allocation of Radio Spectrum,* Hearings before the Communications Subcommittee of the Committee on Commerce, United States Senate, 87th Congress, 1st Session, August 1, 23, 24, 1961, Testimony of Admiral M. E. Curts, pp. 185-186.

[20] *Ibid.*

would like to use mobile stations which could be quickly transported to any part of the world, set up and be in operation with high quality communications in a very short period of time. Since all the frequency bands with the exception of the 50 megacycles, are shared with other services, it is necessary that these mobile stations operate in this exclusive band-otherwise, before the station could be turned on, extensive coordination would be required in order to insure that the operation of the transmitter would not have deleterious effects on other communications facilities in the region where the station was located."[21]

According to the testimony of Dr. Charyk and other experts, the exclusive frequencies agreed to at the international meeting in Geneva, *are of military value only*.[22] The conference's approval of the American proposal for exclusive frequencies in space simply brushed aside the efforts of many years to exclude the arms race from space. The mobile transmitters that are of such interest to the National Communications System are, of course, the communications instrumentation of counter-insurgency.

Requirements for this new electronic alarm system, as Washington and the Pentagon foresee them, are most likely to arise in the underdeveloped areas of the world where conditions of life are most intolerable and popular dissatisfaction vents itself in armed actions. Some of the places mentioned at random, by government officials appearing before congressional committees, where mobile units might prove useful were Lebanon, Laos, Vietnam, Zanzibar, Tanganyika (before the creation of Tanzania) , Panama and Algeria.[23]

## The Military Industrial Complex in Space

The 1963 Geneva Space Communications Conference provided the United States Armed Forces its 50 megacycles of exclusive space communication frequencies while at the same time it established the frequency allocation for more generalized space communications in non-exclusive bands. The results were most gratifying to two domestic interest groups. For industry, there was encouragement to develop satellite communications where they would be commercially profitable. For the Armed Forces, no technical obstacle remained to hamper

---

[21] *Satellite Communications—1964, (Part 1), op. cit.*, pp. 109-110.
[22] *Ibid.*, Statement of W. I. Pritchard, Aeróspace Corporation, p. 193.
[23] *Ibid.*, pp. 149 and 198.

their counter-insurgency technology. American industry and the U.S. military establishment enjoyed, at least temporarily, a comforting complementarity in their space communications aims. This neat division of interest was pointed out by the legal adviser to the State Department, Mr. Abram Chayes: ". . . the main requirements of the commercial part of the system, at least in the early years ahead, will be in the northern latitudes while the main requirements for the National Communications System are to places where existing telecommunications don't go or there aren't rich markets for telecommunications."[24]

Space communications are considered by the Communications Satellite Corporation as a commercial venture which limits their market for the time being to Western Europe, "the northern latitudes." There is also, the perhaps more interesting proposition, that the southern latitudes, the geographical arc that includes most of the poor people in the world, are of concern primarily to the Department of Defense's National Communications System. This amounts to saying that the United States' Armed Forces have been allocated the supervision of the impoverished segment of the globe. That the "have-not" world has the attention of the American military establishment speaks poorly for its future prospects. Profit-taking from the industrially-advanced Northern and Western portions of the world and patrolling and intervention for the impoverished Southern and Eastern sectors, the apparent scheduled division of labor in the United States space communications program, is hardly a basis of long-term stability.

## Current Implementations of Communications for Counter-Insurgency

Events since the 1963 Geneva meeting have confirmed these prospects. While space communications carrying commercial traffic have expanded steadily in recent years under Comsat's direction and control, the *first,* truly global system of space communications to become operative has been for military purposes exclusively.[25] What is more, the system's operations have been concentrated in the "southern latitudes", the world's misery band, and of the initial eight ground sta-

[24] *Ibid.,* p. 266.
[25] *Telecommunications Reports,* June 20, 1966.

tions that have been set down for the use of the Armed Forces, two are in Vietnam. Fulfilling the counter-revolutionary role claimed for them, the commander of the Army's Satellite Communications Agency announced that "We have [ground] stations where the action is."[26]

At the same time, weather satellites are guiding American bombers to targets in North Vietnam[27] and fifty-pound radio backpacks that can fix a soldier's position precisely by signals from a satellite have been developed and may already be in use in Vietnam. With this equipment, "a forward observer could call down accurate artillery fire from as much as 100 miles away."[28]

Satisfaction with space satellite espionage has led President Johnson publicly to assert that though the costs of the entire space program are estimated at about 40 billions through 1967, "an expenditure ten times as large would have been justified."[29]

Conventional broadcasting too, with some special tricks thrown in, has been employed by American forces in Vietnam. Transmitters located along the northern coast of South Vietnam broadcast several hours a day to both North and South Vietnam. And "to make sure the other side hears these messages, the U.S. has dropped more than 10,000 cheap little transistor radios into enemy-held territory both south and north. These specially constructed sets can receive only on frequencies used by U.S. and South Vietnamese stations."[30]

The military utilization of communications, space and conventional, goes beyond the surveillance and pacification of unruly insurrectionists in far-off hunger spots. In a troubled world, instantaneous intelligence which can elude uncertain allies, to say nothing of identified adversaries, also has a high value. A proposed sharing of the U.S. Defense Department's military satellite communications system with its North Atlantic Treaty Organization (NATO) associates had the advantage, its proponents suggested, of by-passing France and other "obstructive land-masses."[31]

The worldwide disposition of United States military communications, in the air, on land and under or in the sea for purposes never

---

26 *The New York Times,* January 19, 1967.
27 *Ibid.,* April 14, 1967.
28 *Ibid.,* March 22, 1967.
29 *Ibid.,* March 17, 1967.
30 *The Wall Street Journal,* March 15, 1966.
31 *Telecommunications Reports,* October 3, 1966.

made explicit, was spotlighted briefly during one curious episode in the 1967 six-day summer war in the Middle East. This was the Israeli attack on the American communications intelligence ship, *Liberty*. The vessel, 15 and a half nautical miles off the Sinai coast, apparently was intercepting Israeli and Arab messages with grand impartiality. A U.S. Navy court of inquiry later claimed that such neutrality was hardly a reason for attack and that the ship had a "right to be where she was."[32] The capture of the *Pueblo* off the North Korean coast is another case in point. The vessel, according to general accounts "was one unit in a vast network of electronic eavesdropping devices that the United States operates on land and sea, in the air, and in space."[33]

## Resources Employed in Military Communications

The resources pouring into the communications effort of the Armed Forces are impressive. Excluding expenditures of over $1.5 billion on equipment for tactical purposes (ships, planes, etc.), communications costs of the Department of Defense for the fiscal year 1965 probably exceeded $1 billion,[34] and the annual costs for military communica-

---

[32] *The New York Times,* June 29, 1967.

[33] *Ibid.*, January 24, 1968.

[34] The following represents the long-haul, point-to-point communications and other communications costs for the Department of Defense, and the long-haul, point-to-point communications of other Government agencies as identified to date with the National Communications System:

|                                                                                                                                                 | Year Fiscal 1965 |
| --- | --- |
| (In millions) | |
| Defense Communications System: Long-haul, point-to-point communications networks of the Department of Defense | $ 664 |
| Defense Communications Agency: Defense Communications Agency headquarters and field activities and elements of the national military comand system | 95 |
| Other defense communications: | |
| Procurement for new aircraft and aircraft modification | 451 |
| Procurement for new ships and ship overhaul and retrofit | 264 |
| Procurement of ground equipment | 870 |
| Research, development, test, and evaluation | 216 |
| Other Government agencies: Long-haul, point-to-point communications networks of other Government agencies that have been identified to date as a part of the National Communications System | 148 |
| Total | $2,703 |

Hearings February 5, 1964 before the Subcommittee on Department of Defense Appropriations of House Committee on Appropriations, 88th Congress, 2nd Session, Department of Defense Appropriations for 1965, p. 706.

tions have been increasing from 10 to 15 percent per year.[35] An informed estimate in 1967, put Defense Department annual expenditures on telecommunications at $2 billions.[36]

The greatest part of this enormous effort is aimed at achieving a state of readiness in the United States' Armed Forces enabling them to move precipitously into the so-called "trouble spots", actual and potential, in the disadvantaged regions of the world. The facilities already in place are indications of the "solutions" that the "haves" are preparing for the "have nots". Communications are being developed as the supporting instrumentation for the global enforcement of the status quo.

The military absorption of resources has overshadowed and reduced to pitiful proportions communications' role of enlightenment in the developing world. The Director General of the United Nations Education, Scientific and Cultural Organization (UNESCO) put the cost of overcoming two-thirds of the adult illiteracy which plagues many of the organization's one hundred and eighteen member states at $1.9 billions, *over a ten-year period*.[37] Though totalling less than $200 million a year, to developing societies, with so many other claims pressing against discouragingly limited means, this continues to be an unattainable expenditure. Seen from a different perspective, it amounts to only ten percent of *one year's* budget allocation for U.S. military communications spending.

## The Department of Defense's Domestic Communications Apparatus

The present allocation of resources between military communications "preparedness" and educational improvement in the poor world, taken over the long run, can only be self-defeating and therefore menacing to the national interest. Equally threatening is a different facet of military communications capabilities. The Armed Forces'

---

[35] *Satellite Communications—1964 (Part 1), op. cit.,* p. 297.

[36] J. D. O'Connell, Director of Telecommunications Management, Office of Emergency Planning, Hearings, Independent Offices and Department of Housing and Urban Development Appropriations for 1968, Subcommittee of the Committee on Appropriations, House of Representatives, Ninetieth Congress, First Session, Washington: 1967, p. 78.

[37] *Mass Media and National Development,* Wilbur Schramm, Stanford University Press, Stanford, California, 1964, p. 205.

enormous communications capacity can also be employed to "inform" and "persuade" an American public unaware of the character and origin of the messages that are made available to it.

In the spring of 1967, the Associated Press reported on what it called the "U.S. government's big public relations and information programs [that] cost taxpayers more than a million dollars a day." In a study that, with some few exceptions, was given little space or attention in the newspapers of its subscribers, the Association released these findings from its "prolonged digging:"

—"The Survey showed that the biggest domestic publicity network is maintained by the military, with about 3,000 employees in this field and an annual budget of at least $32.3 million.

—The National Aeronautics and Space Administration (NASA) is next with 300 employees and a tab of $11.5 million.

—"The sums spent by the individual branches and agencies of government are dwarfed by the slice of taxes laid out for public relations by companies holding defense and space contracts. These firms can charge the government for public relations just as they do for other general management costs. One estimate is that the taxpayers directly pay at least $200 million a year for such press agentry on behalf of private companies." These companies, one recalls, are those most intimately linked to the defense expenditures of the Pentagon. Their press releases and media advertising bestow legitimacy and rspectability to the entire military program.

The AP further reported that the Defense Department, the "home of whirring computers and precise cost analysis" became very vague when asked and "professed almost utter ignorance of the scope of its public relations set-up."

The figure of 3000 employees is a constructed estimate by AP researchers. The Association noted that "Nobody in the Pentagon would even approximate how much money the military spends to tell its story around the world." What this story is and who tells it are equally mysterious. According to the AP, one ghost writer assigned by the Defense Department to write speeches for a general, reports: "In the year and a half I was there, I got to see the general only once. I asked him what his thoughts were and he replied. 'I'll be damned. I don't know what my thoughts are.' "[38]

---

[38] *Associated Press*, Washington, D. C., March 19, 1967.
   See also, *The New York Times*, March 19, 1967.

What comes through this foggy account is heavy taxpayer support for an informational apparatus that is used to convince the public that its outlays are necessary. In this inverted arrangement, the apparatus, serving the Armed Forces, goes about the task of securing public and congressional acceptance for the almost self-determined budgets of the Defense establishment. Civilian control is replaced by public ratification which is induced by an Army-manipulated informational network.

Twenty years ago, before space communications had become a reality, and electronics was still an infant industry, the Commission on Freedom of the Press declared:

> "Recent improvements in the machinery and methods of international communications have made possible, for the first time in history, direct communication across national boundaries to the masses of the people of the world. These mechanical improvements offer at once a new hope and a new danger. The choice is not between the use or the neglect of these new instruments of communication. The instruments exist and will be used in any case. The choice is between their full, purposeful, and responsible use to enlarge the mutual comprehension of peoples, on the one hand, and, on the other, their incomplete, undirected, and irresponsible use, with the risk of an increase in international hatred and suspicion as a consequence."[39]

American communications efforts since 1945 seem to have opted for the second course.

# CHAPTER 6

# The Global American Electronic Invasion

Canada's radio and television air waves are dominated by American programs. Many Canadians feel, consequently, that much of the broadcasting they see and hear is not serving Canadian needs. Such is the finding of a government-appointed Committee on Broadcasting published recently in a report named after its chairman, R. M. Fowler.[1]

In a symposium intriguingly titled "American TV: What Have You Done To Us?", another Canadian, Henry Comor, makes the same point, a little more emphatically. He writes:

> "Canada is in contact with the United States along a great and undefended border, and by the process of osmosis America is destroying not only our television, but our values and our very culture . . . American television has made the development of a Canadian cultural identity almost impossible. . . . Through its own faulty development, American television has negatively influenced the development of a worthy native television in Canada. American television has destroyed television as an art. Canadians are often told that their potential enemies are Russia and China. In my view, the United States is a much more dangerous enemy . . . I am serious when I say this. Partly serious."[2]

Are these harsh words justified?

The heavy exposure of Canadian audiences to American radio-TV culture is to some extent a matter of geography. After all it is esti-

---

[1] *Report of the Committee on Broadcasting*, Ottawa, Canada, 1965.

[2] H. Comor, "American TV: What Have You Done To Us?", *Television Quarterly*, Vol. VI, No. 1, Winter, 1967, pp. 50-51.

mated that almost three-fifths of the Dominion's households are within range of American stations. Certainly the three thousand mile common boundary offers no barrier to electromagnetic impulses originating in U.S. broadcasting studios. But the American mass media's penetration (perhaps saturation is more accurate) of the Canadian scene cannot be explained fully as merely a matter of adjoining real estate. The Canadian experience only represents a sector, and a small one at that, of a staggering global invasion by American electronic communications.

How completely the international community is being blanketed by radio-television programming produced in the United States or in U.S.—financed facilities overseas, has never been fully documented. An inventory would soon become obsolete because the use of American materials and American foreign broadcast holdings are expanding rapidly and continuously. Each new electronic development widens the perimeter of American influence, and the indivisibility of military and commercial activity operates to promote even greater expansion.

The Department of Defense, for instance, possesses a broadcasting network across the world with 38 television and more than 200 radio transmitters. Philip Coombs, former Assistant Secretary of State for educational and cultural affairs, reported that "the foreign audience is believed to outnumber overseas American listeners by about twenty to one."[3] There is, in addition, a huge civilian governmental broadcasting establishment, the United States Information Agency (USIA), which concerns itself, among other things, with transmissions to foreign audiences. The Voice of America, the radio arm of the U.S.I.A., transmits some 845 hours in 38 languages weekly to an overseas audience of unknown size. The Agency also distributes taped programs and scripts to local stations throughout the world and estimates that its materials are broadcast by more than 5,000 stations for some 15,000 hours a week.

Besides forty-three powerful domestically-based transmitters, the Agency operates 59 transmitters overseas, including broadcasting installations in Liberia, on the Isle of Rhodes and in England. The Agency's Berlin radio, RIAS, located in the middle of the German

---

3 P. H. Coombs, *The Fourth Dimension of Foreign Policy*, Harper & Row, New York, 1964, p. 63.

Democratic Republic (unrecognized by the West), operates around the clock with an annual budget exceeding $3,000,000. More than half its broadcast time is occupied with political commentary, news, and cultural programs that are transmitted to and heard by an East German audience 24 hours a day.[4] Additional facilities are being constructed in Greece, Thailand and the Philippines.[5]

Regular TV series programs are prepared for Japan, Nigeria, Thailand and all of Latin America, though "most of the U.S.I.A. programs . . . are not identified as such in the 97 countries in which they are shown."[6] Some of the shows are commercially sponsored by American or local companies and enjoy prime evening television time. Latin Americans, for example, receive *Panorama Panamerico,* a weekly fifteen minute news review presented over 114 stations in the hemisphere. Japan used 8000 U.S.I.A. programs and news clips in 1966.

But official broadcasting efforts, military and civilian, are only a limited side of America's international communications activities. The private sector has come along rapidly in recent years. Former National Association of Educational Broadcasters' president, Harry J. Skornia, not too long ago wrote: "Probably few Americans are aware of the extent to which American television programs, films, advertising agencies, and other communications and entertainment efforts and activities now encompass most of the globe."[7]

The American interest in overseas communications extends from direct ownership of broadcast facilities (still limited but expanding), to equipment sales, management service contracts, and program exports. The magnitude of the involvement is illustrated best perhaps, but by no means exhausted, in the foreign activities of the major United States broadcast corporations.

No one needs to be persuaded of the domestic communications importance of the Columbia Broadcasting System (CBS). Its inter-

[4] Hearings Before a Subcommittee of the Committee on Appropriations, House of Representatives, 89th Congress, First Session, Washington, 1964, *U.S. Information Agency,* Appropriations for 1966, p. 146.

[5] Hearings Before a Subcommittee of the Committee on Appropriations, House of Representatives, 89th Congress, Second Session, *U.S. Information Agency,* September 13, 1966, Washington, pp. 345, 368, 625.

[6] *The New York Times,* March 24, 1967.

[7] H. J. Skornia, "American Broadcasters Abroad", *Quarterly Review of Economics and Business,* Vol. 4, No. 3, Autumn, 1964, pp. 13-20.

national efforts may be less familiar. According to its 1966 Annual Report, "CBS has become a worldwide communications enterprise whose services and products are distributed in 100 countries. . . . Its products are distributed through 72 overseas subsidiaries . . . 10 per cent [of its employees] are foreign nationals . . . distribution of [its] programs expanded to 94 countries, including for the first time India, Greece, Ghana, Liberia, Aden, Gabon, the Ivory Coast and the Congo."[8] CBS also is providing consultation and advisory services for the creation of a government-operated television network in Israel. It owns investments in three Latin American production companies; *Proartel* in Argentina, *Proventel* in Venezuela and *Pantel* in Peru.[9] Additionally, CBS owns television stations in Trinidad and Antigua and CATV systems in several Canadian communities.

RCA is a two billion dollar giant electronics conglomerate, which serves as the corporate supershelter for NBC, another major domestic radio-television communications system. The global communications interests of RCA and its subsidiary, NBC, already considerable are enlarging annually. In 1965, NBC reported that its international activities included "syndication of 125 film series and services in 83 countries for more than 300 television stations. . . . The leading export was "Bonanza", distributed to 60 countries for viewing by approximately 350 million people every week . . . NBC International dubbed programs in Spanish, Japanese, Portuguese, German, Italian, French and Arabic.[10]

In 1966, NBC Enterprises, the internationally-oriented affiliate, was active in 93 foreign countries. Other involvements included investment in a new television station in Hong Kong and a contract for RCA Communications to install, operate and maintain the first communications satellite earth station in Thailand. Also, "in anticipation of regular color broadcasting in Europe, a new company, RCA Colour Tubes Ltd., was formed in England in association with the British firm of Radio Rentals, Ltd., to produce RCA color picture tubes for the British and European markets."[11]

NBC also has partial interests (over 10 per cent but less than controlling) in two Australian TV stations in Brisbane and Sydney, a

---

8 Columbia Broadcasting Company, *Annual Report,* 1966, p. 2 and p. 19.

9 Columbia Broadcasting Company, *Annual Report,* 1965, p. 22.

10 *NBC Year-End Report,* 1965, p. 28.

11 Radio Corporation of America (RCA), *Annual Report,* 1966, p. 24.

radio and television station in Caracas, Venezuela, a TV station in Monterrey, Mexico, and memberships in consortia that operate a TV station in Jamaica, a radio station in Barbados and Hong Kong's UHF station.

More important to date than its overseas broadcast holdings, has been NBC's provision of technical and administrative expertise to developing (and some developed) countries in the last ten years. "It is in the management-services area, where strictures against government-owned operations do not hold", writes one reporter, "that NBC has had the greatest influence on television abroad." Countries in which NBC has been active in this respect since 1957 included Saudi Arabia, "the largest single TV project undertaken by an American firm", South Vietnam, West Germany, Wales, Mexico, Lebanon, Sweden, Peru, the Philippines, Argentina, Yugoslavia, Barbados, Jamaica, Kenya, Nigeria ("the largest project except for Saudi Arabia") and Sierra Leone.[12]

RCA, the parent company, is also one of the major shareholders, along with A.T. & T., and I.T. & T. of Comsat, the Communications Satellite Corporation, and plays therefore, a considerable role in the international space communications consortium, *Intelsat*.

The American Broadcasting Company, the third major network company in the United States, has been the most active in the international field, perhaps compensating for its somewhat less influential position in the domestic market, where it ranks behind CBS and NBC. ABC has organized an international TV network, *Worldvision*, which, at latest estimate, "can reach 60% of all world TV homes [outside the United States] where sponsorship is permitted (a total of 23 million TV homes)."[13] In the 26 nations where *Worldvision* operates, ABC has some financial involvement in telecasting in the following countries: Canada, Guatemala, El Salvador, Honduras, Costa Rica, Panama, Colombia, Venezuela, Ecuador, Argentina, Lebanon, Japan, Ryukyus, Philippines, Australia, Chile and Bermuda.

Direct financial interest, however, as one writer sees it, is not "the cement that holds *Worldvision's* 56 TV stations [now 64] and 30 radio stations together. The essence of the relationship is a worldwide contract that provides the stations with three major services: pro-

---

12 R. Tyler, "Television Around the World", *Television Magazine,* October, 1966, pp. 32 and 59.

13 *Ibid.*

gram buying, sales representation and networking."[14] ABC itself reports that in 1966 "its programs were sold in over eighty foreign markets."[15] ABC also has interests in production companies in Germany and Mexico and Britain.

Other American broadcasting groups besides the "big three" have moved into the international field. Most important to date is *Time-Life Broadcast Stations,* which is involved in two situations with CBS and former Cuban broadcaster Goar Mestre. These are

> "the *Proventel* production company, which provides programs for Channel Eight network in Venezuela, with headquarters and a station in Caracas, plus additional stations in Valencia, Barquisimeto and Maracaibo, and the *Proartel* production company in Buenos Aires, which produces programs for the city's channel 13. In both cases *Time-Life* and CBS own 20% each, with the rest split between Mestre and local interests. . . . Elsewhere in South America, *Time-Life* is furnishing technical and financial assistance to two Brazilian stations, TV Globo in Rio de Janeiro and TV Paulista in Sao Paulo."[16]

Time-Life's Brazilian tie-in has created concern in that country because the Brazilian constitution prohibits foreign ownership of the nation's communications media, and the link that has been established seems clearly to violate this provision. Moreover, the dollar infusion has encouraged TV Globo to attempt the acquisition of a nationwide chain of radio and TV stations in all the nation's major cities.[17]

Whatever the outcome in this case, the communications penetration is familiar and insistent. National laws are being changed to accommodate expanding American investments in international broadcast communications. New Zealand, for example, which has had only state-controlled radio-tv broadcasting, is preparing to revise its statutes to sanction a private commercial television system. A new group, New Zealand Television Corporation Ltd. of Auckland, which intends to establish private TV stations throughout the country, is

---

[14] *Ibid.,* p. 33.

[15] American Broadcasting Companies, Inc., *Annual Report,* 1966, p. 11.

[16] Tyler, *op. cit.,* p. 33.

[17] E. Blum, "Brazil's Yankee Network", *The Nation,* May 29, 1967, pp. 678-681. See also, *Variety,* June 14, 1967, p. 45.

expecting to have $3.8 million of its initial $7 million capital subscribed by NBC International and Time-Life Broadcast Stations.[18]

A special case of American influence exists in Saudi Arabia where there are two TV services, one of which is government controlled and financed (constructed with the assistance of NBC). The other, ARAMCO TV, is financed and run by the Arabian American Oil Company, the overseas holding company of an American oil consortium comprising the Standard Oil companies of New York, California, and New Jersey and the Texas Oil Company. ARAMCO TV is operated largely for American oil personnel in the area but its signals are picked up by local set-owners.

## Program Exports

Though equity investment in facilities offer American broadcast companies direct outlets, the bread and butter revenues, as well as the significant political-cultural impact of the American overseas involvement, still comes from the export of U.S. programming. Commercial television has become an important and flourishing national export. A former United States Information Agency (USIA) official, Wilson P. Dizard, made this appraisal of such transactions:

> "American TV products, for better and for worse, are setting the tone for television programming throughout the world in much the same way Hollywood did for motion pictures 40 years ago. The United States now leads all other countries combined twice over as a program exporter.... Foreign sales were, until a few years ago, a source of random profits peripheral to revenues from syndication at home. . . . Today, overseas sales account for 60 per cent of all U.S. telefilm syndication activities and represent the difference between profit and loss for the entire industry."[19]

American broadcasters are beginning to complain that obstacles are being placed in the way of U.S. commercial television exports. Examples cited are the United Kingdom's stipulation that a minimum of 86 per cent of air time must be of Commonwealth origin, Canadian air-time must be 55% locally produced and Australia 50%.

---

[18] Tyler, *op. cit.*, p. 58.

[19] W. P. Dizard, "American Television's Foreign Markets", *Television Quarterly*, Vol. III, No. 3, Summer 1964, p. 58.

Broadcasters have noted similar trends in Japan, Argentina, Italy, Mexico, Brazil and many other countries.[20] But the limitations on American programming frequently appear more severe than they actually are. Generous interpretations of permissible import categories and local production that is financed by American companies are two loopholes that have been used successfully in motion picture production to circumvent superficially tough national quotas. Similar arrangements may be anticipated in telefilms.

In any event, U.S. television activity abroad intensifies. USIA official Dizard told a congressional committee in 1967 that

> "The amount of [TV commercial] exports, now approaching $100 million a year, is such that the television screen is becoming the main source of the 'American image' for increasing millions of people abroad." He noted also that "It has been said that TV will replace Hollywood films in this respect. However, television, unlike Hollywood, deals not only in fictional entertainment but also in reporting current developments. This adds a dimension to television that Hollywood has never taken on in its products, and it is one that gives television special meaning in the patterns of our communications with other countries. Because our domestic television system is largely commercial, the quantity and quality of American television exports rests primarily in the hands of private broadcasters."[21]

In 1964, Dizard found that "the daily schedule of a typical Australian television station is, particularly in prime listening hours, virtually indistinguishable from that of a station in Iowa or New Jersey."[22] In 1967, *Television Age* reported that "the majority of the shows still on (the Australian) air are still U.S. imports."[23]

The situation, with local variations, is much the same all around the non-Sino-Soviet world. Even the communist area is not entirely immune to American imagery. Consider the weekly television fare in these widely separated countries. In Argentina, "U. S. imports

---

[20] "The Global Market: Tough Nut", *Television Magazine,* August, 1966, pp. 90-92.

[21] W. P. Dizard, Office of Policy and Research, U.S.I.A., Before the Subcommittee on International Organizations and Movements, "Modern Communications and Foreign Policy", 90th Congress, 1st Session, Washington, May 4, 1967, p. 59.

[22] Dizard, *Television Quarterly, op. cit.,* p. 63.

[23] *Television Age,* global report, July 3, 1967, p. 34.

continue to maintain high popularity. Among the favorites and number one in the top income audience group, is *Man From U.N.C.L.E.*
followed by *The F.B.I., Batman,* and *Peyton Place. Beverly Hillbillies*
continue to get high scores. . ." In Belgium, "current and recent U.S.
network film fare dominates Belgium's Top Ten, with *The Jetsons,
The Fugitive, Dr. Kildare, Love On A Rooftop,* and *Voyage To The
Bottom of the Sea* all up there." In Canada, "it's news when a
Canadian program gets in Nielsen's top 10." In Finland, on the commercial channel, 45 per cent of the shows are live and 55 per cent are
filmed. "Imported U.S. half-hour series account for 85 per cent of
the filmed variety." In Hong Kong, the new Time-Life and NBC
International TV station will use U.S. shows exclusively. In Mexico,
"programming, according to an American syndicator, is a 'carbon
copy' of the United States network fare . . . U.S. shows dominate
Mexican prime time, right through the evening."[24]

Though American telefilms currently are obtaining their largest
revenues from the high-income countries whose audiences are prospective customers for the advertising messages that accompany and
finance the film showings, the developing world receives some attention too. Dizard points out that "Almost every U.S. distributor is
selling films at cut-rate prices (in Latin America, Africa, and Asia)
against the day when these markets will become stronger."[25] *Variety*
reports the range of these prices and the countries to which they are
applicable.[26] (See Table I)

---

[24] *Ibid.,* pp. 34-69.

[25] Dizard, *Television Quarterly, op. cit.,* p. 63.

[26] *Variety,* July 26, 1967, p. 54.

## Table I

### Global Prices for American Films on TV

| | Price Range Per Half Hour Episode | | Price Range Per Feature Film |
|---|---|---|---|
| **CANADA** | | | |
| CBC ..................... | $2,500-$3,500 | (CBC) | $ 8,500 to $12,000 |
| CBC (French Net) ........ | 2,000- 3,000 | | |
| CTV Network ............ | 2,000- 2,500 | | |
| **LATIN AMERICA & CARIBBEAN** | | | |
| Argentina ................ | $ 500-$ 800 | | $1,600-$2,500 (dubbed) |
| Bermuda ................. | 25- 40 | | 75- 100 |
| Brazil ................... | 1,000- 1,400 (Portuguese dubbed) | | 3,500- 6,000 (Portuguese dubbed) |
| Chile .................... | 50- 60 | | 300 |
| Colombia ................ | 150- 200 | | 800- 1,000 |
| Costa Rica ............... | 30- 40 | | 50- 150 |
| Dominican Republic ...... | 50- 75 | | 100- 125 |
| Ecuador ................. | 25- 40 | | No sales |
| El Salvador .............. | 35- 45 | | 125- 175 |
| Guatemala ............... | 45- 55 | | 125- 300 |
| Haiti .................... | 25- 30 | | 75- 90 |
| Honduras ................ | 25- 35 | | 60- 80 |
| Jamaica .................. | 25- 30 | | No sales |
| Mexico .................. | 550- 600 | | 600- 800 |
| Netherland Antilles ....... | 25- 30 | | No sales |
| Nicaragua ............... | 25- 30 | | No sales |
| Panama .................. | 40- 50 | | 100- 150 |
| Peru .................... | 100- 120 | | 350- 575 |
| Puerto Rico .............. | 300- 450 | | 1,200- 1,500 (dubbed) 400- 700 (subtitled) |
| Trinidad & Tobago ....... | 30- 35 | | 60- 100 |
| Uruguay ................. | 70- 90 | | 160- 200 (subtitled) |
| Venezuela ............... | 450- 600 | | 500- 2,500 |
| **WESTERN EUROPE** | | | |
| Austria .................. | 400- 800 (German dubbed) | | 1,000- 1,500 (subtitled) |
| Belgium ................. | 400- 600 | | 1,200- 2,000 |
| Denmark ................ | 175- 250 | | 900- 1,500 |
| Finland ................. | 250- 350 | | 700- 1,000 |
| France .................. | 1,200- 2,200 | | 1,600- 3,500 |
| West Germany ............ | 1,500- 3,000 (undubbed) | | 10,000-12,000 (dubbed) |
| Gibraltar ................ | 26- 35 | | 75- 125 |
| Ireland ................. | 70- 75 | | No sales |
| Italy .................... | 400- 650 (dubbed) | | 2,000- 4,000 |
| Luxembourg ............. | 160- 200 (dubbed) | | 175- 225 |

| | Price Range Per Half Hour Episode | | Price Range Per Feature Film |
|---|---|---|---|
| Malta | | 28 | No sales |
| Monaco | 100- | 130 | 130- 160 |
| Netherlands | 250- | 450 | 1,300- 1,700 |
| Norway | 150- | 175 | No sales |
| Portugal | | 140 | 450 |
| Spain | 300- | 350 | 1,800- 2,000 |
| Sweden | 400- | 450 | 1,200- 1,500 |
| Switzerland | 140- | 160 | 900- 1,500 |
| United Kingdom | 2,800- | 4,200 | 6,000-14,000 |
| **EASTERN EUROPE** | | | |
| Bulgaria | 35- | 50 | No sales |
| Czechoslovakia | 180- | 250 | 1,000- 2,000 |
| Eastern Germany | No sales | | 1,000- 1,700 |
| Hungary | 100- | 160 | 300- 600 |
| Poland | 125- | 200 | 350- 600 |
| Rumania | No sales | | No sales |
| USSR | No sales | | No sales |
| Yugoslavia | 75- | 80 | 200- 450 |
| **NEAR EAST AND SOUTH ASIA** | | | |
| Cyprus | 30- | 35 | 100- 150 |
| India | No sales | | No sales |
| Iran | 75- | 80 | No sales |
| Iraq | 100- | 125 | 175- 225 |
| Kuwait | 60- | 90 | 250- 350 |
| Lebanon | 50- | 60 | 175- 225 |
| Saudi Arabia | | 60 | 150- 200 |
| Syrian Arab Republic | 50- | 70 | 90- 120 |
| United Arab Republic | 65- | 80 | 200- 800 |
| **AFRICA** | | | |
| Algeria | 90- | 100 | No sales |
| Kenya | 22- | 28 | No sales |
| Nigeria | 35- | 40 | 80- 100 |
| Rhodesia & Zambia | 50- | 70 | 100- 175 |
| Uganda | 25- | 30 | No sales |
| **FAR EAST** | | | |
| Australia | | | |

(Under a newly arrived at agreement, the price per episode is closely keyed to the success of the particular vidfilm series in the U.S. The manner in which this is done is illustrated by the price structure. If a U.S. series consists of from one to 25 episodes that brings $1,500 per half hour episode; if an American series represents the episodes of one full season, more than 26 episodes, the price per half hour is $1,750; if the series has gone beyond one season on American tv, that brings $1,900 per half hour. The prices quoted embrace the four principal markets of Sydney, Melbourne, Brisbane, and Adelaide. Another $400 to $600 can be secured from the remaining markets of the country, if sold to commercial broadcasters. The Australian Broadcasting Commission pays a flat $300 for the remainder of the country. Regarding the sale of features, American exporters and Australian broadcasters remain at an impasse. The Australian broadcasters would like to see a flat $10,000 per feature fee for the four principal cities of Sydney, Melbourne, Brisbane and Adelaide. The American exporters are insisting against the imposition of a fixed price. There the matter rests now, with no significant post-'48 American feature sales being made to the Australian market.)

|  | Price Range Per Half Hour Episode | | Price Range Per Half Hour Episode | |
| --- | --- | --- | --- | --- |
| Hong Kong .............. | $ 50- | 65 | $ 160- | 200 |
| Japan .................... | 2,000- | 3,500 | 3,000- | 3,500 |
| South Korea .............. | 40- | 80 | No sales | |
| Singapore ................ | 50- | 75 | 175- | 200 |
| Malasia ................. | 40- | 50 | 175- | 200 |
| New Zealand ............. | 140- | | No sales | |
| Philippines ............... | 100- | 150 | No sales | |
| Ryuku Islands ............ | | | | |
| (Okinawa) ............. | 50- | 60 | 100- | 125 |
| Taiwan ................. | 35- | 40 | No sales | |
| Thailand ................ | 50- | 75 | 125- | 150 |

How rapidly world markets for TV exports are filling out is indicated by the patterns of television set ownership across the world's poorer areas. The number of sets in Africa rose from 577,000 in February, 1965, to 857,000 in July, 1967; in the Near East from 404,000 to 677,000 during these two and a half years. In Latin America, Cuba with 555,000 sets, Mexico with 2,100,000, Argentina with 2,000,000, Brazil with 4,000,000 and Venezuela with 650,000 lead the way.

In the Near East, Iran claims 130,000 receivers, Iraq 177,000, and Lebanon 165,000. In Africa, The United Arab Republic lists 500,000 sets, Algeria 150,000, Morocco 36,000 and Nigeria 33,000. In the Far East, Japan with its 30,000,000 receivers comes closest to United States standards of set ownership. Thailand has 250,000 sets in use, the Philippines 240,000, Indonesia 45,000, Pakistan 2,700 and India 6,000.[27]

The small number of television receivers in Pakistan and India is a result of government caution concerning the introduction of television. There have been many pilot surveys in India to determine whether to open the door to the great economic and social burdens that could be created by widespread ownership of sets. In countries that cannot feed all their people, and whose per capita income is only a fraction of the cost of a single television receiver, the purchase of sets hardly rates as a public necessity, *unless very special utilization is made of the new medium.*

---

27 *Television Age,* July 3, 1967, pp. 37-38.

Bilateral arrangements for U.S. telefilm exports are being extended and consolidated into regional and even intercontinental associations. The establishment of the *Worldvision* Corporation, under the aegis of the American Broadcasting Company, links 27 countries in a venture that introduces commercial broadcasting to some hitherto virgin overseas territory and provides, at the same time, additional outlets for American shows and programs. ABC modestly claims that Worldvision is ABC International's worldwide television network, as well as being the fastest growing advertising medium in the world. It sees its chief task as "serving the international advertiser."[28]

The creation of an international communications satellite consortium, *Intelsat,* in which the privately-owned Comsat corporation is the dominant shareholder and decision-maker, adds still another agency for United States enterprises' attempt at worldwide broadcast hegemony.

## Similar Trend in Motion Picture Industry

The global expansion of American radio-tv ownership interests and the utilization of U.S. programming overseas occurs alongside of and is one element in a general extension of American business activity abroad. In the film industry, a closely related field, the development is much the same, if somewhat more advanced. A recent study of the British film industry, for example, found that

> "close to half of the films currently made in Great Britain are made by subsidiaries of American companies or by British producers working with American money. A majority of total financing for British production comes from American sources. As much as three-quarters of the production subsidy from the Film Fund Agency, a government-sanctioned public body, is paid to subsidiaries of American companies for their production in Britain. Almost half of all films shown in Great Britain are distributed by American companies or companies in which there is an important American interest. Considering the number of new films entering into distribution each year in Great Britain, American films outnumber British films."[29]

---

[28] "The Known and the New", *Worldvision,* ABC International Television, Inc., 1966.

[29] T. H. Guback, "American Interests in the British Film Industry", *The Quarterly Review of Economics and Business,* Vol. 7, No. 2, Summer, 1967.

A similar situation is overtaking the French film industry despite governmental concern and resistance. The requirement of an international market to recover climbing production costs makes most local producers dependent on outside capital assistance. In 1964, it was estimated that "one in three French films is now being distributed outside France by American companies", and, "American companies that have French subsidiaries can now benefit from French Government aid in the same way as purely French production companies, as long as the films they are making conform to the official designation of "a French film."[30] In this respect, in the newer television industry, production companies of American broadcast corporations have already been established in Mexico, England, West Germany, Canada, Argentina, Venezuela and Peru.

The cultural consequences of growing American influence in global communications will be considered further along. The economic benefits of wider markets to U.S. broadcasters and film-makers are apparent. Yet more significant, if less well understood, is the vanguard role American commercial communications media assume in the propagation and extension of the American business system and its values to all corners of the international community. This is taken up next in the discussion.

---

[30] *The New York Times,* November 15, 1964.

CHAPTER 7

# The International Commercialization
# of Broadcasting

The United States communications presence overseas extends far beyond the facilities owned, the exports, and the licensing agreements secured by major American broadcasting companies and electronics equipment manufacturers, considerable as these are. Equally, if not more important, is the spread of the American system, the commercial model of communications, to the international arena. How readily a large and growing part of the world community has succumbed to communications arrangements patterned after the United States style and how these developments have been engineered is a story of relatively current vintage.

The electronics revolution that has transformed communications since the first world war also has provided the instrumentation of saturation advertising. Radio and television, almost from their inception in the United States were preempted to fulfill the sales objectives of the business community. Though cautioned in the 1920's by Herbert Hoover not to disfigure the exciting potential of the new natural resource that had been discovered, commerce unhesitatingly turned radio into its untiring pitchman.

Twenty years ago, against the advice and judgment of those who wanted to experiment carefully with the new medium and to discover its most fruitful capabilities, television prematurely was hurried into the economy by impatient equipment manufacturers and broadcasting networks, eager to sell sets and screen time.[1] To no

---

[1] "Television Network Procurement," Report of the Committee on Interstate and Foreign Commerce, 88th Congress, 1st Session, House Report No. 281, March 3, 1963, U.S. Government Printing Office, Washington, 1963, p. 49 and footnote 9.

one's surprise, television followed closely in radio's commercial footsteps.

## The Global Commercialization of Communications Systems

In the pre-television era, the United States stood alone amongst advanced industrialized nations in having its radio broadcasting unabashedly commercial. In no other society did advertisers pay the bill and direct the destinies of the medium so completely. State broadcasting authorities in Europe were the rule and the American arrangement was the exception.

With the advent of television, but not because of it, many national broadcasting structures adopted one or another variants of the American style. Dizard, author of *Television: A World View*, has written about this shift:

> "Television has developed primarily as a commercial medium. This was to be expected in the United States and a few other countries, notably in Latin America, where broadcasting was traditionally a private venture. Elsewhere, however, broadcasting was a state monopoly without commercial connections. Theoretically, television should have followed in the established pattern; significantly it did not. . . At present, television systems in over fifty countries are controlled, in whole or in part, by private interests under state supervision. Commercial advertising is carried by all but a handful of the world's ninety-five television systems."[2]

For the new countries the emerging pattern is the same. Dizard notes "the virtual domination of local television in developing nations by commercial interest."[3] UNESCO reports the same finding. A 1963 study concludes, after presenting evidence that television has been less subject to state control than radio that "this might seem to show that the tendency towards commercial operation is becoming more accentuated in television services than in radio broadcasting."[4]

---

[2] Wilson P. Dizard, *Television a World View*, Syracuse University Press, 1966, Syracuse, New York, p. 12-13.

[3] Dizard, *op. cit.*, p. 239.

[4] UNESCO, *Statistics on Radio and Television*, 1950-1960, 1963, Paris, France, p. 20.

Even strong, industrialized nations have been forced to modify their longtime stabilized broadcasting services and accept commercial operations. Britain yielded in 1954. France teetering on the edge of advertising-sponsored support for years has just moved across the line. The Russians, a special case to be sure, advertise in American newspapers their willingness to accept commercial material over their state-owned TV system.[5]

What has powered this almost universal push toward commercialization in the electronics communications media? Its advocates claim that commercial broadcasting is the most satisfactory method of meeting the financial and programmatic needs of the new media. Dizard, for instance, asserts that "The change [to commercialization] confirmed the effectiveness of American-style broadcasting both as a revenue producer and as a highly acceptable form of entertainment and persuasion."[6]

The revenue-producing capabilities of commercial broadcasting cannot be disputed. The acceptability of the entertainment offered is another matter that will be considered further along. But neither reason faintly suggests the more fundamental forces that are operating. *Nothing less than the viability of the American industrial economy itself is involved in the movement toward international commercialization of broadcasting.* The private yet managed economy depends on advertising. Remove the excitation and the manipulation of consumer demand and industrial slowdown threatens. *Broadcasting* magazine puts it this way: "In this country, where production capacity exceeds consumer demand, advertising has become more than an economic force—it is an influence on our quality of life."[7]

The continuing and pressing requirements of United States manufacturers to reach annually higher output levels to sustain and increase profit margins activate the process that is relentlessly enveloping electronic (and other) communications in a sheath of commercialization. What happens, of course, is a continuing interaction. The direct intrusion of American influence catalyses developments in the affected nations. Also, those countries with similar industrial structures and organization feel corresponding, if at first weaker, impulses themselves in the same direction.

5 *The New York Times,* January 16, 1967.
6 Dizard, *op. cit.,* p. 13.
7 *Broadcasting,* June 26, 1967.

The international dynamics resulting from the explosive force of private enterprise industrialism's market requirements find expression in ordinary trade accounts. *Television Magazine,* for instance, describes the interconnections between the advertising, manufacturing and broadcasting industries:

> "About 1959 a gentle curve representing the expansion of American advertising agencies overseas started an abrupt climb which hasn't yet levelled off. . . The growth of television abroad had something to do with this upsurge, since the head-start American agencies had in dealing with the medium commercially has given them a highly exportable know-how. But television wasn't the prime mover. *That role belongs to the client: The American consumer goods industry."*

The magazine explained this process with a simple illustration:

> "Take a giant corporation like Proctor and Gamble with sales over \$2 billion a year. Its position on the open market is based partly on the corporation's growth rate. But to add, say, 10% in sales each year becomes increasingly difficult when already over the two billion mark. *Where do you find that additional \$200 million? The answer, for more and more American corporations, is overseas."*[8]

American companies have been crossing the oceans regularly, either through direct acquisition or new plant expansion or leasing arrangements or combinations thereof. United States private direct investments in manufacturing across the globe have spurted in the twenty-four years beginning in 1943, from \$2,276 millions to \$22,050 millions. In this period in Western Europe alone, manufacturing investments have increased from \$879 millions to \$8,879 millions. To assist in marketing the output of their expanding foreign facilities, U.S. advertising agencies have been accompanying the industrial plants overseas. McCann-Erickson has 70 offices employing 4,619 persons in 37 countries. J. Walter Thompson, "The grand-daddy of international operations", has 1,110 people employed in its key London office alone. England has 21 American-associated ad agencies,

---

[8] Ralph Tyler "Agencies Abroad: New Horizons for U.S. Advertising," *Television Magazine,* September 1965, p. 36. (Italics added)

West Germany has 20 and France 12. In Latin America, Brazil has 15 American ad agencies and Canada has more U.S. agencies than any other nation. Even the developing world has begun to be penetrated. "Three enterprising U.S. agencies have tackled the huge market of India . . . (and) Africa, too, may be part of a future wave of agency expansion overseas."[9]

The advertising agencies rely on the communications media to open markets for their patrons—the American and Western European consumer goods producers. The state-controlled broadcasting structures which resist commercialization are under the continuous siege of the ad-men and their cohorts in public relations and general image promotion.

Once the privately-directed manufacturing enterprises have begun their goods production, all energies are concentrated on securing the public's ever-widening acceptance of the outpouring commodity streams. The insistence of powerful American sellers, temporarily allied with their local counterparts, on obtaining advertising outlets abroad is overwhelming state broadcasting authorities, one after another. The successful campaign to introduce commercial television in England was largely a matter of industry ad-men manipulating complex political wires. The former director of the BBC's television explained with some understatement, what happened in Britain:

> ". . . there was an unusually strong demand from large sections of British industry in the early nineteen fifties for more opportunities for advertising their goods. Wartime restrictions especially on paper had only recently been lifted, and a real boom in consumer goods was developing, but industry felt that there were insufficient opportunities for telling the public about the large range of new goods which were becoming available. Television was obviously an excellent medium for this, and industry was not averse to harnessing the television horse to the industrial chariot."[10]

Raymond Williams, also generalizing from the British experience, writes that "It is almost a full-time job to work for democratic com-

---

[9] *Ibid.*, p. 65. In 1967, according to *Printers Ink*, there were "at least 46 U.S.-based ad agencies abroad, with a total of 382 branch offices beyond the U. S. boundaries." Forty of these agencies, reported *Advertising Age*, claimed overseas billings of $1,138 millions.

[10] Gerald Beadle: Television A Critical Review, 1963, George Allen and Unwin, Ltd., London, p. 82.

munications against the now fantastic economic and political pressures of managed capitalism."[11]

What is emerging on the international scene bears a striking resemblance to the routine in the United States, of uncoordinated expansion of goods production, their promotion through the communications media, higher sales, further plant expansion and then the cycle's repetition. The symptoms that Fromm finds endemic in America are spreading across oceans and continents. Industrial society's troubled individual who seeks release in goods consumption is appearing throughout the expanding orbit of the international free market. According to Fromm,

> "Twentieth century industrialism has created this new psychological type, *homo consumens,* primarily for economic reasons, i.e., the need for mass consumption which is stimulated and manipulated by advertising. But the character type, once created, also influences the economy and makes the principles of ever-increasing satisfaction appear rational and realistic. Contemporary man, thus, has an unlimited hunger for more and more consumption."[12]

The man in the market economy has become a message receiver beyond all imagination. This individual is the target of the most effective communications media devised by modern technology. Bombarded in the United States by an estimated 1,500 advertising messages a day,[13] and exposed to 4,000 hours of TV viewing before arriving in grade school[14] "contemporary men" are multipyling rapidly in the North Atlantic community. In fact, *homo consumens* is beginning to be discovered as well in Africa, Latin America and Asia. In fourteen industrial private enterprise countries in 1964, twenty-one billion dollars were spent on advertising, two-thirds of which were expended in the United States.[15] Financing much of this

---

[11] Raymond Williams, "Britain's Press Crisis", *The Nation,* April 10, 1967, p. 467.

[12] Erich Fromm, "The Psychological Aspects of the Guaranteed Income" in *The Guaranteed Income,* edited by Robert Theobold, Doubleday and Co., Inc., New York, 1966, p. 179.

[13] *The Wall Street Journal,* November 3, 1965.

[14] *Television Magazine,* July, 1967, p. 37.

[15] "Advertising Investments Around the World," *International Advertising Association,* October, 1965.

staggering budget for global commercial message-making are the powerful multi-national corporations whose plants and service installations are spread over several countries. The major United States advertisers are, as might be expected, the most prominent consumer goods producers. Tobacco, drugs, cosmetics, beer, automobiles, gasoline, and food products are the chief sponsoring industries of commercial television in the United States. Table 1 is an abbreviated listing of the largest American TV advertisers in 1966.

Table 1

Television Advertising Expenditures of U.S. Companies, 1966[16]

| | | |
|---|---|---|
| 1. Proctor & Gamble | | $179.2 million |
| 2. Bristol-Myers | | 93.6 |
| 3. General Foods | | 93.3 |
| 4. Colgate-Palmolive | | 67.1 |
| *5. Lever Brothers | | 58.0 |
| 6. American Home Products | | 57.1 |
| 7. R. J. Reynolds | | 49.8 |
| 8. Gillette | | 41.9 |
| 9. Warner-Lambert | | 41.3 |
| 10. American Tobacco | | 40.8 |
| 11. General Mills | | 39.1 |
| 12. Sterling Drug | | 39.0 |
| 13. Coca-Cola Co./Bottlers | | 38.8 |
| 14. General Motors | | 38.4 |
| 15. Kellogg | | 35.1 |

* Lever Brothers is British-owned.

The engines of commercialization in the West are these "big spenders". Long ago they captured the radio spectrum in the United States. Now they are waging successful campaigns to extend their conquests to Europe, Africa and Asia. One advertising agency predicts that in 1976, American advertisers will be spending as much abroad as they do in the United States.[17] *Television Age's* annual survey of television around the world, offers country by country progress reports of the multi-national companies' advertising penetration. For example, in Argentina, "gasolines and automobile manufacturers, such as Shell, Esso, General Motors, Ford . . . are major advertisers . . . Ponds, Philips, Gillette, Nestle and Colgate are also heavy advertisers. . ." In Australia, "Coca-Cola and Chemstrand are major advertisers along with Ford, Lever Brothers, Alcoa, Ansett Air-

---

[16] *Broadcasting*, April 17, 1967, p. 38.
[17] *Ibid.*, December 19, 1966, p. 23.

lines, The Australian Biscuit Co., Beecham Products, and Bristol-Myers." In Finland, "Ford, Coca-Cola and General Motors are about as active here as they are in the U.S."[18] Wherever big company influence penetrates, electronic communications are subverted to salesmanship.

> "Three soap companies," Fred Friendly notes, "Proctor & Gamble, Colgate-Palmolive, and Lever Brothers, account for about 15 percent of the nation's total television sales. This is one reason why Americans know more about detergents and bleaches than they do about Vietnam or Watts. The three great printing presses in their seven-day-a-week continuous runs are so oriented to advertising and merchandise that after a single day of viewing television, a visitor from another planet could only infer that we are bent on producing a generation of semiliterate consumers."[19]

It is not only a matter of the ubiquitous, jarring commercial. The entire content that illuminates the home screen is fitted to the marketeer's order. "TV is not an art form or a culture channel; it is an advertising medium," states an American TV writer. Therefore, ". . . it seems a bit churlish and un-American of people who watch television to complain that their shows are so lousy. They are not *supposed* to be any good. They are supposed to make money . . . (and) in fact, 'quality' may be not merely irrelevant but a distraction."[20]

Admittedly, the situation of radio-television in the United States is the extreme case. In Western Europe, the tradition of state broadcasting authorities exercising some social responsibility has not yet been demolished. But the striving of the consumer goods producers to gain the attention of large audiences is unrelenting, and as Fromm observes, once the contact is made, the audience itself searches out further stimuli. If commercials are still controlled and compressed into special slices of the viewing time in some national systems abroad, the shows themselves often follow the dictates, directly or indirectly, of their sponsors. Certainly, this is the case in the popular

18 *Television Age,* July 3, 1967, pp. 33 and 61.

19 Fred Friendly, *Due to Circumstances Beyond Our Control,* Random House, 1967, New York, pp. 294-295.

20 Daniel Karp, *The New York Times Magazine,* "TV Shows are Not Supposed To Be Good," January 23, 1966.

and widely shown American productions where the advertising agency may have sat in at each stage of a script's development. Consider this account of a show's gestation: "The writing of a half-hour script takes approximately three weeks. As a first step, Baer (responsible for such shows as "Petticoat Junction", "The Munsters", and "Bewitched") submits several basic ideas for the plot to the producer. If the latter likes one of them, he gives the signal to go ahead. The next step is a five or six-page outline. This is read by the producer, the story editor and sometimes representatives from the advertising agency. On some shows the advertising people only read the finished script."

Whether in at the beginning of the "creative" process or at its conclusion, the advertiser's influence in American programming is paramount. Inevitably, "the writer feels that some of his best and most meaningful ideas have not reached the air because they were not considered commercial enough. Sponsors and producers do not want too radical a departure from what has been done before. Since the financial stake is so large, they want to play it safe."[21]

All the same, American shows, written exclusively to serve the ends of goods producers, are gobbling up the international TV market. ABC, NBC and CBS send their packaged programming to all continents, charging what the freight will bear. In low-income areas in Africa and Asia, old U.S. films and shows are dumped at low prices to secure a foothold in emerging markets, regardless of the relevance or appropriateness of the "entertainment."

In Western Europe, the most stable non-commercial broadcasting structures of sovereign states are unable to resist the forces that are arrayed against them. Here is one description of how "commercials" defy national boundaries, especially in the geographically compact North Atlantic region:

> "Of course, the continued expansion of commercial television, despite powerful opposition, is playing a major role in making unity of diversity. Although many important countries, particularly in Europe, still forbid TV advertising, there is a certain 'spillover' effect that tends to spread commercials even to those countries that originally were adamant. Only this year did the 11-year-old government-controlled Swiss TV service permit commercials on its three regional networks. The move was in large part prompted by

---

[21] *The New York Times*, December 12, 1965.

the concern of Swiss manufacturers who knew their customers were viewing Italian and German TV across the
border. The same process is expected to unfold in the
Netherlands, a large part of which is also open to German
programming and advertising messages. If Netherland TV
goes commercial, then Belgium is expected to follow shortly
thereafter. Then France and Scandinavia will be the last big
holdouts. . . If French television goes commercial, an executive at J. Walter Thompson remarks, then there truly will
be a common market for the TV advertiser."[22]

The pressure on the noncommercial European TV networks to
incorporate private programming and commercials is mounting and
the same forces are at work in radio broadcasting. France was compelled to shift the programming patterns on one of its biggest radio
networks, France-Inter, because of the competition of foreign stations
close to the border. "The change was forced on the non-commercial
network when it realized that it was losing its young listeners to the
Luxembourg Radio and Europe Number One, two stations situated
on the borders of France that adhere to the American-style diet of
pop music interspaced with commercials and newcasts."[23]

If "legitimate" infiltration and demolition of non-commercial state
systems of broadcasting is inapplicable for one reason or another, less
sophisticated techniques are available. Consider the bizarre charades
of the pirate radio stations which were located off the coast of England and some even in the Thames estuary. These illegal transmitters
completely disregarded international frequency allocation agreements. They broadcast pop music interlaced with commercials to
European and English audiences who are apparently hungering for
the entertainment and not at all displeased with the accompanying
consumer messages. Though the pirates were small-scale broadcasters,
behind them stood large-scale interests. In England, until the government actively intervened, both the Institute of Practitioners in
Advertising and the Incorporated Society of British Advertisers lent
indirect support to the pirates. A director of the ISBA stated: "We
recognize they fulfill a need. We would be happier, though, if they
were on-shore and permanent."[24]

[22] *Television Magazine*, September, 1965.
[23] *The New York Times*, February 26, 1967. See also, *Variety*, "Rising Tide of
Monied Interests May Yet Swing 3rd French TV Web", February 15, 1967, p. 38.
[24] *The Sunday Times*, London, June 19, 1966.

Reacting to an impending governmental regulatory bill, one of the pirates, Radio London, commented: "We expect to get sufficient advertising from overseas to enable us to continue. We have four million overseas listeners, *and much of our revenue is from international companies who would not be affected by British legislation.*"[25] Even after Parliament acted against the offshore broadcast facilities, the international connections of commercial broadcasting—the multinational companies, their advertising agencies, wealthy free-booters, and broadcast and record companies—continued to support the pirates in their efforts to weaken the state broadcasting authority.

Piracy apart, programming cannot be contained under present laissez-faire conditions within national frontiers. The flashy show with its lowest common denominator emotional features, styled expressly by commerce for the mass audience, cannot be kept out of one country if presented in another nearby. However questionable the "domino theory" may be in analyzing political developments in Southeast Asia, it is certainly an apt explanation for the march of commercial radio and television in Western Europe. Once a commercial inroad has been made electronically, technology and geography can be relied upon to exploit the advantage in depth.

A similar progression is beginning to appear in Asia. All-India Radio, reversing a thirty-year policy, has acceded, with governmental approval, to commercial advertising. The explanations for the decision are familiar. The government needed revenue, and, more persuasive, "Indian companies have been placing advertisements on the Ceylon Radio, whose light, commercial-studded programs can be heard throughout India." The parallel is striking "Ceylon, an island a few miles off India's southern coast, has been compared in this respect to the pirate radio stations that beam commercial programs to Britain. . ."[26]

Successfully securing control of communications across a good part of the earth's surface, commerce now has turned its attention to conquering space. At the White House Conference on International Cooperation in the winter of 1965, the National Citizens Commission's Committee on Space (whose chairman incidentally was Dr. Joseph Charyk, the president of Comsat), listed as the *first* applica-

---

[25] *The Times*, London, July 2, 1966. (Italics added).
[26] *The New York Times*, January 29, 1967.

tion of communications satellites their future impact on "trade and commerce." The committee's report stated: "It is possible to foresee use of closed circuit television by major companies doing a worldwide business to link together their offices and affiliates in order to kick off a new sales campaign or to demonstrate a new product or to analyze a new marketing situation in the far corners of the world."[27] Admittedly, other applications were proposed but priority went to business.

Similar sentiment exists in other influential places. The London *Economist* views communications satellites as the chosen business medium of the future. Lamenting the British Government's reluctance to participate more actively in ELDO (European Launcher Development Organization), the Europeans' sole hope of matching American communications technological advances, the magazine commented: "But is there only an American or a Russian or a Chinese way of life to be propagated around the world? Will Britain (and Europe) even be able to sell its goods around the world if it cuts itself out of *the advertising medium of the 1970's?*"[28]

Sir John Rogers, president of London's Institute of Practitioners in Advertising and deputy chairman as well of J. Walter Thompson Co., Ltd., an affiliate of the world's largest advertising agency, is more hopeful. Before the 1967 annual meeting of the American Association of Advertising Agencies he declared: "I believe as far as Europe is concerned, where the advertisers need a medium, and the public wants them to have it, they will eventually get it. . . And the projected increase in satellite communications will probably speed both this and the increasing internationalism of advertising in Europe."[29]

Even more indicative of the way utilization of communications satellites is shaping up are the perspectives of two recent conferences concerned with the matter. In December 1965, UNESCO assembled representatives from 19 member states and other interested international organizations to consider the use of space satellites for informational and cultural purposes. A few months later, at the 18th

---

27 *The White House Conference on International Cooperation.* National Citizens' Commission, Report of the Committee on Space, November 28-December 1, 1965, Washington, D. C., p. 27.

28 *The Economist,* London, June 11, 1966, p. 1167, (Italics added) .

29 *Broadcasting,* April 24, 1967, p. 75.

World Congress of the Advertising Association in Mexico City *Worldvision*, a network including 62 television stations in 25 countries, organized by the American Broadcasting Company's international subsidiary, ABC International, ran a three-day workshop demonstrating how "international advertisers could use TV right now." In the words of Donald W. Coyle, president of ABC International, "Global television is not something that we are going to have to wait for a far-off future to implement. It is upon us now."[30]

The contrast in the two approaches to the use of space communications is depressing. UNESCO's vision of international control of communications satellites for cultural use is *in the future*. *Worldvision's* program for commercial utilization of space media *already has begun*. Business and the PR world have swung into action and economic consultants are canvassing clients and informing them of global communications possibilities in marketing their products. A senior vice-president of Young and Rubicam, another giant American advertising agency, explained the new dynamics of selling this way; "I think the time is now, if it hasn't been already", he said, "to consider selling your product everywhere. Not in one country or on one continent, but all over . . . now with subtitles, when you've a good television campaign or a selling idea, and it works in one place, whether England or the United States, Japan, or whatever, then you don't have to test-market it any more, you go right to global marketing immediately and this could happen now."[31]

It is a mistake to view these developments as evidence of an international cabal seeking the global commercialization of communications. The forces are openly at work and the success of "consumerism" rests on a varied mix of human and institutional pressures which are at present very powerful. "Both a consumer oriented economy and commercial television seem to have things going for them at this moment of history in a good part of the globe", is the way one broadcasting publication puts it.[32]

If conspiracy is absent in the American commercial electronic invasion of the world, there is all the same a very clear consciousness present of how to utilize communications for both highly ideological

---

[30] *The New York Times*, May 15, 1966.

[31] Ralph Tyler, "Television Around the World", *Television Magazine*, October, 1966, p. 61.

[32] *Television Magazine*, September, 1965.

and profitable ends. Professor Ithiel de Sola Pool of the Massachusetts Institute of Technology told a congressional committee inquiring into "Modern Communications and Foreign Policy" that "the function that American international communications can serve is to provide people with things for which they are craving but which are not readily available to them." He mentioned world news as one example and added "Another thing that people crave is simply to see what a modern way of life is like—seeing *commodities,* seeing how people live, or hearing popular music." Dr. Joseph Klapper of the Columbia Broadcasting System expanded on the musical theme for the Committee. ". . . the broadcasting of popular music is not likely to have any immediate effect on the audience's political attitude", he noted, "but this kind of communication nevertheless provides a sort of entryway of Western ideas and Western concepts, even though these concepts may not be explicitly and completely stated at any one particular moment in the communication."[33]

The deprivations imposed by the protracted depression of the 1930's in the Western world and the war years shortages of the 40's created a huge longing in Europe and America for goods. The failure of basic social reform in Western Europe after the war to change the motivation and thrust of the national economies toward a public orientation permitted the reconsolidation of the private goods producers' interest. In America, the business system had already recaptured its confidence and authority before the United States entered the war in 1941. Advertising, on behalf of the private interest, whipped the appetite of consumerism higher still. The world outside the industrial North Atlantic enclave has followed the impulses originating in the wealthy core area.

The efforts to hold back the accelerating push toward commercialization of broadcasting communications in Western Europe have relied on the existence of national traditions of propriety unobserved in the United States and even some exclusion or limitation on American programming. Canada and Great Britain, for example, have tried, not too successfully, to keep the proportion of American to domestic shows within certain limits.

Yet the attempts to exclude United States programming and to

---

[33] "Modern Communications and Foreign Policy", Committee on Foreign Affairs, House of Representatives, 90th Congress. 1st Session, May 4, 1967, Washington, D. C., pp. 63-64. (Italics added) .

limit the number and length of national commercials are unlikely to be effective in any one country no matter how influential that society may be in its own region. The subject matter that is denied local transmission reappears in and is broadcast from neighboring states, with transmitters sometimes deliberately established for this specific purpose. Then too, the business system in Western Europe, Canada, Japan and Australia supports the general principle of commercialization and accordingly throws its weight wherever possible behind an advance of salesmanship. After all, the marketing problems in these privately organized industrial states, if not yet at American levels, are approaching them rapidly.

As for the universe of the global poor, the "have-not" nations stand practically defenseless before a rampaging Western commercialism. Impoverished as they are, many developing states are able to afford the new communications complexes only by accepting commercial packages which "tie" their broadcasting systems to foreign programming and foreign financial sponsorship. Time-Life's Vice President Sig Mickelson asserts bluntly: "The various underdeveloped countries are having to permit commercials because they can't afford a television system otherwise."[34] In this way their economic developmental paths are set, regardless of the intentions and designs of their planners, by the pull of market-directed consumerism. Expectations of new roads to national development which *might* foster motivations and behavior different from contemporary Western styles are being dashed in their infancy.

The gloomy and bitter words of Japanese economist, Shigeto Tsuru, seem to take on universality before Western market enterprise's electronic communications offensive:

> "In this world of high-powered communications we may even have to speak of a new kind of 'self-alienation' for citizens living under capitalism. If there were a society on this earth somewhere which would make full use of the highly developed techniques of communication of today for the sole purpose of its inhabitants' autonomous cultural needs, it would be an experience of a life-time for us to visit there—for us who daily, even hourly cannot escape from the onslaught, either subtle or crude, of modern commercialism in a capitalist society."[35]

[34] *Television Magazine*, October, 1966, p. 61.
[35] Shigeto Tsuru, *Has Capitalism Changed?*, Tokyo, 1961, p. 56.

# CHAPTER 8

# The Developing World Under Electronic Siege

So many difficulties beset the poor nations, the Afro-Asian-Latin-American "have nots", that it may seem brutal to suggest still another problem they have yet to face up to. It is not a secondary issue, though, since it concerns the very purpose of national development as well as the destinies of scores of states. What is involved is the cultural integrity of weak societies whose national, regional, local or tribal heritages are beginning to be menaced with extinction by the expansion of modern electronic communications, television in particular, emanating from a few power centers in the industrialized world.

It is understandable that the paraphernalia of modernity, and especially the technology of broadcast communications, should appear strikingly impressive to leadership groups in states still trapped in economic stagnation but desperately striving for improvement. Nor is it all delusion! The informational apparatus now available for national use is much more than glamorous instrumentation; if sufficiently and intelligently applied it is an engine for great forward drives in the developmental process. The positive effects of massive public service communications are still unrealized only because such applications have yet to be undertaken anywhere.

What is less apparent, though no less real, are the negative characteristics of the electronic imagery that is being introduced in poorer communities across the globe. Whereas public service broadcasting is hardly visible, a tidal wave of commercial material is flowing over the earth. And even now, a cultural Gresham's Law seems to be operating internationally whereby the social products with least value receive the widest circulation. The emerging intercontinental television exchange is powered largely by Western commercialism, which

153

up to now has not concerned itself with the disparities in economic levels among states and their correspondingly different communications requirements.

The mechanics that spread this cultural mush globally and the possibilities of diminishing the flow and reducing the ultimate damage demand serious attention.

## The Mechanics of Cultural Levelling

Gunboat diplomacy is now an item in the antiquities showcase but communications diplomacy is a very thriving business of the moment. Consider the rich possibilities for maneuver that accompany the establishment of radio-television broadcast facilities in a society lacking an industrial base.

The actual physical equipment must be secured from abroad. Capital to pay for it usually must be coaxed from reluctant treasuries with tempting promises and enticing conditions. No less a problem to the impoverished state is the matter of trained technicians and personnel to run the broadcast structures once they are in place. Labor that is skilled in these techniques must initially come from or be trained abroad, and the training is usually, as one would expect, in how to run French, English, American style broadcast enterprises.

But the elemental, and barely acknowledged, issue in contemporary communications appears only *after* broadcasting, however it is organized, begins. What messages will the new instrumentation transmit? The content of the programming is all that really matters, for what is broadcast may determine, in large measure, the cultural outlook and the social direction of the new nations for generations.

Mistakes and failures in agriculture and industry, if momentarily disastrous, are still remediable. Cultural patterns, once established, are endlessly persistent. The opportunity to freshly mould a new nation's outlook and social behavior is historically unique and merits the most careful deliberation. Yet in modern mass communications hard and inflexible laws, economic and technological, operate. If these are not taken into account *in the beginning*, and at least partially overcome, courses of development automatically unfold that soon become unquestioned "natural" patterns.

A few examples indicate the character of the forces at work. For instance, the ability to produce local broadcast programming is an extremely demanding business, one which requires skill and experience, not easy to come by. Furthermore, live programming is expensive and the question of how it will be financed becomes critical, not only for the considerable costs involved but for the direction of the medium the character of the financing imposes. Shall broadcast budgets be met by state subsidy with the implicit accompaniment of crippling state control? Can license fees cover the costs, as they hardly do in already-developed Britain and France? Or should commercial sponsorship be permitted? The last is always tempting in countries with empty treasuries, especially since decision makers often seem unaware of the long run *quid pro quo* that private sponsorship exacts.

Though financing is the overriding issue to be settled, another, more mundane, factor cannot be overlooked. Once individuals have made their investments for receivers they will press for longer viewing (and listening) intervals. The pressure to keep the sets playing seems to be irresistible. This demand, if even partly met, creates programming needs far exceeding most local production. This is true even in the most technically advanced societies.

As a result of the limitations to easily expanding the domestic production of programming and TV's enormous appetite for material, the door is opened to foreign program suppliers. The United States is by far the most important of the few states capable of exporting television material. What is more, the program suppliers are willing to distribute their wares at lower than production costs (sometimes at only a tiny fraction of cost) because the foreign sales are bonus revenues, profits made from programs which have already more than covered their production costs. Dumping further discourages domestic program production in all but the richest countries.

Once a developing society gets caught up in the impersonal imperatives of television operations, its broadcast structure rapidly becomes a vehicle for material produced outside its territory with an outlook and a character generally irrelevant, if not injurious, to its development orientation. Already the inroads are vast. For example, Dr. Lloyd A. Free, Director of the Institute for International Social Research, describes this situation in the most heavily populated country in Africa:

"I did a study in Nigeria a couple of years ago. During that time I watched Nigerian television. Do you know that most

of the prime hours of programming time on Nigerian television was made up of filmed television shows from the
United States, many of them of a soap opera variety? . . .
The Nigerians apparently watched because there was nothing else to watch. But of all the sheer waste of program time
in a country faced with very grave problems as we see today,
it just seems atrocious that this medium with the potential
of television was utilized in that way. The reason that it is
utilized that way is that it is cheaper for the Nigerian television networks to buy American films than produce their
own or get other types of material."[1]

In the introduction of his study of Mexican family life, Oscar Lewis
noted the influence of American TV advertising in that country: "The
major television programs are sponsored by foreign-controlled companies like Nestles, General Motors, Proctor and Gamble, and Colgate. Only the use of the Spanish language and Mexican artists
distinguishes the commercials from those in the United States. On
the Quaker Oats program one hears the Mexican lightweight idol
Raton (The Mouse) Macias recommend Quaker Oats as the cereal
of champions. Some commercials do not even trouble to translate
phrases and have spread American linguistic forms or *pochismos*.
Thus, beauty products are announced as 'Touch and Glow', 'Bright
and Clear', etc."[2]

The cultural homogenization that has been underway for years in
the United States now threatens to overtake the globe. Mordecai
Gorelik, long-time student of the theatre, asserted in 1965 that "The
era of mechanized and centralized communication via the syndicated
press, radio, movies and TV, has created a *gleichschaltung* unprecedented in history."[3] Everywhere local culture is facing submersion
from the mass-produced outpourings of commercial broadcasting.
Television in the United States is tailored almost exclusively to fit
the market needs of the consumer goods producers who sponsor and
finance the programming. The program material is designed especially to secure and hold mass audiences in thrall to the delights of
consumerdom.

---

[1] "Modern Communications and Foreign Policy", Subcommittee on International Organization and Movements of the Committee on Foreign Affairs, House
of Representatives, 90th Congress, 1st Session, May 4, 1967, p. 42.

[2] Oscar Lewis, *Five Families*, Basic Books, Inc., New York, 1959, p. 8.

[3] *The New York Times*, April 11, 1965.

Ironically, even the TV commercials, which are themselves, leading contributors to standardized behavior, are losing their national identity and individuality. Wallace A. Ross, director of the American TV Commercials Festival (in consumerdom every artifact has its festival) showed a selection of foreign commercials and noted that "one sad development of the increasingly international market place is that somehow along the way national characteristics . . . have faded away."[4]

A few, but only a few societies have the industrial strength, the technical competence and the national will to resist the electronic onslaughts of commercial television. The Japanese, for instance, have a broadcast law which stipulates that "efforts shall be made to preserve outstanding cultural assets of the past", and Kenneth Adam, Director of British Television, writes admiringly in *The Listener* that "This [objective] has become a key factor in national policy after the powerful Americanizing influences of the years following the second world war. The Japanese have accepted and indeed welcomed a second culture to set beside their own, but they have no intention of allowing their own ways of life and thought to be swamped, and this is increasingly reflected in their broadcasting."[5]

The Canadians, no less eager to retain their national identity, and by no standard a low-income society, are not as fortunate as the Japanese. Ever since the advent of radio in the late 1920's, the Canadians have been waging a losing battle against the American electronic invasion. Public broadcasting in Canada owes its existence to the vigorous and initially successful efforts of a handful of individuals who were aware that "Never before had the 'undefended boundary' presented such an open door to cultural annexation."[6] Television has multiplied the peril. Sixty per cent of Canadian households are within direct reception of American transmitters. Their television is dominated by American programming, and according to the recent government-appointed Committee on Broadcasting

---

[4] *Broadcasting*, November 1, 1965.

[5] Kenneth Adam, "Broadcasting In Japan", *The Listener*, June 30, 1966, p. 943.

[6] M. Prang, "The Origins of Public Broadcasting in Canada", *Canadian Historical Review*, XLVI (March 1965), p. 3. Also, G. Spry, "The Origins of Public Broadcasting in Canada: A Comment", *Canadian Historical Review*, Vol. XLVI, No. 2, June, 1965, pp. 134-141.

(The Fowler Committee), much of the broadcasting Canadians see and hear is not serving national needs.[7]

Still less able to defend themselves against the new communications are the poor, the small and the new states on five continents. Most of these are unable to finance independently the establishment, maintenance, and operation of broadcast facilities. They rely increasingly on either foreign capital to both install facilities and provide programming in a package deal, which quickly turns the broadcast structures into miniature Western (or, Eastern) systems, or on a supply of temporarily low-cost foreign (mostly American) material which originally was produced to the specifications of commercial sponsors. In either case, the programming has not been made with the requirements of the importing nation in view, and if anything, it presents images and styles of life that are wildly out of keeping with the social necessities of most of the "have-not" states.

Furthermore, when developing nations feel compelled by their impoverishment to adopt commercial systems of television broadcasting, which superficially seem to be costless, they become subject inevitably to commercialism's reliance on the mass audience, the standardized appeal, and the want-creating machinery that the consumer goods producers, who sponsor the shows, demand and receive.

But the takeover of communications structures in the developing nations by private enterprise for commercial ends threatens disaster. In the already-developed states, the consumer emphasis, whatever its social cost and however much it distorts individual values, offers at least a more or less effective way of clearing the market of goods produced in highly unstable economies. In the poor states, there are as yet no over-developed consumer goods industries. There are no surpluses of washing machines, TV sets and automobiles. To foster consumerism in the poor world sets the stage for frustration on a massive scale, to say nothing of the fact that there is a powerful body of opinion there which questions sharply the desirability of pursuing the Western pattern of development.

Resources directed into consumer goods in the poorer countries represent materials channelled away from education and capital expansion. The stimulation of personal consumption wants diverts painfully scarce materials from group projects and long range im-

---

[7] *Report of the Committee on Broadcasting*, Ottawa, Canada, 1965.

provement possibilities. Also, it creates or at least intensifies attitudes of individual acquisitiveness that go poorly with the community's desperate need of far-reaching social co-operation.

## Efforts At National Self-Protection

Yet given the strength of the global business system with its powerful roots reaching out hungrily from the North Atlantic basin and utilizing electronic communications to promote its international marketing mission, what means do feeble, backward states possess to follow their own options in economic and cultural decision making?

Some small hope may derive from the tentatively accepted recognition that unrestricted commercial intercourse between nations is not necessarily a benefit to all concerned. What has begun to be apprehended in economics may be recognized eventually as having relevance to culture and communications.

Beginning with the persuasive arguments of Adam Smith, for one hundred and fifty years economists steadfastly have defended free trade. Since Smith, and until most recently, the few dissident voices who saw merit and purpose in limiting and controlling trade came, not surprisingly, from the developing nations of the time. Alexander Hamilton espoused protectionism for the early republic, and in the modernizing German economy of the mid-nineteenth century, Friedrich List saw the problem in terms that are remarkably contemporary. He wrote:

"The loss which a nation undergoes in consequence of protective tariffs consists in any case only in *values;* whereas, on the other hand, it gains *powers* whereby it is enabled permanently to produce values which are incalculable in their amount. This expenditure of values is, accordingly, to be regarded simply as the price of the industrial development of the nation."[8]

The newly-independent countries seeking to "gain powers" at the sacrifice of "values" possess a population numbering perhaps two-thirds of the human race. Singly at first, later collectively, developing societies have challenged the utility of free trade as a means of improv-

---

[8] Friedrich List, *National System of Political Economy,* Jena edition, 1910, Introduction, Volume 1, pp. 63-76.

ing their desperate condition. Skepticism has arisen about the long-standing assumption of the mutual benefits of trade. When the partners to the transaction are unequal in strength, the weaker think they have observed that all too frequently the benefits flow to the stronger side. A world Conference on Trade and Development (UNCTAD), convened under the auspices of the United Nations in Geneva in 1964, noted officially this heretofore only infrequently-admitted phenomenon. The conference accepted, despite headshaking in some quarters, the legitimacy of the efforts of the developing states to impose "unequal" rules on international trade to compensate for their unequal bargaining strength. Advanced states, for instance, were urged to accept high tariffs on their exports (imposed by the developing countries), while they were expected, at the same time, to reduce their duties on the exports of the modernizing states.

The view that complete free trade in goods and services between states unequal in economic strength may be detrimental to the health of the weaker society is now only at the point of partial recognition, certainly not total acceptance, in the powerful industrial nations. Those who are willing to grant *this* possibility have by no means conceded that the proposition can be broadened considerably.

Just as the folklore of commerce supposes that diverse trading groups will be drawn together amicably and beneficially in the exchange of goods, a stronger mythology insists that interpersonal and intergroup communications, whatever their nature, must have a positive and benevolent impact on world-wide human affairs. Open up communications between peoples, the belief goes, and humankind must prosper. The most extravagant claims are made in that connection. Margaret Mead, discussing the survival of man, is optimistic because, among other things, ". . . of the huge recent advances in communications and the possibilities for sharing knowledge."[9] Jerome Frank, similarly, in a different context but also considering the question of human solidarity, writes; "The reason there has not been a feeling for mankind is because we have not been able to communicate fully and intimately with mankind. One of the great new hopes of the world is that the media of mass communications, and the shrinkage of the world in terms of transportation and so on, are going to lead to a rapid buildup of a worldwide network of com-

---

[9] *The New York Times,* April 20, 1965.

munications and of mutual rewards, out of which, I think, can grow a feeling for all mankind."[10]

These are sentiments with which everyone would like to agree, and their commonsense character seems solid enough to be acceptable. But as with conventional trade theory, they set aside the structural and social divisions that now characterize the global community. They assume that everything the well-to-do states have to say is useful and of concern to the destitute nations—an assumption that must be very carefully scrutinized.

The fact and paradox of this age is that technical advances have made electronic communications capable of massive global penetration by the advanced countries, while the socio-economic differentials that still separate nations require, at this stage of world development at least, the maintenance of distance between states and systems. In the poor world, leaderships work frantically to secure domestic integration, to recreate cultural identities, and to maintain national individuality in the face of domestic and internationally-generated resistance.

Communications media could be of great assistance in the realization of these aims, if they functioned in a public educational role. If programming objectives coincided with the nation's developmental goals, massive campaigns of literacy, manpower training programs and honest forums for popular discussion would receive the highest priorities. Broadcasting's responsibility in the emergent states, if identified and accepted, would require a complete reversal of radio-TV's function as it is now performed in America. No such reversal is in sight.

The negative consequences in poor countries of uncontrolled exposure to current Western culture were well appreciated by Frantz Fanon:

> "Young people have at their disposition leisure occupations designed for the youth of capitalist countries: detective novels, penny-in-the-slot machines, sexy photographs, pornographic literature, films banned to those under sixteen, and above all alcohol. In the West, the family circle, the effects of education and the relatively high standard of living of

---

[10] "On the Developed and the Developing", an Occasional Paper, published by the *Center for the Study of Democratic Institutions*, 1965, pp. 18-19.

the working classes provide a more or less efficient protection against the harmful action of these pastimes. But in an African country, where mental development is uneven, where the violent collision of two worlds has considerably shaken old traditions and thrown the universe of the perceptions out of focus, the impressionability and sensibility of the young Africans are at the mercy of the various assaults made upon them by the very nature of Western culture. His family very often proves itself incapable of showing stability and homogeneity when faced with such attacks."[11]

As a matter of fact, Fanon's confidence in the ability of Western youth to shake off the corrosive effects of their own commercial culture is not universally shared in the West. Reporting on a study of children's television, *New York Times*' education editor inquired if TV, as presently carried on in the United States, was not a "form of pollution."[12] The study itself asked "what values are being consistently reinforced by television: helpfulness, caring, consideration? Indifference, malice, cruelty? Sophistication, simplicity, suavity?" "If the decision is to sell", the study asserts, "the most profitable approach is to mesmerize the children with cartoons, add a dash of slapstick humor by an absurd adult, command an audience, and sell a lot of candy."[13]

But as the *Times* editor adds, "much more is being sold than candy—including questionable toys, ranging from destructive weapons to excessively sex-oriented, clothes-conscious dolls, food items which violate proper nutrition, and drugs which as vitamins ought to be used on the recommendation of the health nurse or pediatrician rather than as a result of a child-oriented sales pitch."

The new listeners and viewers in the developing world are beginning to experience what Western audiences have become inured to—commercialism's indifference to the public interest. Western publics have been conditioned to accept and to like the radio-television fare hurled at them daily. Having formed and reinforced popular tastes according to its marketing needs, business turns around and justifies

---

[11] Frantz Fanon, *The Wretched of the Earth*, Grove Press, New York, 1965, p. 156.

[12] *The New York Times*, January 1, 1967.

[13] "Television for Children", Foundation for Character Education, Boston, Massachusetts, 1966, p. 9.

its offerings on the grounds of public demand. Fred Friendly has commented on the peculiarity of this reasoning:

"As this mediocrity, which in the short term is economically profitable, fills the air, it creates appetites; it styles the nation's taste just as advertising influences what we eat, smoke and drive. The stock answer of network apologists for the current television schedules is, 'We give the people what they want,' but what has actually happened is that those viewers who have been brainwashed select their own brand of popcorn, while those of more discerning tastes simply give up watching or listening. If you condition an audience to expect *The McCoys* or *Leave It To Beaver,* of course it will reject the Vietnam hearings or a McNamara news conference when it is broadcast in their place. A Walter Lippmann interview in the weekly time period of *Petticoat Junction* would be greeted with just as much outrage as he would receive if you asked him to lecture between the double feature at any of the Forty-second Street movie houses."[14]

The inescapable responsibility of broadcasters for the influencing of public tastes also was heavily emphasized in the Pilkington Commission's report on broadcasting in Britain in 1960.[15]

## The Necessity of Economic Assistance and National Separateness

Economic assistance and national separateness are the apparently irreconcilable twin concerns of scores of countries. The need of the developing nations for aid is fairly well understood, if not acted upon. Their necessity for social distance has been almost entirely overlooked.

The quest in the emergent nations for separateness is not, as some may believe, a reflection of immaturity. More accurately put, it is a matter of necessity. It is simultaneously the means and the end to providing both domestic improvement and international solidarity, in that order of priority. Efforts to reinforce sovereignty and to enhance bargaining strength are undeniably measures of self-interest, but they contribute also toward a global equalization that must pre-

---

14 Fred Friendly, *Due to Circumstances Beyond Our Control,* Random House, New York, 1967, pp. 273-274.

15 Report of the Committee on Broadcasting, HSMO, London. June, 1962.

cede, however far in the future it may be, genuine international integration.

On the national level, the benefit to the growth prospects of developing states of a degree of isolationism is immediately observable. The elaboration and the implementation of national developmental designs are imperiled by the extent to which incompatible value systems or inappropriate institutional forces are permitted to intrude themselves on the developing economy. The new cultural-ideological structures of an emergent nation are no less vulnerable to the glittering socio-cultural products of the already-developed world than the new industries of the aspiring states are to the established giant corporations of the industrialized West. To meet the threats of the latter, protection is invoked to preserve a frail manufacturing base. In the communications-cultural area, the social fabric which affects the entire economy may be equally in danger, but the threat, much less the means to counter it, is at present hardly recognized.*

Sometimes the issue of freedom is invoked to defend the flow of cultural materials within and across national borders. Tariffs on shoes or woolens or whiskey may be acceptable at times, but, so the argument runs, how can anyone advocate measures which strike at the creations of the human mind? Does not all mankind suffer thereby? If human creativity literally were involved, there could be no other conclusion. But a confusion of individual effort with corporate activity obscures the actualities. It is assumed that films and television and radio programming are the inspired efforts of talented individuals. Yet only in the exceptional case is this so. Most often, the television program or the typical American movie is merely another commodity, designed carefully, in the same sense that soap

---

* If the poor nations are unaware of the attacks being levelled against their cultural identities, some of the initiators of these onslaughts are very conscious of their objectives. For instance, United States Information Agency official, Wilson Dizard told Congress about the difficulties his agency faced in penetrating China: "You know that the Chinese mainland is in effect the toughest nut for us to crack in terms of getting in. . . . The only way we can get in these days is through the Voice of America. We are beefing up our facilities in the Far East right now for this purpose. Unfortunately we are not permitted to go in and put up our own wall posters."[16]

16 "Modern Communications and Foreign Policy", *op. cit.*, p. 73.

and cars and cosmetics are prepared, to satisfy artificially stimulated wants.

Identifying the products of the United States film and broadcasting industries with human freedom can be misleading. Individual expression and talent are difficult to discover in most of the offerings of the information and entertainment industries in the West. What comes out of these faceless complexes today generally are neat packages of stereotyped dramatic ingredients, formalistically arranged. Fortunately, it is not often the artist who is injured if the mass media's artifacts are rejected.

Two decades ago the Commission on Freedom of the Press rejected the easy assumption that the espousal of free speech in the American Constitution was the basis for insisting on an unrestricted international free flow of communication. "The surest antidote for ignorance and deceit", it noted, "is the widest possible exchange of objectively realistic information—*true* information, not merely *more* information; *true* information, not merely, as those who would have us simply write the First Amendment into international law seem to suggest, the *unhindered flow* of information! There is evidence that a mere quantitative increase in the flow of words and images across national borders may replace ignorance with prejudice and distortion rather than with understanding."[17]

Some African leaders are aware of the issues at stake. The Senegalese Ambassador to the United Nations recently suggested:

> "We should, without delay, proceed to take an exhaustive inventory of the artistic and cultural stock of all peoples in order to conserve it so that it may become a part of the universal civilization. . . .
> We must become acquainted with all civilizations and all original cultures of all the races before they perish under the increasingly overwhelming pressure toward the international standardization of man."[18]

If there is a prospect that cultural diversity will survive anywhere on this planet, it depends largely on the willingness and ability of

---

[17] Llewellyn White and Robert D. Leigh, *Peoples Speaking to Peoples*, A Report on International Mass Communications from the Commission on Freedom of the Press, University of Chicago Press, Chicago, 1946, p. 2.

[18] Ousmane Soce Diop, "Communications in Senegal", *The American Scholar* Spring, 1966, p. 221.

scores of weak countries to forego the cellophane-wrapped articles of the West's entertainment industries and persistently to develop, however much time it takes, their own broadcast material.

It is already uncertain whether this remains a serious possibility for the world's "have not" states. Roger Revelle, discussing the biological imperatives of a broadly-based and international scientific ecology, writes that "Especially we need to learn how to avoid irreversible change if we are going to be able to assure future generations the opportunity to choose the kind of world in which they want to live."[19] No less important, in this respect, is the preservation of cultural options to peoples and nations only now becoming aware of their potential.

## Is A Program of Communications Protection Realizable?

The inclination of developing states to protect their weak manufacturing industries against powerful international competition emphasizes the usefulness of even stronger defenses against cultural onslaughts that could prove possibly more disastrous to long run developmental goals. The economic and cultural dangers to national development however, cannot be handled with identical techniques. Keeping goods physically out of the nation, once the will exists to do so, is relatively simple. Excluding electro-magnetic waves is something else again. With the exception of jamming facilities, a decidedly unattractive and highly expensive business in itself, there are no defenses against the speedy electronic impulses which move effortlessly across national frontiers. When the transmitter deliberately chooses to invade an area electronically, protection is practically impossible. These, at any rate, are the experiences of strong national states. If the British, the Swiss and the French have been unable to insulate themselves, what may be said of the chances of the Asians and Africans to achieve protection?

The most promising means of obtaining electronic breathing space for those countries intent on their own specific national needs is an international (though not necessarily an inter-governmental) agreement. Such a covenant would extend the area of regulation in international communications from the existing physical technique of

---

[19] Roger Revelle, "International Biological Program", *Science*, 24 February 1967, Volume 1955, Number 3765, p. 957.

frequency allocation to the character and scheduling of programming itself. Though the possibility of enlarging the scope for governmental control and censorship would be a real threat with such an agreement, it must be balanced against the consequences of proceeding along current lines, where the initiative is in the hands of commercial forces accountable only to company balance sheets. If prevailing practices are unchanged, the laws of the market will secure the global commercialization of electronic communications. If this occurs, the injury, especially to developing economies, may be more real than the threat of potential bureaucratic state censors.

Actually, the prospect may not be so bleak nor so circumscribed. There may be more slack available than the nasty choice of either of two unattractive options. International agreement on programming may, but it need not, be an instrument of state suppression. Independent authorities, responsible to but somewhat insulated from their own governments, may still realistically be expected to offer some security against narrowly nationalistic and censorious tendencies, while at the same time they defend their economies against programming that is antithetical to deeply-felt developmental requirements.

Included in the area of international programming agreement, for instance, might be a daily reservation of time in which only certain categories of programming could be carried. The Fowler Commission's recent suggestion[20] that Canadian television use all morning hours for formal educational material might be considered as the sort of allocation that requires international agreement. It is obvious that Canada, however desirous, is unable to pursue such a course against the opposition of its powerful neighbor with whom it shares a 3,000 mile "undefended boundary". If the United States transmits soap-opera while Canadian stations are carrying educational features, the viewing behavior of the 3 out of 5 Canadian families who are within transmission range of American programming is all too predictable.

Similarly, international programming agreements may assist developing nations to resist the compartmentalization of television (and radio) into educational and recreational components. This artificial separation which in the United States has reduced the educational sector to a threadbare, marginal existence has little meaning

---

[20] Report of the Committee on Broadcasting, *op. cit.*

for the newer nations. For them all programming must be viewed as an entity insofar as national goals are foremost. The integration of television rather than its compartmentalization serves best its application to a developmental use. Otherwise, there is the lamentable and futile effort to minimize and compensate for the excesses of the recreational sector with the offerings of the few educational hours. If the emerging nations choose unified programming, which would be thoroughly in accord with their developmental design, their decision would be reinforced and implemented to the extent international agreements support it.

It is noteworthy that the question of programming control has begun to appear on the agendas of some international organizations. In December 1965, a UNESCO Conference considered the forthcoming impact of communications satellites on the developing world, and one critical point that emerged from the discussion was the need for the protection of national sovereignty by some kind of program control. Indicative of the general sentiment were the introductory remarks of UNESCO's Acting Director-General: ". . . I believe such co-operation (international) must extend beyond the *techniques* of communication to embrace also a common concern with the *content* of what is transmitted."[21]

At the same meeting, the Director-General of *All-India Radio* declared; ". . . a whole world let loose on unsuspecting and comparatively less sophisticated people may have far-reaching consequences. Unless these forces are internationally controlled, it will be difficult to say whether the advantages will outweigh the disadvantages. . . . In the ultimate analysis, freedom may have to be interpreted not merely as a removal of censorship, but as a creation of opportunities."[22]

More recently, writing in the *European Broadcasting Union's Review,* Edward Ploman of Swedish Radio inquired: "Can we really make use of this new medium in a meaningful way on the basis of regulating the allocation of frequencies only, or must we also regulate the use of these same frequencies, in a way and on a scale that has

---

[21] Meeting of the Experts on the Use of Space Communications by the Mass Media, *United Nations Educational, Scientific and Cultural Organization,* UNESCO House, Paris, 6-10 December, 1965, Report of the Meeting, UNESCO/MC/52, Paris, March 31, 1966, p. 9. (Emphasis in the text) .

[22] *Ibid.,* p. 7.

never been done before? This is a new problem and it would demand new thinking and new solutions. I don't think Aldous Huxley was far off the mark when he said that the human race would have to change its ways of thinking more in the next twenty-five years than it has done in the last twenty-five thousand."[23]

More drastic still, some European observers, apprehensive of what they consider to be the present monopolistic character of satellite communications, have cautioned against permitting any space broadcasting until a truly international control organization has been established.[24]

Responsible international regulation of television programming will not answer all the perplexing issues of worldwide economic backwardness. But it is, at least, a step in the direction of reducing rather than intensifying existing difficulties. Also, it is not a matter of action or inaction. If those with a social interest in the peaceful evolution of the international community do not put forward practical alternatives at this point, the onrushing power of market forces in the West will win the field by default. Privately or socially administered, radio-television will not leave the world community as it found it. Its influence, already felt, will leave deeper marks as time goes by. The question before us is the shape of the world we wish to inhabit. The international means still exist, but do we have the will and the energy to resist technology's thrust, abetted by commerce's interest, toward global homogenization?

---

[23] Edward W. Ploman, "Some Observations on Space Communications", *EBU Review*, March 1966, 96B, p. 36.

[24] For an unsympathetic presentation of these sentiments, see Richard N. Gardner, "Space Broadcasting: Problems of International Law and Organization", before the *American Institute of Aeronautics and Astronautics*, May 4, 1966.

# CHAPTER 9

# Comsat and Intelsat: The Structure of International Communications Control

The American postwar imperial thrust is unblushingly evident in space communications. In this entirely new area of human capability and technical achievement, the ambitious commercial-political objectives of the American decision-making elite have been straightforwardly elaborated. The space communications goals and the structures that have been established to achieve them reveal the bold mechanics of American power maneuvering for world position in a strategic sector.

Global communications control, important in the past, today has become indispensable for the exercise of international authority. From the beginning of Western European expansion, centuries ago, Western informational connections with most of the world have been practically one-way circuits. Communications served expansionist societies as order-giving instruments for colonial administrators and for assisting the commercial undertakings of their own nationals. The international network of communications, as it evolved, reinforced the controls of a few Great Powers over subject territories and peoples. Like the fabled colonial railroads that continue to run from raw materials supply centers in the interior to coastal ports and are almost entirely useless for internal transport, nonwestern communications also, were primarily out-going. They served foreign not domestic needs. Even now, though this is changing rapidly, telephone connections in many parts of Asia, Africa and South America continue to be routed through Paris, London or New York because interior lines or exchanges have yet to be established.

The breakdown of *formal* colonialism, the independence movements across the world, the emergence of American power, and a breathtaking new technology are creating new patterns in international communications. Two-way informational flows are replacing the traditional one-way circuits. Regions formerly inaccessible or deemed unimportant to colonial administrators have been or are being drawn into widening informational nets. In the world that is emerging, an absence or shortage of physical communications is rapidly being replaced by total international interconnections. Correspondingly, the contemporary exercise of authority involves at the minimum, a control over the *technical* facilities of global information, and, at the maximum, an influence, short of absolute but far from slight, over the *content* of the informational flow.

The creation, largely as a spin-off from the enormous research expenditures on missiles and rocketry, of an almost instantaneous mode of multi-purpose global communications through space satellites provides the basis for wide-ranging American commercial and national ambitions. At the same time, the unprecedented opportunities for utilization of these same communications for human improvement can hardly be overlooked and are indeed obvious to large numbers of people. The divergence between the aims of the country's decision-making leadership with regard to the utilization of space communications for traditional power purposes, and the goals of the numerous but essentially powerless professional classes, that hope for more constructive uses of the new technology represents the sharp division between declaration and practice which has characterized American space communications policy since its inception in the early sixties.

At the very beginning of the age of sky-borne messages but at the very end of his own presidential tenure, Dwight Eisenhower, on December 30, 1960, declared: "This nation has traditionally followed a policy of conducting international telephone, telegraph and other communications services through private enterprise subject to governmental licensing and regulation. We have achieved communications facilities second to none among the nations of the world. Accordingly, the government should aggressively encourage private enterprise in the establishment and operation of satellite relays for revenue-producing purposes."[1]

---

[1] *New York Times*, December 31, 1960.

Eisenhower's view was, at the time he expressed it, without weight in any juridical sense. It was also, to be sure, no departure from the general philosophy that had prevailed throughout the eight years of his Administration. More surprising was the quick adoption, with some qualifications, of the same outlook by President Kennedy a few months after his inauguration. A statement of presidential policy on communications satellites was issued on July 24, 1961, reaffirming the desirability of private ownership and operation of the U.S. portion of the system.

At the same time, Kennedy declared: "I (again) invite all nations to participate in a communications satellite system, in the interest of world peace and closer brotherhood among peoples throughout the world." He sought the rapid development of international communications, global coverage even "where individual portions of the coverage are not profitable," and foreign participation through ownership in the system. Other objectives were the nondiscriminatory use and equitable access to the system by present and future authorized communications carriers, vigorous competition, compliance with antitrust laws, economical rates, and "a constructive role for the United Nations in international space communications."[2]

The social nature of these policy requirements, juxtaposed with the private character of the basic organizational structure, constitutes the chief source of the incompatibilities imbedded in satellite communications development. A dozen senators recognized the seeds of future conflicts if a private entity was accepted as the instrument for the development of space communications. Despite their efforts the Communications Satellite Act was approved in August, 1962.

Congress based its decision to reject government ownership and management on the following "crucial factual assumptions that remained in dispute to the very end:

1. Private ownership of a global relay is legally possible and desirable notwithstanding the uncertain state of space law and the fact that orbital objects cannot be policed.

2. Private ownership is crucial for speedy development and efficient operation even though the government also has the know-how and resources, and can alone provide necessary booster and tracking capability.

---

[2] *Satellite Communications, 1964* (part 1), Hearings, Committee on Government Operations, 88th Congress, 2nd Session, Washington, 1964, pp. 590-91.

3. Although satellites can accommodate far more varied services than cable, have unique foreign policy implications, and are far more expensive to install, they are essentially an adjunct of existing communications facilities and thus most suitably owned and operated by the international common carriers.

4. The complex international negotiations needed for satellite communication are best handled by the common carriers—even though such negotiations, necessarily multilateral rather than bilateral, involve the State Department and FCC in crucial ways.

5. The great capital and operating costs of any system, added to the need to service uneconomic markets, virtually guarantee losses for a long time, and private common carriers rather than the government should bear these losses.

6. These satellite and ground station components must be jointly owned, even though they are technologically distinct, and common ownership would open the door to government intrusion into both domestic and international communication." [3]

Comsat, the Communications Satellite Corporation, was formally organized as a private U.S. corporation in February 1963. The next summer, the corporation's shares were offered to the public, though foreign purchasers were expressly limited. According to a Federal Communications Commission allocation formula, half the shares were sold to individual investors, numbering 175,000 at the latest count, and half were acquired by 163 authorized (communications) carriers. The four largest carrier stockholders—AT&T, IT&T, General Telephone and Electronics Corporation, and RCA Communications, Inc.—together had 90.9 per cent of the industry segment and 45.4 per cent of the total issue. AT&T, the single largest stockholder, purchased 29 per cent of the total stock issue which constituted 57.9 per cent of the industry allocation. Under the terms of the Communications Satellite Act, three of the board of directors were named by the President of the United States, six were elected by the industry segment, and six by the public shareholders.

The speed with which Comsat was created reflected a conscious decision by the leadership community to extract maximum advantage,

---

[3] Harvey J. Levin, *University of Pennsylvania Law Review*, 113, 3, January, 1965.

in traditional power terms, from its technological advantage in space. McGeorge Bundy, former chief aide to President Kennedy and now President of the Ford Foundation, has given us, years after the fact, the motivation for the establishment of the Communications Satellite Corporation. Testifying before Congress in August 1966, Bundy recollected:

". . . I was myself a part of the executive branch during the period which led up to the establishment of Comsat—and while I do not have the personal familiarity with it which so many of you have on this committee, I do clearly remember what the record fully confirms —that *Comsat was established for the purpose of taking and holding a position of leadership for the United States in the field of international global commercial satellite service.*"[4]

The international activities of the corporation immediately after its organization well bear out Bundy's explanation.

## The Geneva Radio Conference of 1963

Though a two year period elapsed between passage of the Satellite Act and the flotation of the corporation's first stock issue, activities by no means were confined to organizing the domestic financial structure of the new private enterprise. Some essential pre-conditions for operation had to be provided. Interference-free channels were necessary and, though it may sound obvious, sufficient message-receivers had also to be found. For satellite communications, both requirements depend to a large degree on international acquiescence.

Accordingly, long before Comsat was a functioning business, the United States Government began to concern itself with securing radio frequencies for space communications. As early as 1959, the Administration sought and received tentative approval, from an international radio conference under the auspices of the International Telecommunications Union (ITU), for its proposals to use specified channels for space communications. At that time, it was decided to consider the matter more carefully at a later meeting. For the next four years American government leaders and experts drafted papers that were embodied in the official U.S. position to be presented at the Extra-

---

[4] *Progress Report on Space Communications,* Hearings before the Senate Subcommittee on Communications, 89th Congress, 2nd Session, August 10, 17, 18 and 23, 1966, Serial 89-78, Washington, 1966, p. 81. Italics added.

ordinary Radio Administrative Conference, convened in Geneva in October-November, 1963.

The United States delegation was led by Joseph H. McConnell, president of the Reynolds Metal Company, and included representatives from Congress, members of the FCC, the Department of Commerce, NASA, the Navy, the State Department, the president of Comsat, Joseph Charyk, and Leonard Marks, at that time one of Comsat's board of directors, and now the director of the United States Information Agency. At this conference of government delegations Comsat's position, at least on the surface, was strictly advisory.

America's position was simple and single-minded. It sought and secured approval from the 70-nation conference to allocate immediately certain portions of the radio spectrum to space communications. It insisted, further, that the choice of channels be definitive, though many of the countries present argued that communications technology was still evolving and that a provisional allocation should be made in 1963 for reconsideration at a later planning conference. As the leader of the U.S. delegation put it: "you can understand this because many of the countries h⌐re were not as prepared as perhaps some of the rest of us were in the overall space communications field, and we had quite a little discussion about this problem."[5] This discussion included an Israeli resolution which stated in part that space radiocommunications is "both the privilege and the exclusive possibility of great countries only," and that the duty of the "Space Conference is to abandon or at least modify the present practice of first come, first served". It urged that "some form of a Space Communications Administration [may] be entrusted with the responsibility for insuring the global interest . . . of all member states. . . ."[6]

The proposal to consider the decisions of the conference as interim agreements was defeated in committee by an informal vote of 18 to 4, the minority view being taken by the USSR and three Soviet bloc countries.

Though the confused and wasteful allocation of frequencies for radio and television broadcasting in the United States emphasizes the wisdom of unhurried and considered development of new communications media, the American delegation was inflexible in its will to

---

[5] *Congressional Record, House,* January 9, 1964, p. 164.

[6] *Ibid.,* p. 172.

consolidate and extend its technological lead in space communications. At the same time it asserted that its proposals were in the best interests of the developing as well as the developed states.

Harlan Cleveland of the State Department acknowledged that "without the agreement, and particularly, an agreement on satisfactory terms, Dr. Charyk, [Comsat's president] for example, and his corporation would have been in great difficulty in moving ahead."[7] And Dr. Charyk's evaluation was that "there is now a basis for, if you will, an investment based on some assurance that the whole thing isn't going to be upset by another look at the matter in a few years without any positive decision having been taken here."[8]

The global communications program, in this view, could now proceed without endangering the private investment of Comsat's stockholders, even if the directions should later prove unsatisfactory for technological or related reasons. Dr. Charyk phrased it this way: "Who is there first has a priority, so to speak."[9] Whether this was a principle upon which to rest a durable international agreement is, as we shall see, a question which would be reopened at a later date. American delegation leader McConnell noted that "at least 19 European countries with extensive worldwide telecommunications interests had full knowledge and strongly supported all major U.S. proposals. . ." but he was frank to add that "attention is invited to the meager representation from Latin America and Africa south of the Sahara Desert."[10] Among other absentees from the list of participants in this global gathering were a bevy of Asian states including Mainland China, Burma, both Vietnams and both Koreas.

Ignoring these limiting factors, the Geneva Radio Conference was regarded by all Americans concerned as a great success.

## Formation of an International Space Communications System (Intelsat)

Attention now turned to Comsat's second requirement: finding customers who would be willing to use the channels it would be offering, once its satellites were aloft. To secure these, a series of

---

7 *Ibid.*, p. 162.
8 *Ibid.*, p. 165.
9 *Ibid.*, p. 166.
10 *Ibid.*, pp. 167, 175.

loosely structured meetings with representatives from twenty-two Western European states, along with bilateral talks with Canada, Australia and Japan were held in early 1964. They culminated in an agreement in July, 1964, to establish an international communications system, organized as a consortium (INTELSAT). The papers were formally signed and became effective on August 20th, 1964.

Before the substance of the agreement is considered, the novel character of the American negotiating delegation is worth remarking. At these European meetings, according to the State Department's legal adviser at the time, Mr. A. Chayes, "The U.S. delegation was chaired nominally by Ambassador Bruce, but in fact, the laboring oar was carried by Dr. Joseph Charyk, the president of the corporation. . . . Also, on the delegation was Mr. John Johnston . . . in charge of international negotiations for the corporation."[11]

Mr. Chayes was questioned about the curious situation in which a private corporation's president negotiated for his company's advantage, with the authority of a governmental mandate:

> "Mr. Roback (Committee counsel) —Mr. Charyk, as president of the corporation, appeared as a consultant to the State Department or as representative of the company?"
> Mr. Chayes—No; he was a member of the delegation and indeed, vice chairman of the delegation. I do not think it fair to say he represented the company or that he represented the State Department. He represented the United States and in these negotiations the representation of the United States has been affected by a combination of the State Department, other interested agencies and the corporation.
> Mr. Roback—Is it unusual, or is it not unusual for the head of a company to share or speak for the U.S. delegation in an international meeting which affects his company?
> Mr. Chayes—Well it can happen and has happened. In this case, we think implicit in the act itself is the notion that the corporation shall have an important role in international negotiations, although not an exclusive one . . . the objectives that are established in the law are foreign policy objectives of the United States."[12]

Some years later, James McCormack, chairman and chief executive officer of Comsat, defined his company "as a unique concept in cor-

---

11 *Satellite Communications, op. cit.,* p. 344.
12 *Ibid.*

porate structure and purpose. It is a privately owned corporation, but it also serves as a representative of the United States Government."[13]

As for the agreement itself, which established a global commercial communications satellite system, nineteen countries including the Vatican were signatories. With the exception of Australia, Japan, the United States and Canada, the membership originally was exclusively Western European.

Since 1964 participation has broadened considerably and as of this writing 64 countries, including many developing nations, are affiliated with the consortium. Ownership of the system, consisting of the satellites, and the tracking, control and command, and related satellite support equipment, was distributed on an individual share basis to communications entities designated by the signatory nations in proportion to their contributions to the capital costs of the system. An *Interim Communications Satellite Committee* was established, composed of representatives of entities which have at least a share of 1.5%. The original pattern of ownership modified slightly in recent years because of new membership appears in the table below.

| Country | Designated Operating Entity | Percent |
|---|---|---|
| 1. United States | Comsat | 61.0 |
| 2. United Kingdom | Her Britannic Majesty's Postmaster General | 8.40 |
| 3. France | Government of the French Republic | 6.10 |
| 4. Germany | Deutsche Bundespost | 6.10 |
| 5. Canada | Canadian Overseas Telecommunications Corporation | 3.75 |
| 6. Australia | Overseas Telecommunications Commission | 2.75 |
| 7. Italy | To be designated | 2.20 |
| 8. Japan | Kokusai Denshin Denwa Co., Ltd. | 2.00 |
| 9. Switzerland | Direction Generale des Ptt | 2.00 |
| 10. Belgium | Regie des Telegraphes et Telephones | 1.10 |
| 11. Spain | Government of the State of Spain | 1.10 |
| 12. Netherlands | Government of the Kingdom of the Netherlands | 1.00 |
| 13. Sweden | Kungl, Telestyrelsen | .70 |
| 14. Denmark | Generaldirektorat for Post og Telegrafvesenet | .40 |
| 15. Norway | Telegrafstyret | .40 |
| 16. Portugal | Administracao General dos Correlos, Telegrafos e Telefones | .40 |
| 17. Ireland | An Roinn Poist Agus Telegrafa | .35 |
| 18. Austria | Bundesministerium fur Verkehr und Elekstrizitatswirtschaft | .20 |
| 19. Vatican City | Government of the Vatican City State | .05 |
| | Total | 100.00 |

Source: Report prepared by the Military Operations Subcommittee of the Committee on Government Operations, *Satellite Communications*, 88th Congress, 2nd Session, House of Representatives, October, 1964, page 97.

---

[13] "Comsat's Role in Communications", an Interview with James McCormack, *Signal*, May, 1967, p. 32.

The commanding position of the United States in space technology and the insistence that this American dominance should endure are the foremost features of the current international communications system. The ownership provisions in the agreement are illustrative. In the initial allocation, the United States possessed 61 per cent of the shares of the consortium. This proportion has since dropped to about 54 per cent but *it is specified explicitly that no matter how many new members may eventually join the system, the United States share cannot fall below 50.6 per cent.* After the long years of principled opposition by U.S. representatives to the Soviet use of the veto in the UN Security Council, it was distressing if not surprising, to hear Comsat's president reassure a Congressional Committee: ". . . . let me also say a more or less obvious thing, namely that the corporation in any event has a veto on all actions [of the system]."[14]

## The Industrialized World and International Communications

The maintenance of American predominance in future space communications affects both the industrialized and the still-to-be-developed segments of the world, though not in identical ways. United States policy toward the technically advanced economies has developed as an uneasy balancing of solicitude and pressure. Washington and Comsat are concerned that Western Europe associate itself with the global communications organization because there is an obvious need for customers. At the same time, a powerful group sees little virtue in offering generous terms to weaker rivals. The cross pulls in these competing objectives account for the inconsistencies in American policy toward the industrialized states.

Never far from Comsat-Washington thinking, for instance, is an awareness of the earlier British control of worldwide communications through its ownership of transoceanic cables. This inspires a compulsive drive to transfer permanently to American hands the former British communications superiority. Senator Pastore, Chairman of the Senate subcommittee on Communications, in his book, "The Story of Communications", writes emotionally about the threat after World War I, that the British would regain control over radio facilities temporarily lost during the conflict. ". . . We had a definite idea that

---

[14] *Satellite Communications, 1964* (part 2), p. 741.

Britain was planning a round-the-world wireless hookup for its empire that would stifle American competition for good and all."[15] In the 1964 negotiations, Mr. Chayes noted that it was the rapid growth of American satellite technology in the 1950's that undercut Britain's chance to extend control of cable communications for another several decades:

> "It is that very rapidity of movement that has in fact precipitated the European and the British interest in the show . . . British interests and other European interests had thought, at one point, that by delaying this and deferring this, they could get in with . . . another generation of cables and put this whole thing off and put the advantages that we see in it off to the future . . . their early tactics on this issue were designed to preserve not only their existing investment in cables but to project another generation of cables—over which they would have control . . . it was the fact that the corporation (Comsat) was able to mount a program for Early Bird which would supply this North Atlantic capability in 1965, and the Department (State) and A.T.&T. backed them up on it, that broke the resistance of these certain European countries and resulted in what we regard as a highly favorable climate for cooperative participation in an early system."[16]

American advances in space technology made communication satellites a realistic and potentially profitable alternative to cable transmission, and the Europeans were afraid to be shut out entirely of the new developments. Chayes acknowledges this appreciatively: ". . . as the Europeans have seen the determination and speed with which we have been moving, their interest in climbing aboard has intensified. And that is exactly what we wanted. That is exactly what we had hoped for . . . the foreign governments are very anxious, if they are going to get in, to get in. Because they know that every day that passes, we are making more decisions, we are learning more, we are foreclosing other options about the ultimate characteristics of the system. So what the foreign governments want is to get in quickly, and they are pushing us to get in quickly so that they can have some say and some influence on these decisions. . . ." And the legal adviser

---

[15] J. O. Pastore, *The Story of Communications*, Macfadden-Bartell, New York, 1964, p. 67.

[16] *Satellite Communications, 1964* (part 1), p. 364.

made it evident that the pressure was kept on. ". . . We have made it clear . . . to the foreign governments that the timetable was set by the corporation's program and that the foreign governments and entities by failure to agree would not delay the corporation's program."[17]

Success in bringing the Europeans into the new communications system and thereby eliminating the vestiges of English control of global communications carried with it a new problem for Comsat. Though eager to join, the Europeans were not at all willing to become silent partners. From the beginning, they resisted American efforts to negotiate with each nation separately. After a few exploratory talks in the spring of 1963 between Comsat representatives and individual Western European nations, the latter organized themselves into a group known as the *European Conference on Satellite Communications*, "and they chose, after much discussion, to discuss and eventually to negotiate with the United States as a group."[18]

The State Department's special assistant for space communications, William Gilbert Carter, noted with regret that the Europeans had caused problems "for our side" by banding together:

> "The group approach was adopted very strongly and very firmly by the Western Europeans, and I think it is quite fair to say that they did this in order to increase their negotiating strength with us. . . . Also very much with the concept that they would insist on some rather simple, but nevertheless some, intergovernmental agreement rather than purely commercial contractual arrangements as has been characteristic . . . in the cable consortium arrangements . . . this was a very firm position taken unanimously by all of the Western European nations and subsequently by Canada and Australia as well."[19]

The problem of the American side was to establish an international commercial communications system that would satisfy the Europeans sufficiently to enlist their membership and support as customers and participants, while at the same time it prevented their interfering with American control. Since he who pays invariably commands, the matter quickly resolved itself into allowing the Europeans to pay just a little, so that they could establish an identity with the system,

17 *Ibid.*, pp. 364, 360.
18 *Satellite Communications, 1964* (part 2), p. 660.
19 *Ibid.*, p. 661.

but not control it. The thinking that goes into such settlements is worth documenting and we are fortunate to have once more the explanation of the State Department's legal adviser, offered to a member of Congress, Representative Randall of Missouri:

> Mr. Chayes, ". . . in this case our problem is a little bit the reverse of what we usually have. The fact is the Europeans are anxious to put up a greater share of the money than we think they are entitled to."
>
> Mr. Randall—This is novel, isn't it?
>
> Mr. Chayes—It is novel but in a moment you will see why that is the case. We are talking about a $200 million system. But that is only the part of the iceberg that is out of the water. The $200 million system is built on long periods and tremendous outlays of U.S. research and development. If you can get in that $200 million—
>
> Mr. Randall—We are talking the same language. They are trying to get their nose under the tent."[20]

An interesting point arising from Mr. Chayes' testimony, but not brought out in congressional inquiry, is the matter-of-fact assumption that while it would be unthinkable for foreigners to share, without cost, the fruits of United States governmental outlays on space technology, it is completely acceptable for a private domestic corporation, Comsat, to reap such benefits for its stockholders, who constitute the merest fraction of the total taxpaying public.

In the matter of space equipment it was recognized that the new communications system would be a growing and profitable customer.

Understandably, the Western European countries and Japan were not shy about seeking a share of it. Mr. Carter of the State Department reported:

> "It became a highly political issue in Europe as to whether or not there was going to be any provision in here which did not inevitably result in there being complete U.S. procurement for the system for all time. This became a very sensitive political issue in a number of European parliaments. Again I think on balance we came out of the negotiations quite well."[21]

---

20 *Satellite Communications, 1964* (part 1), p. 363.
21 *Satellite Communications, 1964* (part 2), p. 682.

It was agreed that procurement would also be in approximate proportion to the members' respective quotas, assuming that the material met price and quality standards. Since the United States originally had 61 per cent of the consortium's quota and a long technological lead as well, there was little doubt that for years to come American firms would dominate the business stimulated by the new communication system.

## Comsat and the Developing Nations

The European states were not entirely helpless in their negotiations with the powerful Comsat-Washington combination. For one thing, they constituted, in Mr. Carter's words, "the key future partners who must be on the other end of the line if you are to have a system. . . ."22 For another, the Western nations, with precedents to guide them, were able to negotiate with one voice. Finally, their industrialization permitted them alternatives. They could threaten to develop their *own* communications satellite system, or, if necessary, continue to rely on cables. Despite these bargaining strengths, in the first few years at least, the negotiating achievements of the *European Conference on Satellite Communications* were hardly striking—a small voice in current decision making and the promise of some, though not many, future equipment contracts.

Consider then, the plight of the less advanced nations. National policy outlined by President Kennedy in 1961 and embodied in the Communications Satellite Act of 1962, established the desirability of providing communication satellite services to less developed countries even where the costs of such services are not profitable. However, the dynamics and objectives of the privately owned Comsat continue to nullify these declarations of good intentions.

The representation of the global "have nots" was small at the frequencies allocation meeting in Geneva in October-November 1963; in other meetings in 1964, which designed the form and structure of the new international communications system, *the developing nations were excluded entirely.* The twenty-two European states that organized into the *European Conference on Satellite Communications,* along with Canada, Australia and Japan, were the sole participants meeting the Comsat-Washington representatives in the planning and

---

22 *Ibid.,* p. 684.

negotiating sessions. The total exclusion of the nonindustrialized countries from the discussions and the agreement reflected the private commercial orientation of Comsat and was not the manifestation of racial or national discrimination. The results, unfortunately, were the same. When asked whether the interests of the underdeveloped states were being taken into account in the new system, State Department's Mr. Chayes replied:

> ". . . the act (Communications Satellite) also contemplates an economically viable system operated . . . by private enterprise for profit, and therefore, it is important in the early stages to get the system up where it can serve some paying traffic, and then the exact basis on which the system, the facility will become available in underdeveloped countries will have to be worked out. . . ."[23]

By using the existing traffic volume in international communications as a criterion for accepting national participation in the new system, its directors made certain that paying customers would be favored. The countries that engaged in the final negotiations represented among them more than 90 per cent of the world's international intercontinental telephone traffic. Policy pronouncements about the needs of the economically lagging states notwithstanding, Comsat's main concern is to win the communications market in the well-to-do world as it exists today.

The privileges of later accession to the agreement and participation in the system were offered to those not included at the start, though the period of accession was a brief six months, subsequently extended. More indicative of the closed nature of the consortium is the fact that shares reserved for possible new entrants, no matter how numerous, cannot exceed 17 per cent of the total. Assuming the remaining three-quarters of the world were interested in adhering to the agreement, it could never hope to receive more than a 17 per cent vote in the consortium's affairs. In 1968, with 64 nations represented in the system, the United States voting weight rests at 53 per cent. Taking into account the rising dissatisfaction with the system's decision-making structure, one observer who had been active in the organizational phase of Intelsat as the State Department's legal advisor, now notes that ". . . over the next decade [the most important

---

[23] *Satellite Communications, 1964* (part 1) , p. 263.

decisions made about communications satellite systems] will be highly political. . . . This growing political element must find reflection in the allocation of voting power. And the distribution of votes in proportion to use simply does not do that."[24]

Despite its designation, the new communications organization since its formation has been something less than genuinely global. Particularly striking, in light of President Kennedy's statement in July, 1961 that "the U.S. Government will examine with other countries the most constructive role for the United Nations, including the I.T.U., in international space communications", has been the reluctance of the State Department to consider the possibility of an eventual UN attachment for the system. At the very beginning of the consortium's history, the following dialogue occurred between the Congressional sub-committee's counsel, Mr. Roback, and the State Department's special assistant for space communications, Mr. Carter:

> "Mr. Roback—Do you have any idea about what the future evolution of this organization is going to be? . . .
> Mr. Carter—You mean in the legal sense or organizational sense?
> Mr. Roback—Both. That is to say, is it going to become an international corporation?
> Mr. Carter—I do not know.
> Mr. Roback—Is it going to become a U.N. agency?
> Mr. Carter—Well, this phrase, 'U.N. agency' is, I might say, a really loaded one.
> Mr. Roback—Specialized.
> Mr. Carter—No. I think it is not going to become a U.N. agency and will not become a specialized agency of the U.N. I think that is quite clear."[25]

When the plans for a satellite communications system were first formulated, the Russians maintained an attitude of polite interest but indicated little desire to participate. This was hardly surprising when the position of the State Department was taken into account. State's Mr. Chayes expressed it this way: ". . . their (Soviet) international communications are not very great when you take them as a share of world international telecommunications. So whether they will have a real interest in participating in this system *on the kinds*

---

24 Mr. A. Chayes in *Aviation Week and Space Technology*, August 28, 1967, p. 31.
25 *Satellite Communications, 1964* (part 2), p. 682.

*of terms that we would consider acceptable* I don't think you can predict."[26]

More recently, Mr. Chayes, now no longer with the State Department, has conceded that "it seems fairly clear that Russia could not accept membership under a formula that gave her such a small voice compared to the U.S."[27]

Indeed, the Soviets are not alone in viewing Intelsat as an American-dominated system. Despite their inclusion from the beginning, the West European nations have been ambivalent toward the space communications structure. Eager to be instructed in the new technology and to share in the potential profits of the system, they have resisted American efforts to treat each of them as weak individual bargaining units. Though their efforts to expand their influence in the system have thus far met with little success, their ultimate strength resides in the inescapable fact that they are indispensable participants in any intercontinental message system. They reason that no matter how powerful the North American colossus may be, it cannot communicate exclusively with itself.

Indicative of the growing coolness to Intelsat and the related attitude of reserving some independence of action in space communications, have been the recent spate of plans for national, regional and even competing international satellite systems of communications. The Soviet Union has already announced its intention of establishing an international satellite communications system "open to all interested countries."[28] The French and Germans are undertaking a joint satellite communications program which they expect to be operational in the early 1970's. The Japanese are considering a regional system in which they will play a leading role. The Canadians too have announced that their national interest requires a Canadian satellite system. The list will undoubtedly lengthen.

The American space advantage, much like the atomic monopoly before it, is a wasting asset that is depreciating rapidly before a steady stream of electronic advances that cannot be confined to one society. As other nations acquire increased communications sophistication, there is no reason to imagine that they will remain loyal to Comsat's

---

[26] *Satellite Communications, 1964* (part 1), 267. Italics added.
[27] *Aviation Week and Space Technology*, August 28, 1967, p. 31.
[28] *Ibid.*

conception of the American national interest. Proliferation of national systems of communications satellites, if not matching the deadly destructiveness of nuclear spread, will be a poor contribution to international cooperation.

There is a rising global sentiment against the United States' commercial monopoly in space. For example, H. G. Darwin, legal advisor to the U.K.'s mission to the United Nations makes these points:

> "The multiple position of Comsat is particularly open to criticism. It is a majority shareholder of Intelsat, carrying a right of veto and on many issues a right to put any decision through the Interim Committee. It is managing agent, with all the importance that results. And, in addition, it has its independent, quite separate interests as a U.S. corporation, including the TV industry. To the critical eye Comsat is Lord High Executioner and Lord High Everything Else."[29]

FCC Commissioner Nicholas Johnson, reviewing the future of world communications, asks: "Will the entire universe be divided up between Comsat and A.T.&T.—heaven for one, and the earth for the other?"[30]

All the same, Comsat and its Washington supporters, though willing to make some concessions to mounting international criticism, hold firmly to the belief that Intelsat, the system that affords them so privileged a position, is fundamentally sound. President Johnson in his August, 1967 congressional message on communications policy affirmed that "We support the continuation of Intelsat . . . the present arrangements offer a firm foundation on which a permanent structure can be built." In the message, the President took note of the fear that "some nations may feel the United States has too large a voice in the consortium", and he reassured them that the U.S. seeks "no domination of satellite communications."[31] A few months earlier, in his annual report to Congress on the Activities and Accomplishments under the Communications Satellite Act of 1962, the president emphasized ". . . the firmness of the foundation upon which this international partnership (Intelsat) has been constructed" and he noted

---

[29] *Ibid.*

[30] "A Concept of Communications", Nicholas Johnson, *Carnegie Review*, Number 12, July, 1967.

[31] Presidential Message to Congress on Communications Policy, August 14, 1967.

"the expectation of continued healthy expansion in the years ahead."[32]

James McCormack, too, chairman and chief executive officer of Comsat, is satisfied with existing international space communications arrangements. "Intelsat's practical achievements to date testify to the essential soundness of the present organization", he declares. "Improvements can be made, but fundamental restructuring will hardly commend itself to those who are interested in maintaining the pace of progress which has been enjoyed during these initial years."[33] Furthermore, McCormack is cautiously optimistic that the system will develop along the lines that were initially set down because the technical instrumentation already in place compels continued participation of the members. "By 1969", he notes, "when the Intelsat agreement comes up for renegotiation, the global system will be operating. A good many countries will have investments in earth stations designed for use with Intelsat . . . it will be a going concern with a big lead over any possible rival."[34]

Robert Sarnoff, President of the giant Radio Corporation of America, which is one of Comsat's major shareholders, is also confident of Intelsat's future. Sarnoff evaluates the international space communications consortium in ideological terms.

> "The question goes beyond preserving freedom where it now exists—although it is vital that we do so. We must extend it to new systems and services as they come into use—starting today with the new technology of satellite communications. This was the purpose behind American leadership in establishing the International Telecommunications Satellite Consortium (Intelsat). . . . The interim agreement governing the venture will expire in 1969. Hopefully, it will be succeeded by long-term arrangements based on the same principle of cooperation. . . . In the world pattern we hope to achieve, there will be no room for isolated communications satellite systems."[35]

---

[32] *Annual Report,* January 1-December 31st, 1966, p. 1.

[33] "Intelsat, Comsat's Point of View", James McCormack, Bordeau, France, May 22, 1967.

[34] *U.S. News and World Report,* December 26, 1966, p. 62.

[35] "Communications and the Information Revolution", Robert W. Sarnoff, May 1, 1967, pp. 9 and 10.

## Conclusions

The development of both Comsat and Intelsat reveal certain patterns and directions. Whereas a tendency toward wider global representation is observable in several important politico-economic international organizations—the United Nations itself, the UN Conference on Trade and Development, GATT, etc.—space communications to date indicate a retrograde structure. The decisions taken thus far are all based on market considerations emphasizing capital contributions, volume of international communications and expectations of profitability. An inevitable consequence has been the rapid relegation of the nonprofit communications needs of much of the world to the category of afterthought. Contrary to United Nations resolutions and presidential statements, the space communications development under Comsat-Washington auspices has supported an aggressive nationalism, brazenly presenting itself as an international undertaking. The rush to develop space communications seems to indicate, not so much a pressing technological need for expanded communications as a powerful combination of nationalist and commercial impulses to thrust aside competing techniques and secure global economic and military supremacy. The United States National Association of Manufacturers endorses "the communications satellite system (as) one of the finer examples of our country's global leadership in the space age." [36] The intimacy that characterizes the relationship between Comsat and Washington suggests a new and higher form of that curious creature, state capitalism.

To what extent these tendencies may be reversed in the years ahead will be determined by forces already operative. Most important is the rapidly changing space communications technology which even now is providing options to many nations for independent space communications activities. At the very least, the necessity for some coordination in the use of the radio spectrum, as independent users multiply, will increase the pressure for more realistic and less arbitrary international arrangements for space control. At the same time, as the alternatives produced by technology became available to a growing number of states, willingness by these nations to accept subordinate positions in an American system decreases. This too may already be coming to pass and will probably be evident in the renegotiation of the present Intelsat arrangements in the years ahead.

[36] NAM Telecommunications Committee, 1967.

# Chapter 10

## Towards a Democratic Reconstruction of Mass Communications: The Social Use of Technology

Radio and television broadcasting in the United States is largely a private activity that has grown into a powerful industry with far-reaching, though mostly unacknowledged, social consequences. Government control of broadcasting has been limited and, what there is of it, ineffectually implemented. The regulated more often than not impose their will on the regulators.

Operating in a market economy and measuring performance by incoming revenue, broadcasting's internal dynamics, like those of other industrial sectors, move inevitably toward economic concentration. Stations and channels derive their profitability, and therefore their value, from the size of their potential audiences. Time rates are calculated on a listener/viewer per program ratio, and metropolitan signals heard by large numbers are easily the most attractive to prospective advertisers.

Control has tightened in broadcast communications as the economics of radio-television have fostered giantism and concentration. A clutch of corporations (common carriers, manufacturers of electrical equipment, and a few network broadcasting companies) interlock and attempt to arbitrate among themselves, not always with complete success, the domestic communications scene. Meanwhile, as American power has thrust outward in recent years, the authority of this national communications complex has moved into the international and spatial arenas as well.

Mass communications are now a pillar of the emergent imperial society. Messages "made in America" radiate across the globe and serve as the ganglia of national power and expansionism. The ideological images of "have-not" states are increasingly in the custody of American informational media. National authority over attitude creation and opinion formation in the developing world has weakened and is being relinquished to powerful external forces. The facilities and hardware of international information control are being grasped by a highly centralized communications complex, resident in the United States and largely unaccountable to its own population.

The speed of innovation in electronics technology and the already-deployed strength of American communications have produced a spirit of confidence among the leaders of the United States' informational system. Dr. Charyk, the president of Comsat, for example, told a congressional committee in 1966 that he believes "we stand on the threshold of a communications revolution. [The establishment of Comsat and Intelsat] has set in motion technical, political, and economic forces whose ultimate global impact will be profound. Sometimes we hear that satellites afford simply another supplementary or complementary means of communication. But particularly when one talks of international communications and when one looks at the new capabilities which satellites bring into being, there is little doubt in my mind that we are at the dawn of a new age."[1]

If this is so, and it may well be that it is, is there a predictable character to this "new age?" Will it be directed from some imperial center, which unilaterally and arbitrarily decides the course of international events? Inside the "center", are we moving irresistibly toward "knowledge conglomerates", integrated private informational structures which unify the learning and educational process from infancy to the grave, efficiently discarding troublesome messages? Or, is the prospect opening before us a more hopeful one of multiplying opportunities to utilize the new technology for international cooperation, human improvement and individual enrichment? Indeed, *for whom* is this a new age?

The Utopians once enjoyed elaborating designs for social improvement, but they lacked the means for implementing their models. Today the situation is reversed. Utopias are out of fashion just at the time when they are literally attainable. Never before in history have

---

[1] *National Communications Satellite Programs*, Hearings Before the Committee on Aeronautical and Space Sciences, United States Senate, 89th Congress, 2nd Session, January 25 & 26, 1966, Washington, 1966, p. 51.

the basic educational and cultural needs of humanity been so widely appreciated. But while the resources to satisfy these requirements are physically available, they are directed to other ends. The engineering means exist, but the will and the enabling social structure are absent. The resources and the technology, known and available, are capable of monumental physical transformations. The modern obstacles, no less imposing because they are social rather than material, are the institutions which govern human affairs.

Today the fundamental questions concerning communications do not involve process or discovery. Social issues such as ownership, control, financial support, national sovereignty and the character of the programming constitute the unsettled agenda. No longer, as in the past, is there a universal problem of providing every adult and every child with the technical means of receiving information. For poor nations this remains a great concern, but not for the American community. In the United States, the question is *what* message to receive, not *how* to receive it.

Technically-advanced America is socially retarded by institutional machinery which preserves outlooks and practices far beyond their usefulness or applicability. Paradoxically, the most modern sector of the economy, electronic communications, often serves as the chief conservator of outmoded behavior patterns. Yet the mass media's compulsion to reinforce the status quo is understandable. The radio-TV establishments, in their character and structures, are microcosms of the larger social organism. They could hardly not be committed to its survival. If monolithic corporate enterprises command the informational apparatus, this is in keeping with the distribution of power in the economy at large. If the "tube" presents an unending parade of violence and triviality, are these not apt reflections of the wider social environment?

It is possible that institutions eventually may be eroded by changing technology, but this presumes a considerable historical process. Also, the erosion may be uneven, and certain, perhaps vital, institutions remain untouched, while others are altered. Those left intact may still command the overall direction of existence. For the moment, which may endure far beyond an individual's life-span, institutions preside over technology. Operating in this narrower time dimension, can we realistically expect a beneficent social orientation, an appropriate outlook for mankind, simply because the rapidly changing technology of communications make available the possibility of universal coverage, multiplication of services and strikingly effective impact? Are we justified in expecting technology to "wash out" our institutional problems and lift us, almost against our will, onto a higher plateau of existence? It is a comforting notion, but also, I believe, a very misleading one. We will either direct our technology or it will be used to direct us. In communications the second course has been evident for some time.

Now that startling innovations are feasible in the technology of information distribution there is a pause while the technologists reveal the opportunities that their creativity has provided. There is with us, for a moment, the vision of what could be. The routine is broken. The acceptance of unsatisfactory living patterns and popular acquiescence in the shocking underperformance in humanizing the social process are temporarily interrupted. We are given a glimpse of a different social balance in which the prevailing priorities are somehow or other made inoperative. We are left briefly to imagine that a higher standard in the quality of life is attainable because it is physically realizable.

Buckminster Fuller has argued eloquently for years that the world can be engineered into abundance. Even if he is right, and I believe that he is, the institutional structure disregards his blueprints and brushes off his plea for "anticipatory design." The fact of the matter is that the efficient use of global resources, the goal to which Fuller has dedicated his enormous talent, as well as the utilization of communications in the service of man, will not be achieved as an effortless byproduct of advanced engineering processes. The road to the social use of technology runs through the rugged terrain of interest groups, privileged classes, national power, and self-satisfied decision-makers. Prodding, opposing, and perhaps even storming and overturning these ancient but enduring governing coalitions are the means by which the humanistic use of the new technology may be secured. It is willful escapism to believe that technology, by itself, will soon force its way out of the restrictive social web that now surrounds it. The generalized insecurity overhanging industrially omnipotent and economically affluent America is strong evidence of how badly the campaigns to liberate technology have gone in recent years.

The utilization of the new communications technology for human needs requires a thorough reordering of the social process which regulates the informational system at all levels of personal and national existence. The dilemma is, however, that the controlling crust of the industrial state calls on the communications media to resist the social reorganization that must precede the technological reformation.

The development of modern electronic communications illustrates the ability of the prevailing institutional framework to shelter itself from technological subversion. Radio and television have been controlled continuously by the industrial concerns that organized their discovery and development. Television came into the market as the research product of electrical equipment and radio manufacturing corporations and then, incidentally, as a new medium of communications. Corporate interests determined the timing of the product's introduction, the pace of its technological growth, the speed with which it was delivered to the public, the character of its financing and the content of its programming. Consequently, society's cultural process, its deepest concern, has remained largely removed from general consideration and public decision-making. Television, the most educative force in existence has been left almost entirely to private considerations and the vagaries of the marketplace. The cost of overlooking the generalized social need when treating a vital matter of community wellbeing is now only beginning to be appreciated. John Platt's point that what we teach [or do not teach] today may well affect our survival, is a helpful reminder:

"Evidently the time is approaching", he writes, "when our whole society will begin to be self-conscious about what it may become, when we will begin to choose it deliberately instead of accidentally. We now realize that the society we can and will become is shaped by what we teach, by the kind of human nature we are producing day by day in our children. This means that there is a problem of choice in our teaching, a collective problem far larger than any single wise educator can solve for us. The old and yet remarkably new discovery of the plasticity of human nature means that all of us — natural and social scientists, psychologists and teachers, historians and writers, students of economics and politics, government and university leaders, philosophers and citizens — all of us will be deciding and need to be deciding what kind of human nature and what kind of personal and

social relationships we want to teach our children to have so
that they will be able to make a better society in turn for
themselves."[2]

How and where do we introduce into the teaching process social
decision-making when the most effective instrumentation of learning
has been available only marginally for public utilization and collective responsibility? One TV trade journal boasts that "the average
kid has watched four thousand hours of television before his first day
of school."[3] And Federal Communications Commissioner Nicholas
Johnson notes that this "instruction" from [the child's] home set is
"twice as many hours . . . as he will receive in class during the entire
four-year span of his college tenure."[4]

The technology of modern communications must be won away
from its current custodians. It should be generally apparent, although
it is not, that the aims and practices of the commercial market are
not always in step with the social requirements of the human commonwealth. Moreover, in an advanced industrial society, the problem
goes beyond the commercial influence in the mass media. Shifting the
responsibility from private goods-sellers to public (governmental)
authorities, can no longer, if it ever could, be considered a foolproof
alternative which guarantees a socially-minded guardian for the sensitive informational apparatus.

The interdependencies in an essentially privately-run modern nation
have produced a governing coalition that occupies public as well as
private office. Now, in America, governmental control of the communications media could produce a more sophisticated expertise in
audience control than the commercial sublimators ever have managed to construct. It is important to be straightforward about such
a possibility, especially at this time. The American public, having
tolerated for twenty years the impoverishment of "educational television", and accepted what one former FCC Chairman termed an
"electronic Appalachia", now indicates a growing dissatisfaction with

---

[2] John R. Platt, *The Step To Man*, John Wiley and Sons, Inc., New York, 1966,
p. 163.

[3] "The Preteen Market", Caroline Meyer, *Television Magazine*, July 1967, Vol.
XXIV, No. 7, p. 37.

[4] Nicholas Johnson, "The Public Interest and Public Broadcasting: Looking At
Communications as a Whole", September 11, 1967.

the state of affairs of commercial television. The development of space communications technology and the spreading, if still limited, disenchantment with commercial programming, have produced a growing sentiment for a broader public broadcasting authority. A government-supported broadcasting corporation has received congressional authorization. The most obvious defects of unlimited commercialism can be mitigated by this public enterprise, but the prospect is not an unqualified cause for celebration.

It can hardly be disputed that the recent trend in public discussion initiated by the Ford Foundation's proposal for a non-profit public broadcasting corporation has been beneficial. At the very least, it has given the public an opportunity to be acquainted with the monopolistic communications system that presently functions in the United States. It has also restated some forgotten truths. The foremost of these is that the messages a system transmits are inseparably tied to the character of that system's structure and control. The question the Ford Foundation people made central had not been asked for years. It was, Communications for what? Put in self-critical terms, the question becomes, What does it avail a community to possess an instrumentation of miraculous capability if it is placed in the service of mediocrity or irrelevancy or subjugation?

Can a governmentally-financed noncommercial system begin to provide the critical substance that private, advertiser-supported television has rarely offered? The original Ford Foundation plan foresaw informational services which would include the coverage of significant congressional hearings and debates, news interpretations, interviews and discussions with national and international leaders, and political campaigns; cultural programs which would feature the best in the universe of national and international arts and humanities; and a level of instructional service going far beyond anything currently broadcast.

Are these realistic expectations, given the present distribution of income and decision-making in the United States? Furthermore, do these intentions, exciting as they are in comparison with present arrangements, go far enough? Is it possible to create an autonomous structure that will take up the serious and challenging tasks of national education and revitalize the (sadly sagging) democratic spirit in the population? Desperate as we are to answer these questions affirmatively we do ourselves no service by ignoring the realities of contemporary American life. More than a board of honest men, overseeing a public television establishment, will be necessary to reverse the strong anti-democratic tide that has been running in the country for a generation. We are no longer at the point where some modest meliorative changes in our informational fare will suffice. Unfortunately, it is past the time where a little less hucksterism in the programming and a few more hours each week of public service broadcasting will make any substantial difference—either in the popular outlook or in widening the public comprehension of the enormous social problems that have gone unconsidered for so long.

The information process in the United States continues to rest firmly in the grip of tenacious stand-patters. These cannot and will not begin to do the job of meaningfully explaining to their viewers and listeners the revolutionary changes appearing in domestic and international life. It is also doubtful that the creation of a public broadcasting corporation, superior as it unquestionably will be to the present system, will represent the scope of change, either in outlook or allegiance, that the current social situation demands. The chief opposition to a governmentally-financed public broadcast system, incidentally, has come from those sections of Congress and the community which fear that the system will be "captured" by advocates of extreme social change. Sadly, the probabilities are all the other way. It is difficult to imagine a public corporation, with its directors appointed by the President and its money raised through annual congressional authorization, independently criticising, for any length of time, establishment sentiments. Such an expectation would be tantamount to imagining the Voice of America transmitting as its dominant message to Southeast Asia the arguments of the United States peace movement against the American engagement in Vietnam. Yet the state of the contemporary world, and the domestic situation in particular, require an informational apparatus in the United States totally different from what we have grown up with and with which we now feel some, but not enough, irritation.

In many areas of current scientific work, systematic research is producing results that are consciously sought and sometimes even hypothesized well before the inquiry is undertaken. Nature is coming under the deliberate control of the scientific community. This process is least advanced in the social sphere. In the realm of human affairs, a minimal effort is still applied to designing the future. If the reasons for the lag are fairly well known, the consequences are none the less potentially catastrophic. Traditionally, social change has followed one sort or another of social crisis. Slavery, war, mass unemployment have sometimes provoked large scale resistance from their victims. Struggles arising from popular dissatisfaction have on occasion produced reforms throughout the entire social sphere. Change induced in this fashion may not be sufficient to prevent the recurrence of the initial crisis. It always comes after some manifestation of social breakdown. It generally is accompanied by strife and violence. Crisis, therefore, is a very primitive mechanism for creating new social conditions. It is incongruous next to the ordered efforts characteristic of the scientific sphere.

Is there a way for the social sector to emulate its scientific component? Can anticipation and design replace crisis and conflict as the instruments of social change? This, in essence, is the function and the role, if they were to be taken up, of mass communications in the United States today. Radio-television broadcasting, coming into practically every American home, can alert and instruct the disinterested, the ignorant, the misinformed and the apathetic. Communications, subtle yet forceful and entertaining while educational, are the principal hope we have of substituting thoughtful human preventive action for social breakdown and violent, visceral human response. The sense of inevitability need no longer be inevitable.

But to provide invigorating and enlightening communications, the mass media must *lead*, not follow. Commercial broadcasting cannot do this. Public broadcasting, though theoretically capable of such efforts, will probably find its support threatened if it moves resolutely in this direction. What then remains? The answer may have to be found outside the usual terms of reference. The potential exists, I believe, in some forces stirring in the national community itself. An informational apparatus that provides substance, insight and an unshakeable integrity in offering social direction, can develop only alongside of and assisted by the most dynamic elements in the community. Mass communications, if they are to do what has to be done to illuminate the march of events and compel individual awareness and participation in the social process, must be associated intimately with the popular, though unheard-from, agents of social change in the commonwealth.

Linking the mass media with what Gunnar Myrdal calls the

"underclass" and other unaffiliated underdogs is not suggested out of sentimentality. The Establishment is top dog and its outlook, its methodologies, and its behavior have demonstrated their total incapability of extricating us from onrushing disasters, much less of perceiving incipient crises in advance.

Are there centers of dynamism in the American community with which the mass media, set free of their current ties, might identify and, in doing so, lead the way to popular acceptance of social change? Where, in short, is there skepticism in the community toward the prevailing social and political processes? In fact, a few sources of potential change are readily ascertainable.

Some elements in the *public sector* of the economy reveal sharp antagonisms to the status quo. Teachers, social and health workers, and municipal employees in essential services are foci of discontent and dissatisfaction. For the moment their complaints are mostly economic. However, their relatively pinched positions in the affluent society make it likely that their personal demands will be broadened into national policy reassessments. Better conditions for the working force in the expanding public services demand a review of the fundamental (and neglected) issue of public versus private priorities.

The *universities,* too, are beginning to simmer with awareness and a criticism that arises from perceived incongruities. The devotion of staff and facilities to war-related research; the dependence of university funds on the continuing state of war emergency; and, the training, not the education, of students for employment in impersonal bureaucracies, are matters of deep concern to increasing numbers of faculty and students. The most orthodox and insulated campuses are experiencing currents of dissent, still relatively weak, but significant by the fact of their existence.

The most explosive element in contemporary American society is the developing *black social movement.* Emerging from the city ghettoes and the rural slums, thousands of young, articulate militants are questioning the fundamental assumptions of American life that have gone unchallenged for three hundred years. The black rebellion cannot be contained, and each new outbreak produces new layers of involvement. It reveals also unexpected weaknesses and fissures in the governing coalition.

These are the present forceful and forward groupings. Unresolved crises, domestic and international, *already in the making,* are likely to produce additional elements whose allegiance to the now-dominant structure will peel off as the pressures intensify.

Avoidance of social catastrophe necessitates that these emergent forces have the informational apparatus at their disposal. Yet the very suggestion sounds naive and puerile. It is not fortuitous that the governing complex is most concentrated in the communications sector. The mass media, as they now operate, can only be regarded as the strongest support of the ruling estate. Expectations that the communications process will reflect in a significant way the purposes and the outlook of the "other America" have little reasonable foundation.

Though it is important to be clear on the basic structure and orientation of privately-directed mass communications, it is useful also to recognize that the mechanism of information control is far from monolithic. Besides, the system is not averse to engaging in tactical maneuvers that could prove disarming to unwary challengers. Concessions are conceivable. "Tokenism", the technique of coopting a tiny stratum of a dispossessed group into the privileged orders, the device that has worked effectively in the past in splintering "out group" solidarity, is potentially applicable in broadcast communications. Even now there are signs of its presence. For example, there may be one show during the week's 140 hours of programming that presents imagery of realistic conflict. Or there may be the single character in an army of performers who utters an honest line of dialogue.

Beyond these very limited actions to mollify dissidents or to create an appearance of objectivity, there is the wider option of minority broadcasting. This is the market economy's contribution to diverse interests in the community. An entire station (or channel) may be devoted to the views and sentiments of a particular social stratum. Though this may be edifying to the group concerned, most often its consequence is the further separation of that segment from the largest social unit. FCC Commissioner Johnson explains it this way:

> ". . . although a splintered market will assure minorities that their interests and problems will be aired it will not assure that anyone outside of their group will hear . . . a communications system which caters very well to minority views may be to that extent, *less* capable of getting those views across to the public."[5]

_____
[5] *Ibid.*

At this time, there is little cause to believe that student activists, black power leaders, public sector spokesmen and university faculty critics are going to be seduced with the exclusive use of individual channels for the dissemination of their hopes, fears and findings. Still it is not unimaginable, but rather likely, that representatives of these groupings will increasingly find themselves before the public eye. The test of significant impact however, is always the breadth of exposure, the degree of dilution and the extent of continuity. Tokenism and minority broadcasting are insufficient by any yardstick to create the degree of environmental and attitudinal change that we are proposing.

Therefore the basic problem remains. The forces of enlightenment must find means to confront the *general* public with the issues of the times, the options that exist, and the considered consequences of one or another courses of action. Students, blacks, teachers and scientists are not special people, but the matters that distress them go far beyond their personal interests (though these of course are involved). It may seem curious that this should be so, but it is demonstrable that their individual concerns affect the *general* welfare in the fullest measure.

The university's role, for example, which the students are beginning to examine and find wanting, is not a parochial question, limited to the campus enclave. The quality and character of the total educational process are at issue. The aspirations of 20 million blacks cannot be evaluated as a minority matter that is of import to only 10 per cent of the population. The black-white relationship is as critical to the well-being of the national psyche as any other element in the social order. The work of the country's social and natural scientists and how it may be most benefically applied for the community's security and prosperity are not the province of a handful of administrators. More than anything else, it is the substance for general public debate and decision, for, sooner or later, the entire population is to be affected.

It is because the dynamic centers of the society are altering the foundations of social existence that they are in conflict with the power structure, which is itself built on these threatened supports. There is an urgent need for these developing forces to instruct and inform national and local publics of what they are about. Their work is for the most part constructive, their goals, generally desirable. Yet failing to explain and to explore their aims and actions with the popular majority, their efforts may be futile and their objectives will be distorted by their adversaries. They will be swamped by a numerically overwhelming coalition, manipulated by the traditional governors.

Where then is a breakthrough possible? If the informational channels are denied, how may the messages of the creative undergroups penetrate the larger community? It is in this respect that the technologists have a contribution to make. The new communications technology will not of itself overcome the structural order and overturn the levers of control that now limit creative change and prevent adaptation to contemporary needs. It can, however, be of enormous assistance if grasped by the social groups most insistent on restructuring the decision making process. If the groups that are pressing for rationalization of existence in the industrial state and a reconstitution of the social order can claim *massive access* to the new communications, hitherto an impossibility, hope remains that the disasters that a mindless yet powerful economy is provoking may be survived.

The changing character of communications technology could be a saving factor in an otherwise totally negative situation. One of the original arguments which supported the present system of concentrated space communications ownership and control—costliness—is being refuted by a technological flood of communications innovation. Though space satellites are not going to be sold soon at five and dime counters, they are quickly becoming accessible to a wide range of purses and purposes. As a result of massive outlays on space research and hardware, launching expenditures and particularly the costs of the broadcasting "birds" themselves are declining dramatically. The opportunities are expanding for specialized single-purpose satellites.

On the ground, cable television opens the door to a far wider group of program initiators, permitting many more signals into each home set. UHF broadcasting has been extended and additional channels are also being made available in this range of the spectrum. Finally, home video recorders and cameras now are being retailed to a general public. Amateurs have the opportunity to develop skills in the production of material. Set owners with home recorders will be enabled to tape programs and build up libraries of shows they have found compelling and well worth repeating.

Some of these developments may very well move along the familiar road of commercial pre-emption, individual fadism, mass market programming and a system of monopolistic control. But, and this is of critical import, it no longer is technically necessary for communications control to be arbitrarily concentrated. New options, at least for the time being, are open.

The American Telephone and Telegraph Company exercises almost total domination over the country's telephonic communications. Its control of the ground lines and repeater facilities makes the national broadcasting networks dependent on this one corporation for interconnection, vital to national programming. Now, Comsat, already an exclusive and chosen instrument in the international field, seeks to impose its domain over domestic space communications as well. Its argument is efficiency. It claims that a multi-purpose system, under (its own) unified control, will be less wasteful than several individual purpose satellites, each owned and directed by different entities.

There can be no assurance at this early date that individual purpose satellites, individually controlled, will insure the accessibility of hitherto excluded groupings to the newest mode of communications. Indeed it is difficult to imagine the arrangements that would make available a satellite system to social dissidents. The technological barrier still seems formidable. There is, on the contrary, a very good prospect that a multi-purpose system, under the thumb of one, powerful private corporation, will almost automatically maintain social communications in their present unrepresentative and concentrated form. The need at this point is to keep open the technological options for diverse use, even at the sacrifice of some efficiency. Indeed, the concept of efficiency may be in itself a reflection of traditionalism, and the "wastefulness" of alternate systems may be in reality the most promising method of assuring an industrial society some measure of informational liberty.

Turning the new communications technology to democratic advantage will require above all else, continuous aggressive popular pressure on several fronts simultaneously. Individuals outside the established production centers can experiment (as some are already doing) with cameras and TV recorders now coming into their possession. Their efforts, perhaps eventually supported by local, regional or even national social groups, may provide the basis for altogether new sources of communications techniques and programming. Selective taping of the occasional and exceptional program emanating from the commercial system will contribute to libraries of value and substance which can be made available repeatedly for organizational and individual use. Most important of all, requests for new channels and reassignment of stations held by owners indifferent to social needs should become a common and insistent demand of the social "out groups". These demands can be expressed locally as community actions.

The federal and state governments, through their regulatory machinery and the Federal Communications Commission in particular, must be held accountable for the social maximization of the nation's radio spectrum resource. Campaigns to improve mental health and eliminate physical disease generally rely on local initiatives for their support. Similar efforts can be expended in monitoring communications channels and insisting on their utilization for the community's psychic well-being.

Whereas radio and television stations are ranked now according to their market importance—how much they are worth depending on the size and sales potential of their audiences—new criteria can be evolved and applied. In Britain, for instance, the Independent Television Authority has the responsibility for shifting franchises of the most valuable properties if it believes other owners will provide more socially constructive programming. It has done so even at the cost of near-confiscation of heavy private investments. In the United States, commercial licenses have never been revoked on the grounds they have failed to serve the public interest—a case that probably could be made against practically any commercial station now broadcasting. Community pressure can change these rules.

Political action has generally been understood in the United States as the support of one or another candidate for office. This has produced, on occasion, changes in personnel with no corresponding changes in the structure of decision-making. The time may now have arrived for political action which takes up seriously the question of changing underlying structures. Modern political action might find a good starting point in revamping the ownership and control of the informational media at all levels of organization.

It should be evident too that transfers of control can not be regarded as merely one-time actions. No single shift can offer the assurance of perpetual informational flexibility and freedom. Underlying this principle of accessibility to the mass media is the premise that an alert community remains vigilant in respect to its informational needs and retains the vigor and the will to continuously assert itself. The continuing utilization of the broadcasting media for human enlightenment requires the closest attention and participation of all the forces that are engaged in the ongoing process of humanization.

On the international plane, informational needs are enormous, absolutely and qualitatively. There are a billion illiterates in the world. Their education depends on the instructional power of radio and television mobilized for this purpose. Though we are still very far from undertaking such a heroic task, it would be a relatively routine effort insofar as the existing methodologies and educational resources are available. The missing element at this point is the will to act which expresses itself in lamentably inadequate educational budgets. By way of contrast, the Pentagon spends *annually* about one billion dollars for its communications system, a large part of which is designed to alert the military once "trouble" has erupted in the "have not" world.

Much more than money and facilities, however, are required if the mass media are going to assist us to achieve humanity. In his book, *The Wretched of the Earth*, Frantz Fanon wrote: "The news which interests the Third World does not deal with King Baudoin's marriage nor the scandals of the Italian ruling class. What we want to hear about are the experiments carried out by the Argentinians and the Burmese in their efforts to overcome illiteracy or dictatorial tendencies of their leaders."[6]

Will this information come from the international space communications system now being organized under Washington-Comsat's direction?

We return, in conclusion, to our point of departure. The world's desperate communications needs, first for literacy and education but also for meaningful information, are deeply dependent on and influenced by the communications structure and system that operate in the United States. American power, expressed industrially, militarily and culturally, has become the most potent force on earth. Its impact

---

[6] F. Fanon, *The Wretched of the Earth*, Grove Press, Inc., New York, 1965, p. 162.

transcends all national boundaries. Directly by economic control, indirectly by trade and a foreign emulation effect, communications have become a decisive element in the extension of United States world power. Consequently, the link between America's domestic cultural condition and the world's informational-educational requirements can hardly be overstated. The fetters that bind American talent and limit its national engagement are essentially the same as those which are hobbling the social utilization of global communications. Antiquated and narrow perspectives and structures at home and abroad are choking human potential.

More than this, the technological advances that are reducing the world to thimble size, if not assimilated by anticipatory and unselfish behavior on the highest order of international cooperation, can only evoke mean and regressive national responses. This may already be occurring. How otherwise can weak nations defend themselves against globe-girdling satellites that will soon possess the capability of broadcasting messages directly into living rooms throughout the world? What protection is available to developing states against skyborne programming, commercial or nationalistic, that may transmit images and ethics that are incompatible with developmental designs and priorities?

The prospect for a genuinely international space communications system, which operates to satisfy global educational and cultural aspirations, is heavily dependent on the degree to which American domestic space communications are utilized for the social benefit of its own population. The absence of an American model which concerns itself with meaningful programming for its domestic audience deprives the developing nations of an advanced system upon which to draw for support and against which to evaluate their own creative work. Also, a structure of mass communications in the United States that is revised to take into account social needs may spur the changes in the international space communications system that are necessary to provide a similar orientation.

The efforts of our local dynamic centers to assert an increasing influence on the communications media have an international as well as a domestic urgency. Failure to reshape domestic communications to a form which makes room for human development and environmental adaptability can only deepen the disorders already wracking American society. The continuation of the present policy of national hegemony and commercial monopoly in space communications will accelerate in the international community the disintegrative forces of nationalism and competitive chaos. Paradoxically, a viable international order may be attainable only if the efforts of America's present social under-groups to achieve domestic societal restructuring are successful.

# ABOUT THE BOOK
# AND AUTHOR

Originally published in 1969, this book laid out the dimensions of American global domination, emphasizing the role of media-cultural power. It examined how U.S. informational facilities and products were deployed worldwide to support the American empire that came into existence after World War II. A quarter of a century later, although the world has undergone enormous change, U.S. media-cultural power—as a controller of domestic information and a preserver of transnational corporate order—remains unchallenged.

This updated edition of *Mass Communication and American Empire* concludes that the early forms of American cultural imperialism have been transformed into an institutionalized brand of transnational cultural power that propagates and disseminates the ethos of consumption to the world-at-large. The ultimate check on this pervasive phenomenon, the author suggests, is nothing less than the exhaustibility of the earth's resources. Therefore, one important social struggle to come will be the transformation of the international corporate information-marketing system currently in place.

Herbert I. Schiller, longtime information and media critic, is author of nearly a dozen books, including *The Mind Managers; Culture Inc.: The Corporate Takeover of Public Expression;* and *Information and the Crisis Economy.*

# INDEX